Making the Good Life Last

Four Keys to Sustainable Living

Michael A. Schuler

BK

Berrett–Koehler Publishers, Inc.
San Francisco
a BK Life book

Berrett-Koehler Publishers, Inc.
235 Montgomery Street, Suite 650
San Francisco, CA 94104-2916
Tel: (415) 288-0260, Fax: (415) 362-2512, www.bkconnection.com

Ordering Information

Quantity sales: Special discounts are available on quantity purchases by corporations, associations, and others. For details, contact the "Special Sales Department" at the Berrett-Koehler address above.

Individual sales: Berrett-Koehler publications are available through most bookstores. They can also be ordered directly from Berrett-Koehler: Tel: (800) 929-2929; Fax: (802) 864-7626; www.bkconnection.com

Orders for college textbook/course adoption use: Please contact Berrett-Koehler: Tel: (800) 929-2929; Fax: (802) 864-7626.

Orders by U.S. trade bookstores and wholesalers: Please contact Ingram Publisher Services, Tel: (800) 509-4887; Fax: (800) 838-1149; E-mail: customer.service@ingrampublisherservices.com; or visit www.ingrampublisherservices.com/Ordering for details about electronic ordering.

Berrett-Koehler and the BK logo are registered trademarks of Berrett-Koehler Publishers, Inc.

Printed in the United States of America

Berrett-Koehler books are printed on long-lasting acid-free paper. When it is available, we choose paper that has been manufactured by environmentally responsible processes. These may include using trees grown in sustainable forests, incorporating recycled paper, minimizing chlorine in bleaching, or recycling the energy produced at the paper mill.

Editorial, design, and production services provided by CWL Publishing Enterprises, Inc, Madison, Wisconsin, www.cwlpub.com. Copyeditor: Judy Duguid,Proofreader: Marg Sumner, Indexer: Kevin Campbell

Library of Congress Cataloging-in-Publication Data

Schuler, Michael A.
  Making the good life last : four keys to sustainable living / by Michael A. Schuler.
    p. cm.
  Includes bibliographical references and index.
  ISBN 978-1-57675-570-9 (pbk. : alk. paper)
  1. Sustainable living—United States. 2. Quality of life—United States.
  I. Title.
  GE197.S38 2009
  640--dc22

                                                        2009004067

First Edition

14 13 12 11 10 09   10 9 8 7 6 5 4 3 2 1

For Trina, my loving life partner, whose patience, perseverance, input, and constant encouragement were indispensable to the creation of this book.

Contents

Foreword

by Scott Russell Sanders

How shall we live? Humans may be the only species that asks this question, or needs to. Of course, we cannot afford to ask it unless we have answered the prior question of how shall we survive? For the more than two billion humans who lack adequate food or shelter or drinking water, survival is still the overriding concern. But once we can trust that our basic needs will be met, either through our own efforts or through the support of our community, we may feel compelled to ask what we should do with our days beyond merely staying alive. What sorts of skills and knowledge should we seek? What sorts of work should we do? Should we marry and rear children? Where should we make our home? How should we treat one another? How should we treat the earth and its creatures? What responsibilities do we bear toward our neighbors? What do we owe to future generations? Does life have a purpose—for us as individuals, for our society, for our species—and, if so, what is that purpose and where does it come from?

These are perennial questions, which humans have pondered in all ages and in every land. While we can learn from what our predecessors have thought, we must also think for ourselves. If we are to lead examined lives, we must seek answers that accord with our deepest values; we must test those answers in practice; and we must do so not only once but again and again, as our circumstances and outlook change. Now, thanks to this book, we can do our seeking in the cordial company of Michael Schuler, who draws on sources of wisdom that range from the Buddha to Wendell Berry, and who delves into his experiences as husband, father, minister, athlete, and citizen, as he describes how he has chosen to lead his own life.

You can judge what Schuler values by the conduct he recommends. He values fidelity—not only in marriage, but also in pursuit of a calling, in devotion to a place or a cause, in friendship, in dedication to an art or a skill or a spiritual practice. He values equity—not only in the form of legal justice, but also in the compassionate treatment of neighbors and strangers, in the fair distribution of wealth and privilege within society and among nations, and in the due regard for the needs of future generations. He favors deliberation over speed—the savoring of home-cooked meals rather than the gobbling of fast food, an after-dinner stroll instead of a hectic video game, meditation instead of channel surfing. He urges moderation in eating, diligence in exercise, and persistence in all our heartfelt enterprises. He defends the wealth we hold in common, such as parks and schools and unpolluted air, as a counterbalance to an exaggerated concern for the wealth we own as individuals. He supports vigorous local economies as a buffer against remote rule by global corporations. He champions continuity over novelty, simplicity over luxury, thrift over profligacy, quality over quantity, cooperation over competition, conservation over consumption, gratitude over greed.

Schuler is well aware that such values set him in opposition to the main currents in contemporary American society. Free-market capitalism, obsessed with short-term profit and perpetual growth, averse to all constraints, is devouring the planet. Round-the-clock advertising inflames what Buddhists call the "hungry ghost" within us, a craving that gnaws at us constantly. While the malls distract us with endless stuff, the media distract us with endless stimulation. True, electronic technology opens us to new sources of information and new avenues of communication, but it also accelerates our lives, driving us from task to task, swamping us with messages, often forcing us to act without sufficient care.

A faith in technology as a remedy for all our ills serves as an excuse for continuing reckless behavior, such as our looting of the oceans and our destabilizing of earth's climate. The most aggressive form of religious faith in America today, is a millenarian version of Christianity that regards the earth as a warehouse for human exploitation, a mere backdrop for the drama of salvation, a fallen world to be eagerly left behind by the chosen few on their way to heaven. Even humanists insist on "human primacy," Schuler points out, and they tend to deny the reality of anything that cannot be measured by the tools of science or explained by the methods of reason.

Schuler takes on all of these "impediments," as he calls them, challenging widely shared notions about what makes for a good life. Among those he challenges are Americans who call themselves conservative while espousing unregulated markets, unrestrained population growth, drilling and mining in the last remnants of wilderness, property rights without responsibilities, ignorance about science and sex—ideologies and actions that shatter families, undermine communities, crowd out other species, lay waste the planet, and squander resources vital to the wellbeing of future generations. Schuler is a conservative in the root meaning of that word: he seeks to protect and nurture what he cherishes, from earth's bounty to personal health, from loving families to thriving communities, from handsome buildings to worthy traditions. He invites us to live in such a way that our descendants will be able to enjoy the blessings we have enjoyed. If you wish to reflect anew on what makes for a good life, a useful life, a virtuous life, then here is an enlightening book to consult as you ponder these ancient questions.

Scott Russell Sanders studied physics and English at Brown University, graduating in 1967. With the aid of a Marshall Scholarship, he pursued graduate work at the University of Cambridge, where he completed his Ph.D. in English in 1971. Since 1971 he has been teaching at Indiana University, where he is a Distinguished Professor of English. His writing examines the human place in nature, the pursuit of social justice, the relation between culture and geography, and the search for a spiritual path.

Among his more than 20 books are novels, collections of stories, and works of personal nonfiction, including Staying Put, Writing from the Center, *and* Hunting for Hope. *His latest book is* A Private History of Awe, *a coming-of-age memoir, love story, and spiritual testament, which was nominated for the Pulitzer Prize.* A Conservationist Manifesto, *his vision of a shift to a sustainable society, was published in 2009.*

Preface

Ten years or so ago, I decided to take my commitment to a healthy natural environment a step further. Strictly individual initiatives—what former Vice President Dick Cheney once characterized as an exercise in "personal virtue"—didn't go far enough. I wanted to energize and empower more people for this important work.

Several activists I knew had been instrumental in establishing neighborhood "Eco-Teams," and after quizzing them, I concluded that this might be a good place for me to make a meaningful contribution. The project would take some time and effort but, despite a busy schedule, seemed well within my capacity.

First came recruitment. Having compiled a list of possible participants within a four-block radius of my home, I began soliciting door-to-door, offering brief descriptions of the Eco-Team process and distributing invitations. These visits were followed up with phone calls, and within two weeks, six households had made a firm commitment.

At our initial orientation we met with a certified Eco-Team trainer from an organization called Sustain Dane, who patiently outlined the process and answered our questions. At subsequent meetings we discussed a wide range of lifestyle topics: driving habits, refuse and recycling practices, water consumption, dietary conventions, lawn and garden care, the toxicity of the cleaning products we typically used, and more.

Between these spirited sessions, we had homework to do. We timed our showers, weighed the household garbage before sending it into the trash stream, toted up vehicle mileage, inventoried our kitchen and bathroom cabinets, and explored "green" alternatives to conventional products for weed and insect control. Even those who were reasonably savvy about the environment learned a few things—the benefit to the watershed of using less salt in a water softener, for instance.

We also conceded that knowledge alone wasn't sufficient. Even those of us who knew quite well what environmental friendliness prescribed were plagued by inconsistency. However, the application of mild peer pressure made a difference, filling the gap between thought and action. As we discussed each subject, compared notes, and laughed about our foibles, members of my Eco-Team adopted new habits and gradually became more conscientious.

Having completed the assigned curriculum, the group decided to meet one final time for a potluck. We agreed that every dish would consist of locally sourced and/or sustainably produced items, that everyone would either bike or walk to the event, and that no paper plates or plastic utensils would be used. Even the wine was of Wisconsin vintage.

I share this experience for two reasons. First, to underscore the fact that useful information on the subject of environmental sustainability is relatively easy to find. There is no shortage of sources from which to elicit advice on how to shrink one's environmental footprint and adopt more earth-sensitive practices. The advantage of belonging to an Eco-Team is that the material was already consolidated for our use. But every month my utility bill comes with an insert on practical ways to conserve energy. The shelves of bookstores burgeon with titles like *A Hundred Ways to Save the Environment*. And information on the Internet seems almost boundless. Enter the word *sustainable* in your search engine, and in the twinkling of an eye it will provide you with a year's worth of reading options.

Although environmental issues figure prominently in this book and serve as a springboard for a much broader discussion of sustainability, it is not my intention to cover ground into which many others have already carved deep furrows. The particulars—how to choose an Energy Star appliance, maximize auto mileage, build and remodel in keeping with green standards—can easily be found elsewhere. This is not to say that readers won't find specific suggestions and recommendations in the chapters that follow, but for the most part they are embedded in an argument that differs significantly from the ones found in standard environmental literature.

In other words, although the principle that forms the nucleus of this book is sustainability, *Making the Good Life Last* is not a how-to manual in the conventional sense. After many years of thoughtful consideration, I've come to the conclusion that between the overarching concept of sustainability and myriad concrete applications, something has been missing: a set of behavioral "keys" which, when properly identified, defined, and taken to heart, lay the proper groundwork for adaptive action. What basic life skills must be developed and what sort of shift in perspective must occur for people to make constructive use of the nitty-gritty instructions they receive from so many other sources?

While the word *key* suggests that this book is about opening the door to a sustainable future, the term *precept* may give some readers a better sense of the direction I will take. According to *Webster's Dictionary*, a precept is an "intended rule of action." In Buddhism, for example, the foundations of moral and spiritual practice are referred to as precepts. But because that term has an unfamiliar and faintly esoteric ring to our Western ears, *key* is the preferred choice.

Although the public is gradually becoming convinced of the importance of sustainability and is better educated about its details, requirements, and payoffs, resistance to sustainable practices remains stubbornly in place. Until people make a major adjustment in the attitudes they bring to their daily activities, this principle will not become a personal priority for most of them. As Eckhart Tolle has warned, "If the structures of the human mind remain unchanged, we will always end up recreating fundamentally the same world, the same evils, the same dysfunction."[1]

More specifically, I believe serious consideration must be given to four life skills, or core behaviors: *paying attention, staying put, exercising patience,* and *practicing prudence.* Over the years I have found that if I make an effort to put these keys into practice on a regular basis, my choices will be wiser, healthier, and more considerate. What follows, then, is mostly about this "missing middle" and its implications.

The second reason my experience in organizing and facilitating that Eco-Team is relevant to this topic has to do with its social implications. In the end, our efforts proved as efficacious for community building as for environmental stewardship. Although the participants all lived within a quarter mile of one another and had all resided in the immediate area for quite some time, we came together initially as strangers—people who recognized but really did not know each other.

Unfortunately, this is the rule rather than the exception. Modern life keeps us so busy and on the go, television and computers are so seductive, and our fears and suspicions have made us so wary that often we are unable to establish a mutually beneficial bond even with the family at the end of the block. People today lament that they feel less safe, that they find fewer opportunities for interpersonal support and assistance, and that they frequently feel abused by the impersonal way the world treats them, all of which testify to the need for a resurrection of community.

This won't happen just because we want it to. For a community to coalesce, its members have to be more proactive, organizing block parties, Eco-Teams, book discussion groups, child-care co-ops. In the twenty-first century, the human ecology—our towns and neighborhoods—needs help almost as desperately as the natural environment, which means that the principle of sustainability has the potential for wider applications than we might previously have thought.

As a parish minister, my primary job for the past thirty years has been to create, nurture, and strengthen community. Over time, I have increasingly come to appreciate that human beings cannot thrive or be happy in isolation or by the assiduous pursuit of individual self-interest. No living thing can prosper for very long outside of a prosperous community or environment, but in recent decades many of us apparently thought we could.

My own faith tradition, Unitarian Universalism, has long encouraged its members to recognize their social and biological interdependence and to align their values with that fundamental reality. This has been a frequent theme in my own preaching and teaching, and I have written this book to address a long-standing concern—one that was also shared by our third president and professed Unitarian, Thomas Jefferson. A true free spirit in many respects, Jefferson also realized that what benefits the individual must prove beneficial for all. The quest for a just and happy life—the good life, if you will—must of necessity become a *communal* endeavor.[2]

Sustainability has become for me a source of serious interest for other reasons as well. Helping people to discover or make meaning, to become more appreciative, grateful, and giving, has been another focus of my ministry. People come to faith communities because they know something important is missing in their lives, and often they aren't quite sure what it is or how to go about getting it. Spirituality is about that "something more" in life that a material- and pleasure-oriented culture can't provide. Sustainability can, I believe, also speak to this yearning. In our chaotic, increasingly unpredictable world, individuals and families are looking for grounding—a few reliable points of reference to steady themselves.

This book generalizes from observations I've made during three decades of working intimately with individuals and families, at all stages and walks of life, from cradle to grave. It is also the product of someone who has lived and worked in a number of distinctive places: rural Illinois, Florida resort communities, a northeastern industrial city, university towns in the Middle and Far West. During my own lifetime some of these places have undergone radical transformation, and not always for the better. They had not incorporated the principle of sustainability into their developmental road map.

Making the Good Life Last integrates my own personal experiences with insights from a variety of disciplines, from the Eastern and Western spiritual classics, from scientists, novelists, philosophers, and poets. Out of this material I've extracted some common threads that can help us understand where we've wandered astray and what we need to do to get on the right track.

Sustainability is a concept whose time has come. The purpose of this book is to liberate it from the environmental and economic confines where specialists in those fields have placed it and move the discussion to a higher level. Sustainability is a life-affirming principle that ought to be included in any updated list of the cardinal virtues.

As the title implies, what is at stake here is nothing more or less than the "good life"—not the evanescent "good times" that movie theaters, restaurants, and amusement parks provide, but a way of being in the world that delivers regular, dependable satisfaction.

How do people in the world today typically envision the good life? Open your browser and punch in those two words and note the images that appear: photos of people lolling by the seashore, drinking champagne, driving expensive sports cars, being pampered by masseurs, skiing or skydiving. The depictions include big bouquets of long-stemmed roses, diamond necklaces, wads of cash, impeccably furnished penthouses—all representations of over-the-top luxury and once-in-a-lifetime vacations. If this is the principle way in which we conceive of the good life, is it any wonder that so many people feel deprived and dissatisfied?

We need to revise our thinking and our expectations, because the correlation of financial and material well-being with happiness is limited. Beyond a certain modest level of achievement, it largely disappears. What seems, rather, to make human beings reliably happy are good health, dependable relationships, personal integrity, altruistic service, feelings of belonging, a sense of calling, and the ability to savor the moment without regret or anxiety.

The ideas and arguments of *Making the Good Life Last* unfold as follows. The Introduction unpacks the concept of "sustainability" and explains its relevance for the good life. We look at some of the consequences of our cultural neglect of this concept and offer a few brief examples of sustainability's utility for both the person and the planet.

In Chapter 1 the four "keys"—pay attention, stay put, exercise patience, and practice prudence—are introduced, and examples are provided of each one in action. Four very powerful patterns of thought, or belief systems, have helped create adverse conditions for the institutionalization of sustainable principles in our culture. Although Christianity, humanism, capitalism, and what I have dubbed "techno-idealism" contain many positive features, others deserve serious scrutiny. In the interest of a sustainable future, each of these influential systems will need to make certain concessions. This is the focus of Chapter 2.

Chapters 3 through 6 expand the discussion of the four keys initiated in Chapter 1. In each instance, the key is further explained and arguments for its relevance presented. A variety of relevant examples will help the reader see how each key can be usefully applied in both our individual and collective lives and how each contributes to the good life.

Finally, the Conclusion addresses the spiritual advantages of putting the four keys into active practice. Even those who profess not to be religious in the conventional sense crave meaning, a sense of purpose, and a desire to leave an honorable legacy. What person would prefer to feel bitter rather than experience the beneficence of life, or to approach death unfulfilled and, as a result, abjectly fearful? If we can face and come to terms with these deep and difficult questions, the good life is likely to last into and through our old age.

I will argue that this life is available to us right now, with little or nothing added. It deals with the everyday and the unexceptional, attended to and raised to a new level of appreciation. The good life is ours for the making and the sustaining. By the time you finish this book, I hope you'll have a much better sense of how that might be accomplished.

Introduction

Sustaining Ourselves

A Personal Awakening

A four-month sabbatical in late 2005 lent both substance and a sense of urgency to a question that had been nagging at me for quite some time: what would it take, and what would it mean, to move toward a more sustainable way of living?

My wife, Trina, and I were fortunate to have been offered the use of a lovely home in northwest Tucson for this period of writing and reflection. Tucson is the second largest city in Arizona and reputedly the most progressive metropolis in the desert Southwest. Its neighborhoods literally fill the cavity between four rugged mountain ranges. Fast-moving traffic hums along the wide thoroughfares that crisscross the desert, connecting the urban area's growing population to a plethora of strip malls, office complexes, and recreational facilities. New residential and commercial developments continue to spring up at the peripheries, scaling the Santa Catalina foothills and fingering north through the Sonora Desert toward Phoenix.

Over 700,000 human beings now live in the Tucson area, and for Pima County as a whole the numbers climb to almost a million. Historically, the inhospitable climate of southern Arizona made it unattractive to all but the hardiest of indigenous peoples, the

Tohono O'odham. Even the Spanish found little in the area to recommend permanent settlement, at least not on the scale of an El Paso or a Santa Fe.

Tucson is, therefore, a fairly young city by southwestern standards. A settlement of little consequence until the 1880s, it has existed as a viable center of human habitation for less than a century and a quarter. But with the presence of a major university and a nearby military installation, and with a steady influx of legions of sun lovers from the continent's colder regions, Tucson has grown rapidly and somewhat randomly since World War II.

The community's popularity has produced its share of negative results. Gazing south from the Catalina foothills during morning rush hour, one often has difficulty locating the downtown through a low-lying bank of unhealthy-looking yellow smog, a phenomenon created almost exclusively by a flood of auto commuters. The standard of living in Tucson is woefully unbalanced; as a result, crimes against property are climbing, and in their wake, the number of economically segregated, gated communities is growing. Residents express worry about such developments, as well as the steady deterioration of Tucson's unique southwestern ambience and its overall quality of life. Still, any effort to control growth or intelligently manage further development inevitably falters before the irrefutable claims of the free market and the individual citizen's presumed right to personal gain. Prior to the 2008–09 recession, officials estimated that Greater Tucson would gain another half million residents in the next thirty to forty years—a prospect that had local construction and real estate interests licking their lips in anticipatory delight.

However, for a Sun Belt community Tucson does seem relatively enlightened. While Greater Phoenix appears to be determined to *repudiate* its native desert environment, Tucson has chosen to accept and even to embrace it. Houses in Tucson almost without exception eschew green turf and feature natural, desert plantings. Drip irrigation systems are the rule, and per capita water consumption is significantly lower than in comparable southwestern cities.[1]

Furthermore, while its public transportation system is unexceptional, Tucson has established and continues to expand an admirable network of bike routes (of which many citizens take full advantage). The city is reasonably clean, its public parks attractive, and the populace generally friendly and conscientious.

Perhaps because I lived there only temporarily and have no personal stake in Tucson, it was easier for me to size up the situation and ponder the question that too few of the city's residents seem to be asking: Is this community truly sustainable?

Tucsonans could not possibly, in their current numbers, live off the land. The environment itself is capable of sustaining only a very few human beings. The community ultimately and absolutely depends upon imported power and commodities and, most crucially, the wholesale extraction of what in the Southwest is essentially a nonrenewable resource: fresh water. Like that of its southwestern counterparts, Tucson's success has been achieved not by embracing but by defiantly opposing the harsh laws of the local ecosystem. For this community to remain viable, it must receive huge daily transfusions of lifeblood from elsewhere. This explains how it has managed to grow to such staggering proportions and to create an immense oasis of comfort and prosperity in the bleakest of environments.

These facts receive only occasional and cursory mention in the local media, and generally they are rebutted by politicians, entrepreneurs, and journalists extolling the desirability—nay, the necessity—of further growth (the lead editorial in the November 14, 2005, edition of the *Arizona Daily Star* cordially invited Californians fleeing that state and its high home prices to relocate in affordable southern Arizona). Nevertheless, I have the impression that people in Tucson *do* sense the precariousness of their situation and realize how little it would take for the prickly pear and saguaro to reclaim their ancient dominion. But as long as faucets are flowing and the air conditioners are keeping the blazing desert sun at bay, it remains possible to bracket such fears and go blithely about one's daily business, and even invite *more* business.

A Day of Reckoning?
Who can say when the systems of artificial life-support upon which Tucson and a half-dozen other overzealous and overbuilt southwestern communities depend will begin to fail? I am certainly

no authority on such matters, but simple common sense tells me that the day of reckoning is not too distant. The populations have grown too large and are far too profligate for the status quo to be maintained, much less improved upon. Nor are the peoples of arid Arizona the only ones who need to ask this question. Florida has become an environmental basket case. In few places has growth occurred so rapidly and in such haphazard fashion. According to the Environmental Defense Fund, of 3,400 applications for a permit to destroy a Florida wetland submitted in 2003, the Corps of Engineers denied only one. A developer's paradise, Florida has sacrificed so much of its natural heritage and become so crowded and congested that someone like me, who came of age on its southwest coast just three decades ago, barely recognizes his old haunts. Ironically, further development may soon be stymied in Florida and throughout the drought-stricken Southeast by a dearth of fresh water.

Problems in the Heartland

Unfortunately, it is by no means necessary to travel to Cactus Country or to the Sunshine State to appreciate the scope and depth of this problem. My family's home for the past twenty years has been Madison, Wisconsin—a relatively small, stable, and compact city by comparison with sprawling Tucson or Orlando. Nevertheless, the Greater Madison area has grown significantly during my time here, with land-hungry suburbs and exurbs gobbling up prime farmland and air quality advisories becoming increasingly common on sultry summer days. Frankly, I never thought I'd see the day when Madison residents would be urged to curtail outdoor exercise because of high ozone readings.

Equally unsettling has been the deterioration of the local watershed. Historically, Madison has been known and frequently lauded as the "City of the Lakes." Even today, it isn't uncommon for an angler to hook a good-sized game fish within sight of the gleaming State Capitol. Appearances, however, can be deceiving. Groundwater is being pumped so aggressively that aquifers beneath the city are falling rapidly, which has led surface streams in the area to dry up, caused wells to fail, and compromised the quality of lakes already degraded by nonpoint source pollution. By comparison with most other states, Wisconsin is considered "water rich," but both Madison and Waukesha County to the east now anticipate future water shortages and are scrambling to develop contingency plans. One has to wonder whether Greater Madison, a community less than half the size of Tucson, adjacent to several large bodies of water, and situated in the nation's breadbasket, is itself sustainable. The answer is no if current practices remain unaltered. (*Note:* The federal government projects that at least thirty-six states will face water shortages of varying severity before 2012.)[2]

Sustainability: A Concept Whose Time Has Come

It has become increasingly clear that the wholesale development of sprawling, resource-hungry urban complexes is both ecologically unsound and socially problematic. Even the sanguine Thomas Friedman of *The New York Times* has come to realize that the future depends on humanity's willingness and ability to husband the planet's resources. Depletion of natural capital is an "enormously powerful threat," Friedman writes in his book *The World Is Flat*. "Be afraid. I certainly am."[3]

However, I am convinced that this well-documented trend represents but one thread in a broader pattern of unhealthy, short-sighted human behavior. Although this book contains numerous environmental allusions and analogies, the overarching purpose of these chapters is to deepen and broaden our understanding of sustainability in terms of our attitudes, values, and decision making and to demonstrate the relevance of sustainability in resolving personal as well as planetary problems. The basic premise is that substantial improvement in the quality of our lives and livelihoods would be possible if we better understand this fundamental principle and a short list of reinforcing behaviors.

Expanded Applications

Until fairly recently, discussions of sustainability remained largely within the province of certain professions. Ecologists and conservationists have focused on sustainable farming methods and the wise use of natural resources. Architects and engineers have worked to develop protocols for constructing "green" buildings. Concern over persistent poverty in developing nations has led to innovative proposals for the "sustainable development" of stagnant economies— a movement inspired by E. F. Schumacher's now-classic work, *Small Is Beautiful.* Interest in sustainability gradually has spread, moving beyond professional and academic circles into the general population. The term has entered the popular lexicon, and increasing numbers of people now have at least a rudimentary notion of its meaning and significance.

Even so, sustainability today remains a somewhat marginal and, in some quarters, even a subversive idea. Despite growing mainstream acceptance, it is cynically dismissed by some as a manifestation of political correctness or environmental faddism—an impediment to economic growth and a barrier to the optimal performance of the free market.

For example, in a recent opinion piece by Bill Berry, Milwaukeean Patrick McIlheren offered this caustic definition of *sustainable:* "Doing things in a wildly expensive, pointlessly ineffective way for political reasons. Implies an extra $5 a pound."[4]

For some, sustainability may appear more threatening than promising, which is why sustainable products (e.g., green buildings, natural foods, recycled products) still represent a relatively small share of the total market and are, in some cases, prohibitively expensive. Although experts generally agree that prevailing production methods and consumption patterns are untenable, as a culture we are still a long way from hitting the tipping point where conventional thinking about development and the economy gives way and people everywhere begin routinely to factor sustainable principles into their thinking and planning.

A case in point: Until the 2008 Summer Olympic Games caused the world to give the booming Chinese economy a second, closer look, that country received near-constant commendation for its accomplishments from Western economists. It is now becoming apparent that China's rapid and unprecedented industrial expansion has been purchased at a staggering cost to the environment and to the health of its own citizens. Regrettably, sustainable development remains the exception rather than the rule for many of the most "robust" economies of the developing world.

Common Assumptions and Uncommon Associations

Sustainability arose during the environmental movement and has remained closely identified with it. The term is most often used to describe a resource utilization strategy that preserves or even replenishes the earth's natural capital. Care must be taken to keep the ledger in balance, which means planning for renewal and restoration, as well as expropriation and extraction. Sound practices such as reuse, recycling, and the tapping of renewable, nonpolluting sources of energy like the sun, wind, biomass, and geothermal are frequently mentioned components of environmental sustainability. These and similar measures are meant to keep human civilization and the biotic systems that support it viable far into the future.

Because of its frequent invocation by environmentalists, some, like Milwaukee's columnist Patrick McIlheren, associate sustainability with liberal thinking and politics. At a practical level, though, the idea tilts in a decidedly conservative direction. Among primary synonyms of *sustain* found in *Webster's* are these: "to maintain," "to prolong," "to preserve," "to protect or keep safe." There's nothing particularly "liberal" about any of those terms, and no less a figure than Russell Kirk—founder of *The National Review* and patron saint of modern American conservatism—identified "social continuity" as one of the conservative movement's core objectives.[5] A conservative, in other words, has an obligation to protect those assets that ensure the long-term health and dynamism of a culture or community.

Moreover, one of sustainability's earliest champions—the noted conservationist Aldo Leopol—tried hard to convince parties across the political spectrum of the concept's merits. Leopold's supporters included many prominent Republicans, and his own attitude toward the "liberal" conservation policies of Franklin D. Roosevelt's New Deal was ambivalent at best (he distrusted government-mandated

programs because they did little to create the broad cultural consensus he believed was necessary for a conservation ethic to take
hold). Leopold's was truly a nonpartisan position, and his goal was
to build a case for environmental stewardship that both Democrats
and Republicans could embrace. As his biographer Curt Meine
observes:

> Conservation, in Leopold's view, was not bound to any par-
> ticular philosophy. From his earliest days as a forester, he was
> (simply) concerned with keeping ends and means balanced.[6]

Becoming Restorative

As a result of Aldo Leopold's work, recent decades have witnessed
growing sophistication in the field of *restoration biology*. In keeping
with the first principle of Leopold's "Land Ethic"—a thing is right
when it tends to preserve the integrity, stability, and beauty of the
biotic community—the intent of environmental restoration work is
to reverse the deterioration of so many of the planet's critical life-
supporting systems and thus make the land and water healthy and
productive again.[7] Here modern technical knowledge is being used
literally to turn back the clock.

Writer and entrepreneur Paul Hawken also uses the term
restoration to describe a new way of doing business. "The Golden
Rule of a restorative economy," Hawken writes, "is to leave the
world *better* than you found it; take no more than you need; try
not to harm life or the environment; make amends if you do."[8]

By extension, one can easily see how this same "restorative"
idea might be usefully enlisted to resolve some of the serious social
and familial problems that have arisen in recent decades. The
stresses that the typical modern nuclear family faces have clearly
been exacerbated by the sundering of the generations in the late
twentieth century. But what if grandparents were encouraged and
given incentives to live with or near their adult children and growing grandchildren? How much more livable would our major cities
be if greater efforts were made to restore old, pedestrian-friendly
neighborhoods so that people would be less prone to settle in
anonymous, automobile-dependent suburbs? Cities ought to be
attractive for the quality of life they afford, not just because rising

gasoline costs give them an economic advantage. The shift away from extended families and livable cities has largely taken place within my own lifetime, but there is no reason it cannot be reversed. In fact, in certain quarters that's already happening.

The principle of sustainability is truly conservative, then, in that it seeks to protect and preserve those key elements that keep a system healthy and in balance. But that could suggest a steady state in which any new or novel elements are unwelcome. Clearly, insulating a system from outside influences that might produce change isn't always, if ever, advisable. If the "good life" is our goal, something more must be added to our definition of sustainability.

To Support and to Nourish

We have considered one possible meaning of the term *sustainable*: to preserve, protect, and keep safe. But for our purposes, one of the secondary definitions is more appropriate. To sustain, *Webster's* dictionary continues, means "to nourish or support." *Support* is a more far-reaching term than *preserve* and is more in keeping with the fact that it is in the nature of people, social systems, and ecologies to grow, adapt, and evolve. Change is inevitable, and correctly understood, the principle of sustainability accommodates change and invites the human imagination to participate in and intelligently contribute to the overall process.

A sustainable ecology, economy, community, or family system isn't cast in concrete. Balance, not stasis, is the true objective, as Aldo Leopold reminds us. Carefully considered and cautiously implemented change is, he believed, perfectly consistent with sound conservation principles. It's important that we understand sustainability as a dynamic principle. The ultimate objective is to improve life, but with the accompanying awareness that not every change represents an improvement. To disrupt, destroy, or substantially alter anything that retains significant practical or aesthetic value subverts sustainability's intent.

A case in point: In some parts of the world the notion of "sustainable tourism" has lately come into vogue. Its purpose is to ensure that the unique characteristics of perennially popular destinations—the coral reefs of the Caribbean, the wildlife of the

Galapagos, the waterfronts of Charleston and Savannah, the light-houses and orchards of Wisconsin's Door County, and the architecture of Victoria, British Columbia—are made a community priority and maintained in their integrity. Too often, tourist hot spots allow their most notable features to deteriorate or are overrun by the kind of cookie-cutter dining, shopping, and entertainment venues that can be found in Everytown, U.S.A. "Sustainable tourism," Myles Dannhausen writes,

> Is based on the idea of pinpointing the difference between simply attracting visitors at all costs and attracting visitors who won't cost you who you are.... To get there you need to do an inventory of the cultural, natural and human assets that set you apart.[9]

What sustainability eschews, then, are those quick fixes (economic or otherwise) whose long-term consequences have been insufficiently anticipated and for which contingency plans have not been made. It is a principle that challenges the juggernaut of rapid, unreflective growth and development that now poses a bona fide threat to the well-being of the planet and most of its people. It seeks to control the pace at which civilization barrels ahead, refusing to enter into devil's bargains that make the "bottom line" look better at the expense of justice, beauty, and equity.

The intelligent practice of sustainable principles attempts to take the past, present, and future equally into consideration. It is not about clinging stubbornly to an unsatisfactory status quo, but it also refuses to accept the undiscerning assumption that "new is always improved." In fact, a sustainable solution may involve a return to the status quo ante to restore health *and* balance to a system.

The Joie de Vivre chain of boutique hotels in California affords a fine example. Founded by Chip Conley in 1987, the company generates several hundred million dollars of revenue a year. Conley offers his guests the kind of old-fashioned, individually tailored service that other hotel chains dispensed with years ago. As a result, JdV generates more return business than its rivals and has fared better during tough economic times. Its traditional orientation has helped Conley's enterprises prosper in the present.

But this perceptive entrepreneur also has an eye to the future. The average hotel experiences a sixty percent turnover of personnel every year. As a result, extra resources must be devoted to training, and employees never develop sufficient loyalty to do their best work. JdV's turnover rate is just twenty-five percent because management works hard to ensure that everyone on staff—even those who spend their days scrubbing down toilets and shower stalls—feels appreciated, challenged, and valued as part of a meaningful community effort. Conley runs a sustainable operation that "invests in long-term growth based on a strategy of integrity and creativity that aligns with the interests of all stakeholders."[10]

Reassessing Our Priorities

By now it is becoming clear that sustainability offers a useful handle for reorienting our thinking and adjusting our behavior in just about every significant area of human endeavor. It is, in fact, one of those guiding principles that thoughtful people ought to take into account in making any important lifestyle, relational, or ethical choice. When we set goals, establish objectives, or contemplate a new course of action, we would be wise to consider not only the profitability or practical utility of those measures, but also their sustainability. In a world dominated by short-term strategic planning, we need to develop coherent strategies for anticipating adverse reactions and making sure that what we do ensures long-term viability.

It has become something of a cliché to criticize ours as a culture of immediate gratification and momentary impulse, but that doesn't belie the basic accuracy of the complaint. The fact is, even most grocery store purchases are spur-of-the-moment rather than planned. Whether we are choosing a breakfast cereal, a profession, or an intimate partner, a community, a spiritual practice, or a fitness regimen, whether we are investing in a retirement plan or volunteering our services, the horizons of our thinking remain in the near distance. We shake our heads in dismay over the lack of cohesion in our neighborhoods, the fragility of our relationships, the poor condition of our bodies, and the despondency of our spirits; yet we don't do what's required to create a healthier and more stable lifestyle.

Among the many books and articles I've consulted and the numerous conversations I've had on matters of healthy, happy, and virtuous living, the principle of sustainability has received scant attention. Why are we so oblivious to a concept that would seem absolutely central to our long-term best interests? Is the idea so simple and self-evident that most people take for granted that cities will persist, careers continue, and marriages last "until death do us part"? But the fact that sustainability has been an uncommon rather than a common occurrence in recorded history would seem to indicate that, self-evident or not, it has seldom attracted much of a following. So perhaps a clearer explication of the idea and a few suggestions for useful application will help move us in the right direction.

Sustainability: A Means, Not an End

To begin with, sustainability must be understood as an instrumental rather than a terminal value; that is to say, it is a means and not an end. We embrace sustainable principles and adopt sustainable practices because they help produce something else that we deem important. Compassion, justice, peace, beauty, and happiness are generally regarded as ends in themselves whose individual or collective realization defines a good life. Sustainability belongs in another category, for it always invites the further question: sustainable for what?

Geof Syphers works as a sustainability officer for Codding Enterprises, a development firm in Northern California that specializes in environmentally responsible design, and he understands this perfectly. The goal of Sonoma Mountain Village, one of Codding's more notable projects, was to create the conditions for residents to enjoy a healthy, environmentally sound lifestyle. "Sustainability isn't a goal," Syphers insists. "It is a process."[11]

Today's world does not suffer from a dearth of sound, terminal values. Human beings still yearn for beauty, happiness, intimacy, and an honorable legacy, just as our forebears did. However, deeper wisdom and more deliberate effort are needed if we are to gain and maintain the ends we seek.

The Futility of the Hungry Ghost

Buddhist teachings describe perpetually dissatisfied, grasping, overanxious people as "hungry ghosts." As much as they long for happiness and the experience of true contentment, these sad individuals are unenlightened about how an abiding sense of well-being might be secured. Moreover, they haven't acquired the tools or the self-discipline to tap into these wellsprings of nourishment. The "hungry ghost" subsists, therefore, on the deceptively thin fare its culture provides—easily appropriated pleasures that dull the cravings but do not satisfy them. The habit of happiness, beauty that is more than skin-deep, and trustworthy relationships all lie beyond the ghost's reach and are usually beyond its ken.

In the Chinese language, the two words *pin* and *tan* look very similar on the printed page. The first means "greed," and the other stands for "poverty." This, in a nutshell, is the dilemma of the hungry ghost: greedy for experiences and possessions to fill its emptiness; yet for all the effort the ghost expends, it still feels impoverished. The hungry ghost may compensate for its emptiness through the compulsive quest for pleasure and prestige, but it is unlikely to find in such pursuits any antidote for its chronic discontent. This Buddhist metaphor is compelling; it graphically describes a condition that afflicts many Americans.

The promising road maps offered by our hard-won consumerist culture have too often led us down blind alleys and into cul-de-sacs. Novelty, excitement, sensory stimulation, and satiation are supplied in abundance, but in terms of what human beings truly want and need, the systems we have devised have proved less than salutary. For example, at one time a house was truly a domicile, a place of familial interaction and neighborly connection. But in recent years many people have been persuaded to treat houses as investments, places to be occupied only until they can be "flipped" for a healthy profit (though the bursting of the housing bubble has caused most people to reconsider this strategy). Such behavior may or may not make sound economic sense, but it undermines all attempts to establish a sustainable community life. Too many of us have lost our connection to a sustainable life path that leads to treasures of perennial value: a beautiful and healthy earth home, human communities where all are well served and feel secure, work that makes a genuine contribution to the common good, play that restores one's body and lifts one's spirits, to mention only a few estimable goals. "To live lightly on the earth with simple, joyful elegance" is how one writer characterized the overarching purpose of sustainability.[12]

Timeless Elements of the Good Life

From a historical standpoint, our contemporary, consumer-oriented culture's conception of the good life is probably the exception rather than the rule. As cultural geographer Yi Fu Tuan's studies indicate, physical comfort "is without doubt a component of the good life," but by itself is hardly sufficient. Moreover, only a modicum of comfort is required for human beings to experience a sense of physical well-being. Yi Fu Tuan cites the example of a traditional Mongolian family, the day's chores accomplished, enjoying the evening meal together in the snug confines of their yurt. They play music, sing, tell stories, and are grateful for protection from the outside elements. By contrast, many of the royal and very rich have learned to their dismay that "comfort and splendor are incompatible."[13]

Cultural conceptions of the good life do vary, but certain features remain fairly consistent. Robust good health and vitality—even physical exuberance—are an unalloyed blessing. Intimacy—physical, emotional, or intellectual—makes a big difference. Remember the last time you had a deep and meaningful conversation with someone and how satisfying that felt? "A meeting of minds can be as . . . intoxicating as a meeting of bodies," Yi Fu Tuan writes.[14] Rendering service, enhancing the well-being of others, also contributes to our sense of life's goodness. In this respect, self-aggrandizing behavior may actually prove counterproductive, compromising rather than complementing our happiness. Yi Fu Tuan quotes a repairman who contrasts the experience of fixing a television for a house full of appreciative children with other jobs where fee-for-service is his only reward. "Knowing that I made a family happy" magnified the repairman's sense of accomplishment.[15]

Yi Fu Tuan also mentions "having a home base"—an attachment not just to people but to place—as something most humans associate with the good life. Even nomadic peoples and wanderers acquire a deep knowledge of the wider regions through which they move, and thus they feel closely connected to their environment. Engaging in productive labor that serves a valid purpose can be deeply satisfying—particularly when performed in the company of others who are also invested in the enterprise.[16] These and other aspects of "good living" will be treated in greater detail in the pages that follow.

Certainly not all human aspirations and endeavors are worth sustaining. Those who created and successfully maintained a brutal culture of apartheid in South Africa may well have found the concept useful. Likewise, the Fascist tyrants who boasted of establishing a "thousand-year Reich."

As an instrumental value, sustainability can certainly be applied to any number of projects, not all of them life-affirming. My purpose, however, is to align this principle with positive outcomes that serve to support, enhance, and dignify life. As such, it can operate as a counterweight to maladaptive public and private policies that support short-term private interests to the detriment of the long-term welfare of both the person and the planet.

Therefore, rather than remain a regretful afterthought, sustainability needs to move to the forefront of our thinking. This is how we will create lives that work not just for ourselves but, more critically, for the many generations that succeed our own whose interests we have inexcusably betrayed. David Brower, former executive director of the Sierra Club, once said that conservation should be a matter of conscience, and thus a consideration in everything we do and in every field of endeavor.[17] Similarly, it should be our aim to place *sustainable* precepts (or keys) and protocols at the forefront of our thinking and to apply them as consistently as possible.

What Do We Have to Lose?

For more than a few people, the word *sustainability* suggests the need for sacrifice and the likelihood that at least some of the amenities to which we have been accustomed will have to be reduced, if not given up altogether. That possibility makes the principle less palatable to some and raises the hackles of others. Because of its historic connection with environmentalism, sustainability may also be faulted with placing nonhuman interests above legitimate human needs. Such perceptions create a major problem, for if people worry that sustainability will lead to deprivation rather than to a noticeable enhancement of human life, they are likely to balk.

There is no use denying that some moderation of expectations, some deferral of gratification, some cultivation of new interests, and some consideration of healthier alternatives will need to occur if the serious problems confronting us are to be successfully resolved. For a new door to open, an old door will need to close. The prospects, however, are exciting provided we take the time to explore the concept thoroughly and thereby come to realize how preferable a secure, sustainable future would be to the "anxious age" with which we are presently trying to cope.

The whole purpose behind sustainability is to spare humankind the experience of scarcity and the need for major sacrifices. It is the sturdy thread which, when woven daily into the relational, vocational, and spiritual fabric of our lives, ensures that future generations *will* enjoy a quality of life superior to our own.

New Relevance for an Ancient Story

Aesop's venerable fable of the grasshopper and the ant is worth reviewing here. The grasshopper, you may recall, spent his summer days in leisurely fashion and couldn't be bothered to put away provisions for the winter ahead. Moreover, he laughed at his industrious neighbor the ant, who took the necessary precautions. To put it bluntly, ours has become a nation overpopulated with grasshoppers—impetuous adults who have been so conditioned and are so eager to "grab the gusto while they can" that many now lack sufficient restraint to establish a college fund for their children or to make adequate provision for medical emergencies or for their own retirement. Like the grasshopper, we are determined not to miss out on the good life (defined almost exclusively in terms of material possessions and physical pleasure) and are perfectly willing to let the future take care of itself. Deceptive lending practices aside, the lingering home mortgage crisis and burgeoning credit card balances reveal just how incautious many Americans have become. To be sure, through no fault of their own, single working parents and low wage earners may have found themselves in a bind. But when the savings-to-debt ratio for the *average* family falls into the negative range, it is hard not to conclude that many otherwise intelligent men and women have lost touch with economic reality. Whether we describe it as irrational exuberance or cockeyed optimism, it hardly reflects a sustainable sensibility.

Aesop's ant was neither a puritan nor a drudge, but I would hazard that in remembering this cautionary tale, most Americans would describe that wee creature as uninspiring—risk averse and not much fun to be with. The logic of the ant colony runs counter to much that we have been taught and are encouraged to do. Indebtedness is a privilege, not a problem; and without the grasshopper's uninhibited quest for instant gratification, the whole world economy would collapse. No matter what those finger-wagging ants might say, "the American standard of living is simply not negotiable," as former President George H. W. Bush famously put it.

My own bias is toward the ant, and not just because I see the wisdom of making prudent provision for the cold winter ahead. I've learned that despite the modifications it requires, a sustainable life really is the *good* life. When a person manages to get it right—that is, when it becomes more or less second nature to use this principle as a touchstone in one's daily endeavors—the quality of mental, emotional, and moral satisfaction that's achieved more than compensates for any perceived sacrifice of short-term stimulation or pleasure.

Environmental writer Bill McKibben admits that, for him, "sustainability is a vexed term" because even its advocates can't agree on what it means. But having said as much, he offers this ant-like assessment:

But we know, instinctively, what it *doesn't* mean. It doesn't mean fast, and it doesn't mean cheap, and it doesn't mean easy. Those are the hallmarks of our economy at the moment, the things we hold up as our highest goals. ... We want a planet that is deeply rooted and patient and solid, a world that we can count on, and an economy that's mature.[18]

Sustainability at Work

There is hardly any area of human endeavor to which we cannot usefully apply sustainability, but let's look for a moment at work—an enterprise to which most people, of necessity, devote considerable time and energy for upwards of 50 years. Having pursued the same line of work—parish ministry—for a third of a century, I often feel like something of an oddball. Yes ... people in professional fields like mine probably enjoy greater vocational longevity than some others. And yes ... the vagaries of a volatile job market do make it more difficult for many workers to stay in place. Still, planning for and pursuing a career is by no means as commonplace as it was even a few decades ago. Job-hopping and retraining are becoming the rule rather than the exception both because economic changes require it and because people are reporting lower levels of intrinsic satisfaction from the work they do and are thus eager to move on. Even the ministry—historically a remarkably stable profession—is seeing fewer and fewer "lifers." Only a handful of those who prepared with me for parish service have remained committed to their calling.

Bouncing from one workplace to the other may be advantageous in some respects, but it can reduce the individual's opportunity for making career advancements, for mastering a particular set of skills, for acquiring good health and retirement benefits, and for establishing a stable home life. Careful and thorough consideration of potential drawbacks is always in order before accepting a new opportunity.

Maintaining a career is by no means easy and has undoubtedly become more difficult in an uncertain, global economy. But all things being equal, it does make sense to choose and stick with work that will provide not only financial security but, in the long run, a real sense of accomplishment. I happen to think that a sustainable career is one of life's great blessings, and recent research suggests that it also contributes significantly to good mental health.[19] Following the four keys of sustainability—Pay Attention, Stay Put, Exercise Patience, and Practice Prudence—may allow that to happen.

Sustainable Relationships

An analysis performed recently by the Institute for American Values indicates that for the first time since World War II, women and men who married in the late 1970s had a less than even chance of still being married twenty-five years later.[20] From my own observation, it appears that civil unions between same-sex couples fare no better than heterosexual marriages.

My wife, Trina, and I have been partners for considerably more years than I've served as a minister, and we feel fortunate to have shared so much of our lives together. We met as juniors in high school and began "going steady" after only a few months. We attended different colleges but tied the nuptial knot following four years of lengthy weekend commutes. (We were lucky that gas was dirt cheap in those days.) In 2005, joined by family and a few close friends, Trina and I celebrated thirty-two years of marriage and eighteen years of successful parenting with a sunrise renewal-of-vows ceremony on a bluff overlooking Lake Mendota.

How do you make love stay? That straightforward question also happens to be the title of a song composed by a friend of mine for his fiancée. I had the honor of presiding at their marriage, and as far as I know, John and Katie's relationship—like ours—is still going strong. But in an era where relationships topple like ninepins and "serial monogamy" has gained universal social acceptance (how many people today are really concerned about the number of spouses a candidate for president has had?), one does have to ask: what keys can help us enjoy a relationship that is stable, supportive, and mutually fulfilling?

I am not, by the way, either an idealist or an absolutist when it comes to marital commitment. I do believe the bond is sacred, but experience has certainly convinced me that marriage is too great a blessing for incompatible partners to remain shackled to each other for superstitious or unsound reasons. I've conducted hundreds of happy weddings, but also counseled scores of con-flicted couples and tried to help fracture families pick up the pieces of their broken lives. While not a certified expert on rela-tional issues, I have seen enough couples through tough times and have faced enough complications in my own relationship to be sensitive to the issues involved.

Nevertheless, having reached my late fifties, with a well-adjusted son tucked safely away at college and a modicum of finan-cial security, I appreciate more than ever the reliable presence of a partner whom I know intimately, love deeply, and trust unre-servedly. Maintaining a healthy intimate relationship is hard work, and Trina and I have probably faced and overcome as many obsta-cles as any other couple. In addition to the daily pressures of min-istry, we've coped with life-threatening illness, troubles with our families of origin, money worries, work pressures, parenting prob-lems—the kind of stuff that can send an unstable marriage into a tailspin. At midlife, however, we have learned gracefully to let go of those immature longings for an unblemished partner and an unruffled love life which we harbored in our younger years. Today we gratefully accept each other's full-but-frail humanity and cher-ish our ability to be present for each other.

Bo Lozoff, founder of the Human Kindness Foundation, said something that accurately reflects Trina's and my own experience and provides further insight into the true character of a sustainable partnership. The traditional wedding vow includes the phrases "for better and for worse, in sickness and in health, for richer or poorer" and ends with that powerful affirmation "until death do us part." If a couple considers this vow closely and takes it seriously, the part-ners realize that marriage will expose them to the ugliest and pet-tiest as well as the most admirable parts of their respective personalities. "Strong wedding vows are meant to help us stick around long enough to come out the other side," Lozoff says. It gives a couple the opportunity to strip away every illusion and see each other whole. In this sense "marriage becomes a tool in the service of the spiritual journey, a way of combining forces and help-ing each other become enlightened."[21]

Our rich and varied experience has convinced Trina and me that families, communities, and individuals all benefit from strong, healthy primary partnerships. Sustain a marriage, same-sex union, or close friendship, and you are in a better position to sustain both the person and the planet.

Sustainability and Personal Well-Being

Speaking of the person, sustainability is also pertinent to the project of maintaining mental, emotional, and physical fitness. Too many people today are frustrated by their seeming inability to develop healthy patterns of exercise, stress reduction, eating, and spiritual deepening. If the good life is to be our goal, this is an excellent place to begin.

In a study of thirty-one different long-term diets, UCLA researchers saw participants losing, on average, five to ten percent of their total body mass. Most, unfortunately, regained all that weight over the longer term, and some even put on more than they had initially lost. Only a small fraction of those studied kept the extra pounds off, and those were people who had established a sustainable pattern of simply eating less and exercising more. Nothing complicated or mysterious was at work here, just the cultivation of sound, sensible habits.[22]

My own experience in this area has been similar. A few simple practices, consistently followed, make a big difference. I've been able to avoid illness and chronic injury, control my weight, and maintain mental acuity and emotional stability into and through late middle age by attending to the basics. I enjoy a sensible "flexitarian" diet, engage in vigorous aerobic exercise six days a week, work periodically on balance and flexibility, try to get adequate sleep, and make time for meditation. It isn't necessary or desirable to be obsessive about such practices, just reasonably committed.

Surviving and Thriving

As I see it, sustainability promises much more than the mere *survival* of a community, an economy, a marriage, or a sentient being. Its purpose is to help individuals, as well as natural and social systems, genuinely to *thrive*. Again, it supplies an effective means to realize a desirable end.

Even in a country as materially blessed as the United States, depression, apathy, interpersonal violence, divorce, vocational dissatisfaction, restlessness, and anxiety have reached epidemic proportions. Young people seem disproportionately afflicted by these maladies. In these economically perilous times, most of us are still comfortably surviving, but we do not feel we are living the good life. For all our gadgets, gimcracks, and 120 TV channels, we are not happy campers. A more mature civilization would be conscious of what its own members require in order to thrive.

A number of years ago the Dalai Lama participated in an extended discussion of mental health issues with a group of prominent Western psychologists and was brought face-to-face with this apparent paradox. During the conversation, one of the professionals observed that poor self-esteem was a persistent, underlying problem for many of his patients. These outwardly successful Americans, he reported, often didn't feel very confident or capable and held a rather low opinion of themselves. The Dalai Lama was astounded and asked others in the room whether this description accurately reflected their own clinical experience. All nodded in assent. The Tibetan shook his head. This, he said, is not an infirmity from which my own countrymen suffer.[23]

Although the symptoms are perhaps more obvious and better documented today, the malady is hardly a new one. More than a century and a half ago, that astute visitor from France, Alexis de Tocqueville, anticipated this development when he reflected on the "strange melancholy which often haunts the inhabitants of democratic countries in the midst of their abundance."[24] So are we ready to wise up, or will we remain stuck in patterns of behavior that ultimately are inimical to human happiness?

A culture committed to sustainability, to creating a social environment where people can thrive emotionally and spiritually, as well as physically, would be eager to expose and treat the underlying causes of the condition. It would realize that mood-altering medications and psychotherapy, while useful in treating symptoms, do not address the pathology itself. The latter requires a more aggressive, nonmedical approach. Some of the Dalai Lama's insights could prove useful here, as well as those of the ancient Greek lawmaker Solon, who once described the happy person as one who "is moderately furnished with externals, but has done noble acts and acted temperately."

Our culture's crude equation of material abundance with happiness presents a real problem. Despite the demonstrable fact that rich people are no more satisfied with their lives than those of modest means, most Americans still hunger for wealth—even if that means putting additional strain on an overburdened planet and placing more of their fellow human beings at grave risk.

Even if we could have it all, is it possible to be happy with an uneasy conscience? At least a third of humanity—over two billion people—lives at or below subsistence level. Those who are well-off cannot help but be aware of what their lifestyle really costs and whom it affects. The question is, can human beings truly thrive as individuals if the social, economic, and natural systems to which they belong are not also doing reasonably well? That is why Episcopal theologian Matthew Fox declares in his *A New Reformation* that "sustainability is another word for justice, for what is just is sustainable and what is unjust is not."[25]

Sustainability is a practical principle, but it also has moral implications. For a culture to thrive and for there to be a general increase in happiness, measures to ameliorate inequality and injustice must be taken. A mountain of physical amenities is no substitute for a clear conscience.

Part One

Reimagining
the Good Life

Chapter 1

Embracing New
Rules of Conduct

I f life and love are to endure, if better health and greater happiness are to be obtained, and if the communities and ecologies that sustain us are to thrive, society will have to reappraise its values. More specifically, the principle of sustainability now needs to move to the forefront of our planning and problem solving.

What, then, would this entail? As I've already pointed out, most of the commentary on sustainability focuses on technical solutions—specific, scientifically determined measures meant to solve particular social, environmental, or economic problems. What have been missing are a few basic behavioral norms that can provide the initiated and uninitiated alike with the insight and proper incentive to accomplish some very important goals. What I recommend is the application at both the individual and collective level of four deceptively simple and straightforward rules of conduct, or "keys." Their ultimate purpose is to ensure that the efforts we make to create the good life will produce the desired results. The rules are these:

- Pay attention.
- Stay put.
- Exercise patience.
- Practice prudence.

Pay Attention

The first key—pay attention—may strike you as somewhat puzzling. After all, doesn't every reasonably observant, healthy individual know how to attend? Perhaps those afflicted with some perceptual malady may find the task difficult, but otherwise this is an ability most of us take for granted.

In this department we undoubtedly give ourselves more credit than we deserve. Is the *quality* of our attention such that we accurately perceive what's going on around us and inside ourselves? The sad fact is that many of us are eminently distractible, noticeably preoccupied, and solidly entrenched in a pattern of preconceptions and prejudicial thinking that seriously compromises our ability to see clearly.

This is not invariably the case, of course. Most people are quite able to pay close attention when engaged in an activity they really enjoy or feel passionate about. That quality is clearly displayed in the demeanor of a professional poker player or a pinball wizard. It is also an ability most new mothers develop, such that even the faintest cry from their baby's crib will bring them to instant alertness. A computer game, a concert, or a compelling research project can all produce rapt attention in their respective participants.

And yet many aspects of personal, interpersonal, and planetary life don't receive sufficient attention. If an enterprise, a relationship, or an environment isn't sufficiently engaging, we tune out and turn our attention elsewhere. Why? Because paying attention requires energy and self-discipline—a greater expenditure of sustained effort than most of us want to invest. But if we restrict our powers of attention only to those areas that seem likely to pay immediate dividends in terms of pleasure or profit, much that is critical to our well-being won't be given the serious consideration it deserves. The quality of a person's attention will decisively affect that person's performance as a parent, an employee, a citizen, or a steward of the planet.

Paying Attention on a Farm

My own upbringing on a modest working farm in the upper Midwest has helped me as an adult to appreciate the critical role that attention plays in the practice of sustainable agriculture. Apart from a few rudimentary practices like crop rotation, neither we nor our rural neighbors consciously adhered to sustainable standards. We almost certainly did not pay the kind of close attention to what we were doing that the noted Kentucky farmer-writer Wendell Berry advocates. Berry, whose observations of Amish culture and his own determined efforts to make a small, hardscrabble farm productive have made him something of a sustainability guru, can help readers appreciate the difference between his and our own more conventional approach to agriculture.

Farmers of the "old school," Berry writes, are always alert to what Alexander Pope characterized as the "genius of the place." They are guided in their work and their ambitions by the natural contours of their property, by the presence of certain wild plants and animals, and by subtle variations in the soil. Marketability and mass production are not the only or even the first consideration for the sustainable farmer. Plants and animals are raised according to what best suits the land and its resources.

The farmers that Berry cites recognize the indissoluble connection between the land's aliveness and their own livelihood; they strive to be conscientious stewards as well as successful producers. Berry finds appalling those industrial-style farmers and absentee owners whose hunger for profit and reliance on technology have led them to abdicate their responsibility. Their jaded sensibilities and unwillingness to pay attention to the consequences of their actions have undermined the health of rural ecologies and communities alike. "The inability to distinguish between a farm and any farm is a condition predisposing to abuse," Berry writes, "and abuse has been the result. Rape, indeed, has been the result, and we have seen that we are not exempt from the damage we have inflicted. Now we must think of marriage."[1]

Peter Martinelli, who operates a small, coastal farm north of San Francisco, offers an instructive example of how attention and intuition can be used to solve an agricultural problem. Farming in this region is an ongoing challenge; in contrast with

California's sun-soaked central valley, the weather is less predictable and soil conditions are less uniform. The environment
demands an opportunistic and flexible orientation and a willingness to explore many possibilities. Consequently, Martinelli is
always looking, questioning, and rearranging the pieces of his
farm to obtain better results.

A few years ago he decided to make a stab at growing strawberries—a common coastal crop. He studied the subject and
learned from the literature that because the fruit's sweetness is
directly affected by heat and sun, strawberries should be planted in
his warmest field—a flat, treeless expanse of valley real estate.
Accordingly, he planted his berries "by the book," but the resulting
product wasn't what the literature had promised. Martinelli ended
up with small, excessively tart berries that were barely edible. To
make matters worse, during the ensuing winter most of the plants
in that "prime" location died. Nevertheless, the persistent farmer
wasn't ready to throw in the towel. He still had a gut feeling about
those strawberries.

Laying "science" temporarily aside, Martinelli thoroughly rein-
spected his property, walking and looking and, as Wendell Berry
put it, trying to get a sense of its "genius." Finally, on a hunch, he
planted a second crop in a hillside clearing surrounded by woods.
Although experts would hardly have considered it an ideal spot for
domesticated strawberries, Martinelli felt confident. The plants
did well, and when the berries ripened, they were simply exqui-
site—"delicious in a way that forces you to stop and consider each
one deeply," as Martinelli himself reported.

There was really nothing all that mysterious or magical about
this unexpected success. Rather than allow his judgment to be
clouded by his previous assumptions and prevailing agricultural
opinion, the farmer simply resolved to pay close attention and let
the land speak directly to him. On one of many saunters around his
property, something had made Martinelli pause: on a hill at the edge
of the woods he discovered a few wild strawberries stretching their
tendrils across a litter of leaves. In the lower field where the crop

had failed, no wild berries were present. There was something about the higher elevation that seemed to suit the plant. The farmer only needed to notice what was already there.[2]

Going about our daily lives, how often do our own decisions and actions reflect close attention? Our behavior might reflect ingrained habit or standard operating procedure. Often we feel obliged to follow the guidance of experts or conventional wisdom. But there is also a lot to be said for the power of simple attention as we search for the optimal place to sow the seeds of happiness.

The Tao of Attention

Traditional Eastern philosophies have always placed a premium on this quality of perception and the practices that promote it. Over 2,400 years ago the Taoist sage Chuang Tzu provided a holistic description of "attention" that remains relevant:

> The goal ... is inner unity. This means hearing, not just with the ear; hearing, but not with the understanding; hearing with the spirit, with your whole being. ... Hence, it demands the emptiness of all the other faculties. And when the faculties are empty, then the whole being listens.[3]

Taoism teaches that by fully attending to things as they are, we can enjoy a harmonious relationship with the Tao—that ineffable, all-pervading principle that governs and gives coherence to the cosmos. In the process, we gain the ability to move through life mindfully, with ever-greater poise and equanimity and free from the need to be always "in control" of others and the environment.

Philosopher-anthropologist David Abram has reached a similar conclusion. Despite the rapid expansion of our knowledge about the world, the incredible amount of information literally at our fingertips, and the sophisticated technology we now command, awareness of and sensitivity to our surroundings have eroded. Knowledge derived from secondary sources causes us, as it did Peter Martinelli, to make assumptions and often as not to draw the wrong conclusions. Technology keeps us at arm's length from that which nourishes us. Abram believes that our best hope for moving from estrangement back into relationship is to take our cues from pretechnical, nonliterate traditional peoples who still know how to pay attention. Statutory codes, cool rational appraisals, and philosophic principles, while important, are not sufficient. If a more compelling environmental ethic is to gain widespread acceptance, "*a renewed attentiveness to this perceptual dimension that underlies all our logics* (my emphasis) and a rejuvenation of our carnal, sensorial empathy with the living land that sustains us" will also be required.[4]

Or as the British philosopher John Gray succinctly put it: "Why do we need to have a [definable] purpose in life? Can we not think of the aim of life as being simply to *see?*"—seeing being just another way of saying "Pay attention!"[5]

Stay Put

In addition to improving the quality of our perception, we have to get better at controlling our restlessness. Novelist Wallace Stegner was a close observer of American culture, and he once observed that people in this country can generally be assigned to one of two categories: they are either "boomers" or "stickers." He lamented that the former—folks who with very little forethought will pull up stakes and head for the latest boomtown—were becoming increasingly dominant. Modern society, Stegner complained, schools its citizens in discontent and encourages us to "get up and get out." The itch for greener pastures or greater adventure—symptomatic, perhaps, of an unresolved frontier fixation—is one we just can't resist scratching. But, Stegner wrote, "Neither the country nor the society we build out of it can be healthy if we don't stop raiding and running. We must learn to be quiet part of the time and acquire the sense not of ownership, but of belonging."[6]

Stegner first voiced this concern a half century ago, and today the average American pulls up stakes and heads for a new home, neighborhood, or community about once every seven years. Underscoring Stegner's point, Scott Russell Sanders observes that "from the beginning our heroes have been vagabonds of every stripe." Rather than create viable livelihoods and livable communities where they already are, Americans have continually hankered for a new environment more suited to their needs. "The promised land has always been over the next ridge, or at the end of the trail, never under our feet," Sanders writes.[7] The problem has reached such proportions that environmental writer Terry Tempest Williams has even suggested that "perhaps the most radical thing we can do these days is to stay home."[8]

Why We Don't Stay Put

The reasons for all this meandering about aren't necessarily trivial, and boomers sometimes protest that they don't have much choice. The explanations people give include loss of local employment, educational opportunities elsewhere, environmental health issues, and the need to live nearer to close relatives. Nevertheless, a good bit of this transience appears to be based on internal restlessness rather than real necessity. People "get up and get out" for the sake of a more congenial climate, an upscale lifestyle, or a more child-friendly atmosphere. I'm familiar with these rationales because earlier in life we ourselves made similar choices. At this stage of the game, however, I'm pretty well convinced that the American reluctance to sink our roots too deeply in any native soil has had a negative impact on families, communities, and ecologies.

The Dividends It Pays

I have become a convert to the second key of sustainability: *stay put.* For the past two decades our family has lived in the same tightly integrated neighborhood. We have watched our son and his friends move from infancy to adulthood and then leave home, and we have marveled at the many changes that have occurred in our surroundings and in ourselves. While it is certainly conceivable that circumstances might eventually cause us to move elsewhere, we would take that step with great reluctance and with a genuine sense of loss. Trina and I enjoy our status as stickers and wish more Americans shared our own appreciation for its pleasures.

People come to the city where we live, Madison, and swoon over its most obvious assets: four beautiful lakes, Frank Lloyd Wright buildings, the nation's best and biggest farmer's market, its expansive park system, and its funky State Street shopping area. They say that they "love" the city, but what they're really describing seems more like infatuation than real devotion. Commitment comes when residents become curious and attentive enough to develop a deep sense of identity, after which they begin seriously to care. For a bona fide sticker, the fate of self and the fate of community are felt to be intertwined.

Communities owe their health and beauty to those with the fortitude and faithfulness to stay put—those who, as Stegner wrote, are prepared to place homemaking ahead of profit making. For stickers, a house is first and foremost a home and only secondarily an investment. Such residents are thus more likely than most to protect a community from those whose paramount concern is their own enrichment.

These are people who've been around long enough to know that their community actually has character and that this is one of the qualities that makes it habitable. As time passes, stickers inevitably learn something of their local history, recognize important landmarks and artifacts, and come to understand who and what makes the community tick. The economic, cultural, and environmental forces that have shaped and reshaped the region are obvious to stickers, and they are eager to do what they can to maintain continuity with the healthiest aspects of the past. When Terry Tempest Williams urges us to "stay home," it is for this express purpose: to deepen our knowledge of and commitment to the place and the people we are part of.

Of course, sticking doesn't guarantee that the special identity of a community will be preserved and its long-term interests well served. Often the developers, real estate brokers, and investors who are most responsible for altering its character can cite long residency and routinely express great pride in their community. But because their first priority is profit making, actors such as these tend to think and perform more like boomers than stickers. Despite their status as homegrown products, they have nevertheless aided and abetted a development process that has rendered many of America's towns and cities culturally sterile and commercially homogenous. These communities are "purposely held in bondage by a local network of moneyed families, bankers, developers, lawyers, and businesspeople" who are not the least interested in community values or the health of its citizenry, journalist and gadfly Joe Bageant complains.[9]

To be a sticker is not to be an obstinate opponent of change, but it is to be a person who understands his or her community thoroughly enough to know what deserves to be left undisturbed, what needs to be restored, and what is, in fact, dispensable. In the absence of persons with this level of sensitivity, indiscriminate profit seekers and indifferent newcomers will sap a community's strength.

We Need More Stickers

So Wallace Stegner is surely right about society's need for more stickers, by which we mean persons who are willing to make a spiritual as well as a physical commitment to a place. Equipped with in-depth knowledge and an appreciation for its "genius," they pay attention to the things that really matter to their community and thus are able to offer the necessary resistance to those whose vision has been clouded by the lust for personal power and profit.

Iowa native John Price recently penned an open letter to the young people of that state, many of whom are eager to settle elsewhere. In that missive he acknowledges that Iowa is probably not the most stimulating place to live, and he understands a youngster's restlessness. Still, give your home a second look, Price urges. Don't be so eager to rush off before you've considered what you might be leaving behind. "By staying put," he writes, "the place I once wanted to escape has taught me to see the world in a new and better way, with a degree of hope I could've hardly discovered on my own."

Most of all, Price promises, if you stay, you will never feel alone, for you will be surrounded by a dependable network of family, friends, and, yes, even strangers "who are bound to you by the land we share and by the vow of all committed love: to be there, to try."[10] Staying close to home isn't always an option, and it isn't always desirable; but if we are feeling antsy to get up and get out, let's at least be aware of what we may be leaving behind and how our own departure may affect a community's future.

The present discussion has concentrated on the most obvious physical implications of this key, *staying put*. When we come to consider our labor, relational life, health and fitness, and spiritual well-being, its relevance will become even more apparent, for this key also suggests traits of character like perseverance, fidelity, and self-discipline. Modern culture has made it too tempting and too easy to opt for a succession of spouses rather than our first love, to experiment with multiple spiritual paths instead of deepening our understanding of one, to move from job to job without ever developing a true sense of "calling."

While circumstances may sometimes make it difficult to stay put in the ways I've described, it's important to understand that by *choosing* the lifestyle of a perpetually restless boomer, we forfeit the many subtle pleasures that require continuity and that are part and parcel of the good life.

Exercise Patience

The ability to stay put implies patience, but casual observation of people's behavior in checkout lines and eating establishments suggests that the latter has little standing in any recent catalogue of American virtues. It is on the thoroughfares we use to reach our dining and shopping destinations where the absence of patience is most noticeable. Both civility and safety concerns evaporate the minute we settle into the driver's seat and hit the gas.

Tucson is an example of a city that is, from a planning standpoint, well designed to accommodate cyclists. Clearly designated bike lanes provide easy access to most important destinations for commuters and casual riders alike. But as some bicyclists quickly learn, appropriate infrastructure offers no real protection against impatient and incautious drivers. A surprising number of people behind the wheel honk, shout obscenities out their windows, and seem to relish playing "chicken" with those who opt for peddle power. Serious and fatal injury to riders occurs all too frequently in Tucson and in other hypothetically bicycle-friendly cities.

The problem is compounded by the fact that hardly anyone observes the posted speed limits, which are a generous forty-five mph on Tucson's main arteries and seventy-five mph on Arizona's limited-access highways. Driving less than the posted upper limit is to risk being rear-ended. To be fair, conditions aren't all that different on East Coast arteries like the Massachusetts and New Jersey Turnpikes or even Chicago's Eisenhower Expressway. Not only does such impatience produce a higher number of fatal accidents, but it represents a gross waste of resources.

Excessive speed, jack-rabbit starts, and quick stops are the primary culprits in loss of fuel economy, and it has been amply documented that if the typical driver relaxed a little and resisted the temptation to press the pedal to the metal, the result would be a marked reduction in overall gas consumption (in this respect, every vehicle sold should feature a dashboard display similar to the one on the Toyota Prius, which provides the operator with instant miles-per-gallon feedback). If we think that by simply going faster we'll somehow capture the "good life," we're probably on the wrong highway. To paraphrase those ubiquitous road signs: "Slow down and live well."

Patience and Appreciation

The heedless waste of an increasingly costly nonrenewable resource is one compelling reason for cultivating patience. A second has to do with the quality of our human relationships and the character of our communities. No matter how cordial and considerate folks might be within the charmed circle of family and friends, on the streets they too often act like chariot drivers in the Circus Maximus or stock car jockeys at Talladega. I'm not even talking about road-rage—a relatively rare phenomenon. The aggressiveness of the typical hurried, harried driver has created an adversarial atmosphere on the nation's roadways and seriously compromised our consideration for one another. Comedian Steven Wright's humorous remark that "God is going to come down and pull civilization over for speeding" makes a valid point: when a culture runs out of patience, it also falls out of grace.[11]

People who are constantly in a hurry lose the capacity to reflect meaningfully on their own actions, and thus they find it difficult to uphold their core values in challenging circumstances (e.g., lambs at home become lions behind the wheel). If we made a more deliberate effort to take our time, we might also become more proficient, as author and essayist Mark Slouka puts it, "at figuring out who we are and what we believe." If our desire is to maintain a more consistent ethic of care, we simply have to slow down.[12]

Patience is also a must if we desire a deeper understanding of and appreciation for the world around us. Naturalists from Henry David Thoreau to Annie Dillard offer cogent reminders that the sentient universe is so much more sublime when we take time to savor it. Too often their soulful appeals fall on deaf ears.

Consider the simple process of preparing and consuming a cup of tea and how the experience is enhanced by adding an extra dollop of time and attention. "Just a cup of tea," Stephen Levine concedes, but liberated from our usual habit of haste, tea-tasting can provide a genuine opportunity for healing.

> Just this moment of newness. Just the hand touching the cup. Just the arm retracting. The fragrance increasing as the cup nears the lips. ... Noticing the first taste of tea before the tea even reaches the lips. The fragrance and heat rising into the mouth. The first noticing of flavor. The touch of warm tea on willing tongue. The tongue moving the tea about in the mouth. The intention to swallow. The warmth that extends down into the stomach. What a wonderful cup of tea. The tea of peace, of satisfaction.[13]

No matter how suggestively such voices ask us to reconsider our addiction to speed, most of us still have trouble setting a healthier and holier pace for ourselves. Soon after the day begins we shift into high gear and from there our own momentum carries us forward. We rarely will stop either to smell the roses or appreciatively to sip the tea.

The tragedy of too much haste struck me forcefully one early October evening in Tucson. Trina and I had returned from an excursion to Mt. Lemmon, where we had spent the day high above the valley's scorching heat. We were welcomed by one of the most dramatic sunsets either of us had ever seen. Storm clouds were slowly receding, and both the western and eastern horizons displayed a palette worthy of the great Venetian painters Titian and Tintoretto. The two of us spent the better part of a half hour strolling to various vantage points, trying to capture just a bit more of the evening's glory before darkness fell. Cars and bikes whizzed by, but no one slowed down, much less stopped, to gaze toward the firmament. Perhaps most Arizonans are so accustomed to spectacular sunsets that they are no longer moved by them. For us, however, it was soul food of the most satisfying sort.

The late Sigurd Olson, a noted naturalist and prolific essayist, described a similar experience he had many years earlier. At the other end of the state lies the majestic Grand Canyon. When Olson and several friends arrived at the southern rim on an excursion, the sun still hung well above the horizon. Their timing was deliberate, for that company had come to savor the subtle color shifts in the canyon walls as the evening progressed. "For over an hour," Olson reports, "we feasted on a panorama unequaled anywhere in the world, and over it was a silence and timelessness that gave added meaning to the scene."

Olson's party had suspended all peripheral needs and personal agendas to be fully present for this delectable experience. They were content to nibble slowly at a visual feast rather than gluttonously try to take it in at a single glance. Then, as the canyon was at its most colorful, two vacationing parents and their children roared up to the lookout spot where Olson and his comrades were sitting. The family noisily piled out of the car, walked quickly to the guardrail, and peered out over the abyss for a few moments. "Well, we've seen this one," Dad pronounced. "Let's try to make it to the next vista point before we call it a day."

In telling this story, Olson expressed sympathy rather than irritation over the intrusion. He felt that this family, like so many casual visitors to the canyon, had to have come away disappointed. "They are so imbued with the sense of hurry and the thrill of travel that they actually lose what they came so far to find," he remarked.[14]

Many Americans have become accustomed to living in the fast lane and feel so pressured to meet their obligations and work into their schedules an ever-expanding array of activities that patience is a luxury few feel they can afford. We have created an economy and a culture that fairly demands that we keep quickening our pace. Many also equate patience with excessive caution, lack of ambition, inefficiency, and lagging productivity. Any attempt to promote its practice is likely to be regarded as unfeasible, if not downright subversive.

And yet the epidemic of fretfulness and anxiety that has spread through the country, and that is the proximate cause of so much personal and interpersonal distress, would seem to indicate the need for a change of pace. Sedatives and sleeping pills (prescriptions for which have increased dramatically in recent years) are not a sustainable solution. In the words of the Vietnamese Zen Buddhist teacher and peace activist Thich Nhat Hanh: "We must organize a resistance. ... We have to resist the speed, the losing of ourselves."[15]

Practice Prudence

The fourth key, *practice prudence*, is contingent upon the three already discussed—pay attention, stay put, and exercise patience. Unsound or imprudent behavior often reflects failure in one or more of the other areas. People are more likely to act and live prudently—that is, with due caution and foresight—if they are willing to abide and take time to attend. Easier said than done, however. In a brief discussion of personal finances, environmental and social commentator Bill McKibben highlights the problem: "Only twenty percent of Americans are currently 'planners' who save toward a quantitative goal." The rest, McKibben asserts, leave their future more or less to chance. They are "strugglers," "impulsives," and "deniers." Often as not, the issue is lack of will power rather than awareness. Americans generally agree that they know *how* to cut back on household spending — sixty-eight percent, for instance, indicated they could save by eating out less often—but they have difficulty putting that knowledge into practice.[16]

McKibben's research indicates that even though a majority of Americans acknowledge the importance of being prudent, four out of five concede that they are not self-disciplined enough to make prudent decisions. This is hardly surprising given the constant encouragement we receive to consume our way to happiness. Living on credit, never putting off until tomorrow what can be purchased today, has become the accepted way of doing business. For many Americans, shopping has become the primary recreational activity. Without it, we might not know what to do with ourselves. Even former President George W. Bush told us at one time that a trip to the mall should be considered a patriotic act!

The word *prudence* has an old-fashioned ring to it, and for some it may evoke images of men in starched collars and or tight-lipped schoolmarms in petticoats. Further explication of its relationship to the good life is, therefore, in order.

Helpful Synonyms

One suggestive synonym for prudence is *mindfulness.* While this word appears often in the literature of meditation and spiritual development and is closely related to *attention,* here mindfulness carries a different connotation. Apropos of the signs posted in British subways advising riders to "mind the gap," it means to "be careful." Prudence, then, suggests the exercise of due care.

Before embarking on an adventure or beginning a new enterprise, the prudent person makes a patient and mindful attempt to anticipate problems and lower the chances of mishap. If we don't see prudence displayed often enough, it may be because a culture that countenances and even encourages high-risk ventures would equate it with timidity. The brave, self-confident person seizes the day and lets tomorrow take care of itself. If the choice is between the impetuous and the prudent, it is all too probable we will opt for the former.

Prudence can also be equated with common sense, which the futurist Marilyn Ferguson has defined as "an attitude of continuous investigation." The problem is that common sense isn't all that common any more. Our resistance to a consumer culture that continually tickles our appetites and discourages due deliberation has grown weak. In the spring of 2008, as his quest for the presidency was getting under way, Barack Obama warned his New York audience of an impending financial disaster. "A complete disdain for pay-as-you-go budgeting," he presciently observed, "... allowed far too many to put short-term gain ahead of long-term consequences."[17]

The fact is, we just can't have it all. We need to do our homework, carefully consider our options, and exercise sound judgment. Healthful and happy living requires a prudent disposition.

Sometimes prudence substitutes for words like *economy, thrift,* and *husbandry*. The prudent individual or community keeps close tabs on its resources and resists the temptation, as the *Tao Te Ching* puts it, to "overreach, overuse, overspend."[18] Defined in this fashion, our fourth key can be directly applied to the quest for economic and environmental sustainability. When *Small Is Beautiful* author E. F Schumacher offered his "first principle" of sustainable economics, he was making a pitch for prudence. An economic practice is life affirming, he wrote, when it produces maximum well-being with minimum consumption.[19]

Cautious But Not Compulsive

I come from a long line of farmers and businessmen who seem to have sworn some sort of oath to the idea of prudence, which may explain why I am also drawn to it. My paternal grandfather, Harry Schuler, died of work-related emphysema in his early sixties (OK, maybe he wasn't all *that* prudent!), well before we could sit down together and discuss his values. But according to family lore, Harry's cautious approach to investment served him and his loved ones well during the Great Depression, when so many Americans lost most of their hard-earned assets. I remember my grandfather as a hard-working man who sewed patches on his old khakis and drove sensible cars. Since they were moderately well-to-do, the family could have afforded more luxuries. But in the end Harry's prudence paid off, making it possible for his widow to live comfortably and securely to the enviable age of 102.

In this regard, Harry's son, my own father, is a chip off the block. Dad has always declined to invest in the stock market (a casino, he complains, where clever brokers, inside traders, and big investors control the outcome) and has placed most of his and my mother's assets in instruments that produce modest but dependable returns. Hedging their bets against the high cost of future medical care, my parents have forgone the temptation to buy the new cars and lavish furnishings they could certainly afford. Now in their mid eighties, they indulge moderately and are content to enjoy comfort rather than splendor.

Trina and I began setting money aside for our son's college education while he was still a toddler, so we're obviously following in my forebears' footsteps. We avoid buying on credit whenever possible, pay off our balance immediately, and carefully monitor our discretionary spending. We live well, but well within our means. Prudent planning has put us on a solid financial footing, and it has also kept our stress level low, given our son a healthy head start, and laid the groundwork for a sustainable retirement.

The prudent person is levelheaded and not anxious, deliberative and cautious but not hypervigilant. Indeed, if equanimity and peace of mind are what we are after, prudence is the name of the game. By assessing the future and establishing sensible priorities, we eliminate a lot of unnecessary worry. To the extent that we allow the impulsive side of our personality to dominate, we may feel satisfied one day, only to wake up the next troubled and anxious. As the world's social, economic, and environmental problems mount, Americans would do well to explore more sensible avenues to the good life because the road we are running on seems likely to end in a cul-de-sac.

Confronting a Fatal Flaw

A pioneer in the emerging field of bioethics and an eminent University of Wisconsin biochemist, Van Rensselaer Potter spent a good bit of time in retirement thinking about the future of the planet and trying to understand why human beings exhibited so little common sense. Ultimately, he concluded that our species suffers from an inborn deficiency, or "fatal flaw," that threatens to undo all that we have achieved. The problem, he observed, is that most men and women lack prescience; they have lost—or perhaps never acquired—the ability to anticipate the long-term consequences of their actions.[20]

But Potter merely updated a thesis presented several centuries earlier by that bleak English philosopher Thomas Hobbes. Hobbes lamented that the insistent physical and emotional urge to satisfy our immediate wants prevents us from "foreseeing the greater evils that necessarily attach" to the goods we seek.[21]

Years of inaction on critical planetary issues like climate change, resource depletion, and species losses would seem to confirm the fatal flaw thesis. Even repeated, forceful admonitions from the world's most respected scientists haven't convinced the average person to make more prudent choices. Ours may be an extraordinarily clever species, but we are also experts at rationalizing our irresponsible behavior and selectively ignoring mounting evidence that we are on the wrong track. One hopes that enough of us will recognize the aforementioned defect and correct it before the planet's slow sickening becomes acute and irreversible.

Fortunately, the shortcoming that Hobbes and Potter identified doesn't afflict everyone. Although eighty percent of Americans are impulsives, the remaining twenty percent do plan deliberately for the future. They consider the odds and make decisions with one eye trained on the distance. These are the people we need to listen to, aspire to become, and promote to positions of leadership. Panderers who proclaim that "the American way of life is not negotiable" and that even token sacrifice for the sake of the future is unnecessary can no longer be tolerated and must be vigorously challenged.

If technical arguments and dire warnings have proved insufficient to overcome the fatal flaw, perhaps sober consideration of the ugly legacy we are preparing will give us pause. It certainly has had an effect on Bill Moyers, a distinguished journalist with six grandchildren. Their sweet visages serve to remind him of the need to reflect upon his own responsibility:

> I look up at the pictures on my desk, next to my computer … and I see the future looking back at me from those photographs and I say, "Father, forgive us, for we know not what we do." And then the shiver runs down my spine, and I am seized by the realization: That's not right. We do know what we are doing. We are stealing their future.[22]

Chapter 2

Releasing Old Habits of Thought and Belief

Before exploring the four keys of sustainability in greater depth and connecting them more explicitly to the "good life," we should seek to expose the cultural and ideological forces that might hinder any serious attempt to apply those keys. It has been argued that sustainability ought to be placed at the forefront of our values, its transformative potential recognized and affirmed. But for that to happen, other ideas and principles long deemed important have to be reconsidered, altered, and, in some instances, retired. Once we understand what inhibits sustainability, we will be in a better position to investigate its promise.

Echoing Van Rensselaer Potter, British philosopher John Gray attributes humanity's failure to formulate and practice sound sustainable principles to a stubborn, ineradicable flaw in our species. He argues that the profound environmental damage humans have caused has been due to something other than the institutional mechanisms that are usually blamed—global capitalism and industrialization, for instance. Even before the modern era, Gray points out, human advance has "coincided with ecological devastation." Something more deeply ingrained is at work here. "The mass of humankind is ruled not by its intermittent moral sensations, still less by self-interest," John Gray concludes, "but by the needs of the moment. It seems fated to wreck the balance of life on earth."[1]

Gray supports this pessimistic assessment with evidence indicating that otherwise sophisticated, "premodern" societies in the Middle East, North Africa, the Yucatan, and the American Southwest consistently failed to come to terms with environmental realities. Civilizations have been overturned and ecosystems overtaxed because the human reach has repeatedly exceeded its grasp. The big difference between those ancient cultures and our own is the scale of the problem: what was once a regional concern has morphed into a global emergency.

Nevertheless, some civilizations have persisted and prospered longer than others. By applying appropriate technologies, bringing life into alignment with the ebb and flow of the Nile River, and keeping the population in check, Egyptian culture grew strong and its people enjoyed relative prosperity for better than two thousand years. Similarly, recent archeological data suggest that Native Americans in both the Northern and Southern Hemispheres developed unique agricultural and husbandry practices that met the needs of large human populations without despoiling the natural environment. Collapse of those long-standing systems occurred only after European diseases decimated the Indian populations and destabilized hundreds of thriving communities.[2]

Even more suggestively, experts in the field of Paleolithic cave art have been astounded to discover an amazing continuity of style and subject matter persisting for twenty-five millennia—four times as long as recorded history. Such a profoundly conservative tendency in art, Gregory Curtis notes, is one of the hallmarks of "classical civilization" and betokens a mode of existence that was both stable and deeply satisfying.[3]

Evidence for a "fatal flaw," then, is mixed. Nevertheless, it seems undeniable that for quite some time now humans have been botching the game. Is this because rapaciousness is basic to our human nature, or have we invested too heavily in certain powerful thought patterns or ideologies that are incompatible with sustainability? Both theses are probably true to a degree, but what seems indisputable is that certain cultural values can help to check humankind's worst proclivities while others only reinforce them. Christianity, humanism, capitalism, and techno-idealism are four intellectual and belief systems that have had a profound impact on Western civilization, but each supports ideas that conflict with those that reinforce sustainability. The purpose of the present chapter is to expose and scrutinize a few of their less-than-salutary features.

The Christian Conundrum

Christianity, the most influential intellectual force in the Western world for well over a millennium, has conditioned us to look at the world and ourselves in a particular way. This powerful religion comes in many flavors; it is not now, nor has it ever been, truly monolithic. That being the case, we need to exercise caution and offer appropriate qualifications in discussing the subject unless we wish to be consigned to the same "culture of complaint" to which disparaging writers like Richard Dawkins (*The God Delusion*) and Christopher Hitchens (*God Is Not Great*) belong.

My Unitarian and Universalist forebears proudly identified themselves as "Christian" despite the strenuous efforts of more conventional believers to deprive them of that label. To the extent that personalities like Jesus, Saint Francis, Hildegard of Bingen, and Thomas Merton have instructed and inspired me, I, too, feel kinship with Christianity. Still, there is ample cause for concern. Across history, Christianity has promulgated certain doctrines that make the establishment of sustainable standards considerably more difficult.

The Unfortunate Fall

There is, within the history of Christian doctrine, a devaluation of the material in favor of the immaterial. The physical world is understood to be "fallen," corrupted, and the defective human body merely a shell, a temporary abode for the imperishable spirit. Material creation—the devil's playground—is the proximate source of sin, a place where evil flowers and all sentient life is tainted. Matter and spirit exist in perpetual tension and, short of the Second Coming, cannot be reconciled. It is imperative, therefore, for human beings to resist the gravitational pull toward matter and turn their attention and energies to elevation of the spirit. As Saint Paul clearly and unequivocally states in the seventh chapter of his Epistle to the Romans: "For I know that nothing good dwells within me, that is, in my flesh. ... Wretched man that I am, who will deliver me from this body of death?" (Rom. 7:18, 24)

To be sure, the Bible does not consistently support spirit-matter dualism. Paul's Epistles and those books bearing John's autograph betray this quality, and they have decisively influenced subsequent Christian theology. On the other hand, many passages in the Old Testament, or *Tanakh*, wholeheartedly extol and show appreciation for a physical cosmos that God created and then declared to be "good." From scattered references in Genesis, Isaiah, Job, and the Psalms, contemporary theologians have formulated a scripturally based ethic of planetary stewardship and "creation care." Even some of those on the conservative end of the Christian spectrum have been reexamining old assumptions. According to Richard Cizik, vice president of the National Association of Evangelicals, in just a few years environmental stewardship has "gone from being irrelevant to being at the center of action" for some of his associates.[4]

Still, many members of the Christian community remain wedded to a metaphysic that discourages people from making too great a commitment to the planet and their own communities. A Platonic-Pauline perspective, which, in David Abrams' words, "denigrates the visible and tangible order of things on behalf of some absolute source assumed to exist entirely beyond or outside the bodily world," continues to dominate much Christian thinking.[5] It's hard to find a suitable place for sustainability in such an outlook, and Christianity has only recently begun to confront the scriptural and theological inconsistencies that have for centuries prevented it from entering into a more wholesome relationship with God's good creation. As Loren Eiseley glumly commented on the eve of the world's first Earth Day: "Primitive man was still *inside* the world, [but] Christian men in the West drove Pan from his hillside and rendered him powerless."[6]

Obsession with the End Times

The linear view of history common to the three Abrahamic traditions—Judaism, Islam, and Christianity—presents another problem.
The Christian understanding of this theory holds that the human
story commenced with a deliberate act of creation, has been unfolding in a purposeful way, and will terminate when God's plan has been
fulfilled. The world as we know it will then cease to exist. All gross,
corrupted matter will be utterly transformed into a purified and
immortalized substance subject to neither pain nor harm.

A considerable number of Christians believe the earth we
know is merely a temporary abode, a place where we are challenged to demonstrate our fitness for salvation and eternal bliss.
Within the larger scheme of things, our planet and its various institutions and structures have been assigned to play a pre-arranged
and limited role. Ultimately, they are not meant to be taken all that
seriously. "We know that while we are at home in the body we are
away from the Lord ... and we would rather be away from the
body and at home with the Lord" (2Cor. 5:6-8).

At the end of time and following a series of cataclysmic events
["For then there will be great tribulation, such as has not been seen
from the beginning of the world until now." (Matt. 24:21)], all
things will miraculously be made new and the planet will become,
by God's design not ours, a place of perfect peace, absolute harmony, and unlimited abundance—for the elect, that is; those who
have been "chosen."

The branch of Christian thinking briefly outlined above
attempts to make sense of human history by creating a compelling
narrative line. No genre of Christian writing is as enduringly popular as millenarianism, which describes the "end times." Apocalyptic
pot boilers from authors like Hal Lindsey and Tim LaHaye fairly
leap off the shelves of Christian bookstores. The appeal of such literature is obvious: behind the seeming capriciousness of history—
the random rise and fall of religions and civilizations—a cosmic
drama is unfolding.

The problem this poses for a program founded on sound sustainable principles is significant: the present planet and its systems

will always play second fiddle to the project of helping God lay the groundwork for a post-tribulation paradise. Not all Christians hold millenarian views. Many even find them quite distasteful. But the views are particularly prevalent among Pentecostals, evangelicals, and fundamentalists—the fastest-growing segments of the Christian movement.

Humankind—A Privileged Species

A third element of conventional Christian thought that militates against sustainability is the "separate and unequal" status accorded to human beings. Our species is described as a "special creation" bearing a "likeness to God." With our superior ontological position comes the authority to manage, subdue, and freely consume the resources of the planet. Despite an occasional nod to the notion of responsible stewardship, the Bible clearly suggests in its opening chapters that God intended for the plant and animal kingdom to serve the sole purpose of sustaining human life (Gen. 1:29–30). This has, in fact, been the position taken by successive generations of Christian thinkers and theologians. Far from being citizens within a biotic community, Christians have long regarded themselves as the natural world's rightful and presumptive overlords. In past centuries only a very few eccentrics deviated from this position, figures like Francis of Assisi and Henry David Thoreau. Not many would have agreed with U.S. President James Madison's enlightened view of the matter: "We have no reason to suppose that all of earth's resources which support so much living diversity, can rightfully be commandeered to support mankind alone."[7]

Expressions of awe, admiration, and gratitude for the natural world are not uncommon in Christian literature. Still, the orthodox doctrine of "special creation" introduces significant ambiguity and makes it that much more difficult for humans to recognize their embeddedness in and dependence upon natural systems that require conscientious maintenance and a considerable measure of restraint. In certain quarters, support for sustainable principles is regarded as evidence of bad or weak faith. According to evangelical writers Mark Beliles and Stephen McDowell:

> A secular society ... has a limited-resource mentality and views the world as a pie (there is only so much) that needs to be cut up so that everybody can have a piece. In contrast, the Christian knows that the potential in God is unlimited and that there is no shortage of resources in God's earth.[8]

The recent upsurge of interest in creation care notwithstanding, environmentalism is regarded with suspicion by many at the conservative end of the Christian spectrum. Earth-centered principles are associated with paganism and on that basis are condemned as idolatrous. Attempts to place humans and other sentient beings on a more equal footing are dismissed as dangerously Darwinian and a threat to the authority of scripture. If sustainability has been slow to gain acceptance within certain segments of the Christian community, it is often for these reasons.

Fortunately, persuasive writers on social and environmental issues such as Thomas Berry, Wendell Berry, Bill McKibben, and Annie Dillard are having an impact on American faith communities. Church-sponsored eco-fairs, "eat-local" campaigns, and community wellness projects are springing up across the country; and as already mentioned, increasing numbers of evangelical Christians are gingerly climbing aboard the sustainability bandwagon. Wheaton, a theologically conservative college outside of Chicago, offers a strong program in environmental biology and has sponsored a Creation Care Summit. More and more evangelicals are finding their way into Rocha, a Christian organization devoted to conservation.[9]

A particularly positive development has been the enthusiastic embrace of a stewardship ethic by an otherwise orthodox and conservative Roman Catholic pope—Benedict XVI. In 2007, the Vatican began installing the first of one thousand solar panels on the main auditorium of Vatican City, and Benedict himself has added polluting the earth to the church's list of serious sins. Some have dubbed Benedict history's first "green" pope, although the Holy See has yet to alter its inflexible position on reproductive choice or admit its own complicity in the scandal of human overpopulation.[10]

While a growing number of influential Christians understand that we can count on no deus ex machina to save us from the consequences of our own planetary mismanagement, only a small portion of the religious community has made creation care a high priority. It still generates far less passion than abortion, homosexuality, or school vouchers. A virtual revolution in mainstream Christian theology will be required for an ethic of sustainability to become embedded in our faith communities. Canadian theologian Sallie McFague has issued this challenge to her co-religionists. "A just and sustainable planet is the great work of the twenty-first century to which all religions … are called," she writes. The issues of climate change, species loss, and resource depletion are no longer debatable even among Christians. We all must "do what is necessary to work with God to create a just and sustainable planet, for only in this way will we all flourish."[11]

Humanism's Unconfirmed Optimism

Humanism, a thought tradition that emerged in the wake of and in concert with Darwin's intellectual revolution and whose tenets many in the scientific and technical community find attractive, has often taken positions seemingly at odds not only with Christianity but with revealed, supernatural religion more generally. Serious supporters of the humanist position would find little to quibble with in the foregoing critique of Christianity; yet humanism itself (whether secular or religious) betrays biases that in some cases are remarkably similar. Despite its commitment to empirical problem solving, humanist thought has not always complemented or encouraged an ethos of sustainability.

Improper Pride

In the first place, until rather recently humanism has echoed Christianity's claim that human beings and their interests are and ought to be paramount. Although humanism has no use for the Christian doctrine of a "special creation" and prefers to quote science rather than scripture, it ends up in approximately the same place: with a clear declaration of human primacy. The superior status of Homo sapiens (anthropocentrism) has long been one of the touchstones of humanist writing and rhetoric and gives us license to do largely as we please. Barbara Kingsolver conveys the spirit of humanism with this pungent comment: "It's hard for humans to doubt, even for a minute, that this program of plunking down our edifices ... over the entire landmass of planet earth is overall a good idea."[12]

Whereas the Christian perspective on humanity is grounded in scripture, humanism points to certain observable qualities that set human beings apart from the world they inhabit. What other creature possesses the ability to reflect, to recall the past and anticipate the future, to invent and use complex symbol systems, to create sophisticated cultures and consciously affect the course of evolution itself? All such attributes are thought to belong to humans exclusively and, taken as a whole, prove conclusively that one species only occupies a proprietary position in the great chain of being.

As an ideology, humanism arose to challenge the assertion of divine sovereignty made by the Abrahamic religions. In other words, humanism sought to replace theocentrism with anthropocentrism. The first (1933) and second (1973) Humanist Manifestos made this clear. Unfortunately, like Christianity, humanism positioned humankind outside rather than "*inside* the world," where biocentrists like Loren Eiseley felt we rightfully belonged. Furthermore, by putting human beings rather than God in the driver's seat, humanism inadvertently encouraged hubris and overweening ambition.[13]

Humanism presumes that we are clever enough to manipulate and remake the cosmos to better serve our own interests. Since humans are demonstrably "smarter" than nature, it makes sense that we have the right not only to tweak the existing order of things, but to radically rearrange it. Like Christianity, humanism has assumed ipso facto that human needs trump all others in the biotic community.

Until recently, only a few writers had the courage to expose this bias and question the assumptions of Christianity and humanism. Mark Twain was one, and late in life he delivered this stinging parody of the latter:

I have been studying the traits and dispositions of the lower animals (so-called), and contrasting them with the traits and dispositions of man. I find the result humiliating to me. For it obliges me to renounce my allegiance to the Darwinian theory of the Ascent of Man from the Lower Animals; since it now seems plain to me that the theory ought to be vacated in favor of a new and truer one, this new and truer one to be named the *Descent* of Man from the Higher Animals.[14]

What the prescient Twain recognized, and what the rest of us are slowly grasping, is that the planet requires greater humility on our part and a more patient and prudent approach to a host of humanly produced social and environmental problems.

Compared with Christianity, humanism is a relatively minor philosophical movement, and not many people in the Western world would self-identify as humanists. In most cases, it signifies an underlying attitude or a set of semiconscious assumptions. A clearer understanding of humanism is critical because of its close relationship to science, which, as John Gray notes, "encourages us to believe that, unlike any other animal, we can understand the natural world and thereby bend it to our will."[15]

Fortunately, as in Christianity, something of a shift is taking place among those of a humanist bent. The unqualified confidence of computer pioneer John von Neumann is less common than it once was, and his confident prediction to Congress in 1956 that humankind would soon be able to control the weather is not one many scientists would now make.[16]

While continuing to assert humanity's prerogatives and its right to a lion's share of the earth's resources, humanist commentators seem to have accepted Aldo Leopold's verdict that ecosystems are far more complex and self-organizing than we've given them credit for. We tamper with them at serious peril to ourselves, as a recent spate of catastrophic floods and wildfires has demonstrated. Nevertheless, true believers, whether Christian or humanist, still regard planet earth as a resource to be carefully utilized rather than as a community of sentient beings possessing intrinsic value and entitled to respect. The word *restraint* has been slow to enter the vocabulary of both parties.

Blind Faith in Progress

In keeping with the foregoing, humanism has maintained a consistently optimistic tone with respect to the planet's prospects. If any single phrase suitable in length for a bumper sticker captures the essence of humanism, it would be this one: *Onward and upward forever*.

Now, it is one thing to feel positive or hopeful about the future, and quite another to declare that the human condition is destined to improve or that there is no limit to what humans might achieve. The problem is compounded by a predilection for measuring progress using a strictly anthropocentric yardstick. Declines in the health and well-being of the nonhuman universe while humanity advances triumphantly forward are too often downplayed or overlooked. Such a restricted view of progress confounds attempts to instill sustainable values. "For a long time," Wendell Berry complains:

> ... we have understood ourselves as traveling toward some sort of industrial paradise, some new Eden conceived and constructed entirely by human ingenuity. ... Now we face overwhelming evidence that we are not smart enough to recover Eden by assault, and that nature does not tolerate or excuse our abuses.[17]

The criteria or "metrics" one uses to measure progress can make a profound difference. Humanists and scientists have historically exhibited a clear bias in favor of that which can be most readily quantified: calories consumed, cars on the road, years of schooling attained, dollars earned. Less obvious trends—higher incidents of substance abuse, mental and emotional illness, stress-related diseases, and anomie—have often escaped their attention. Only in recent years have researchers begun paying attention to a host of symptoms signaling a civilization in distress. Belatedly we have come to appreciate that as a country or a community "develops," quality of life may paradoxically suffer a setback.

An upwardly mobile Chinese family living in a village sixty miles from Beijing provides a snapshot of the problem. "In seven years," Peter Hessler writes, "the Wei family's income had increased six-fold." The head of the household smokes more than a pack of cigarettes a day and, because of the stress he's now under, has begun to drink heavily. His wife is probably addicted to amphetamine-based diet pills and has turned to a superstitious form of religion for solace. The couple's son is seriously overweight. The family's previously tranquil household has become the scene of heated arguments and bitter silences. Statisticians would undoubtedly declare that this family, representative of the emerging Chinese middle class, is making progress despite the heavy toll it has taken on the family's health and relationships.[18]

A Preference for Novelty

Humanism exhibits a strong preference for innovation over tradition, and that presents a third potential problem. The march of humankind is naturally and inevitably forward, and progress presumes that what is new and innovative will replace what is old and outmoded. This means that whatever virtues a stable, indigenous community might possess (self-sufficiency, less pressure, greater leisure, a clear sense of mutual responsibility, intergenerational connection, etc.) hold little value for those harboring a humanist bias. The members of such a culture might well be described as "happy in their ignorance" because they remain unaware of the wonders of fast food and digital TV.

To their credit, humanistic values have helped pave the way for rapid scientific, technological, and economic progress. But at the same time, humanism has often failed to anticipate or find ways to mitigate the undesirable side effects that have accompanied material and social development. The last century witnessed billions of people abandoning their traditional customs, stories, aesthetics, vocations, and communal commitments for the sake of a Happy Meal, employment in a sweatshop, or the opportunity to view *Baywatch* on TV.

Once appetites have been aroused and people begin to believe what the exponents of progress tell them—that the "old ways" no longer make sense—it's hard to turn back. A few, like the Wei family, will achieve their middle-class dream only to find it more of a burden than a blessing. The vast majority are not even that fortunate. The urban slums of the Third World teem with souls whose link to the past has been broken and who have very little on which to pin their hopes. If we are not more prudent in our planning, the great march forward may well land us in purgatory rather than paradise.

The humanist assumptions outlined above have owed their persuasive power to a faulty understanding of evolution itself. As Richard Lewontin points out, the disciplines of biology and paleontology provide little support for the thesis that with the passage of time "inferior" forms of life give way to ones that are qualitatively "superior." All we can really state with confidence about the natural world is that it ceaselessly changes—an observation that would have made perfect sense to both Heraclitus and Lao Tse, humanists of a sort who lived 2,500 years ago.

Nineteenth- and twentieth-century humanists incorrectly assumed that evolution produced "better" organisms, and from this they surmised that social and economic systems developed in similar fashion. Lewontin advises that we give up on this idea because it is problematic from both a moral and a practical standpoint. Cultures and creatures adapt, but they don't necessarily progress.[19]

And indeed, some cultures—even sophisticated ones—regress. As a host of recent anthropological and archeological discoveries have shown, the early inhabitants of the Americas knew more about the practice of sustainable agriculture—and a few other important things—than our best scientists do.[20]

The Western humanistic tradition has emphasized the progress of human civilization, commended the complete taming of nature, and forecast an increasingly comfortable life for those who come after us. Ironically, a more satisfying and sustainable way of life will quite likely require us to question each of these claims and step back a pace or two. Geologist Marcia Bjornerud's perspective reflects her work with materials that have been around for millions of years, and hers are words worth heeding: "Perhaps the greatest challenge we face in attempting to fathom the earth is to gain a proper sense of our own size as a human species; like spoiled children, we routinely overestimate our importance on the planet but underestimate the destructiveness of our self-absorption."[21]

Capitalism: Have We Made Too Many Compromises?

The modern free market system provides an enormous range of affordable goods and services for large numbers of people. In partnership with advanced technology, free enterprise capitalism has provided human beings with an unprecedented degree of physical comfort, a plethora of laborsaving devices and alimentary options, increased mobility, and mind-blowing entertainment. During the last century, we have created for ourselves a veritable elysian field of physical and sensual satisfaction. And yet troubling questions arise about the system's current methods and objectives.

A significant percentage and perhaps even a majority of the world's inhabitants are not being served by the present arrangement. The disparity between the haves and have-nots continues to widen, and our economic system (as presently constituted) seems ill equipped to redress this growing imbalance. Wealth continues to accumulate at the apex of the economic pyramid, while the number of underprivileged human beings worldwide who form the base of this pyramid grows even larger.

Recent government statistics show that 1.1 million more Americans fell below the poverty line in 2004, and the percentage of Americans living in poverty rose to 12.7 percent—a mark that has stubbornly refused to budge since the Great Society of the late 1960s despite a booming economy. According to economist Paul Krugman, the median real income of full-time, year-round male workers fell more than two percent in 2004—a year touted by *The Wall Street Journal* as one of solid economic growth.[22] Moreover, these figures probably understate the problem, because the federal government's official threshold for poverty is so low that it excludes another forty million individuals who can legitimately be described as "disadvantaged."[23] Since those figures were released, overall poverty rates have remained unchanged, and wages for all but the top tier of workers have failed to match the rising cost of fuel, food, and other basic commodities. As noted by the Economic Policy Institute, the first seven years of the new millennium have been extremely weak for the living standards of most households.[24]

A Small Town's Decline

If you grew up in one of thousands of America's smaller cities and towns and have tracked its economic performance over the course of the last three or four decades, chances are that conditions have not changed for the better. As a child in the 1950s and early 1960s, I perceived the lower Rock River Valley and my hometown of Dixon, Illinois, as a peaceful, reasonably prosperous, and more or less stable culture, somewhat analogous to Frodo Baggin's friendly Shire or the quietly proud rural Midwest depicted in the film *Hoosiers*. What my own community lacked in excitement and novelty, it made up for in charm, neighborliness, a shared sense of responsibility, and modest ambition. My interest in social and cultural sustainability emerges not only from literature on the subject but from vivid memories of these early years as well.

A child's eye undoubtedly overlooks much that is not so pleasant about small-town, country living—the parochialism, hypocrisy, and intolerance of difference that are often encountered in such communities and that adults are generally more aware of than children. Moreover, despite their innocent, friendly façades, towns like Dixon were often "sundown towns"—racially exclusive and antagonistic toward minorities.[25] But if my hometown wasn't exactly the idyll I perceived it to be, profound social and economic changes have made it less desirable than it once was.

Like most American communities whose economic well-being was vitally linked to modest, owner-occupied family farms, Dixon has stagnated in recent decades and taken on a somewhat forlorn appearance. Its principal employer is now a large state prison, recently converted from a home for the developmentally disabled, just beyond the city's boundaries. And while there are fewer empty storefronts on Main Street than in many other Illinois cities of similar size, patrons are few in number, and the sidewalks are seldom crowded. What was once a high-quality community is visibly struggling.

A major shift in patterns of ownership and economic exchange has been the proximate cause of decline among towns, villages, and even small cities throughout the United States. Like most of its counterparts, Dixon today is dominated by businesses whose stake in the community is minimal. Its major highways are lined with all-too-familiar food franchises and chain stores, and the number of family farms in the vicinity has dwindled. In an economy increasingly dominated by service-sector jobs, purchasing power has declined, and a cursory inspection of the city's older neighborhoods reveals peeling paint, missing shingles, and neglected landscaping. Even the properties adjacent to Ronald Reagan's boyhood home are a little on the scruffy side (the Reagan property itself remains a well-groomed local shrine).

Dixon is merely a microcosm and, despite its decline, remains more prosperous than many comparable cities between the Appalachian and Sierra mountain ranges. It illustrates a growing concern about the fateful erosion of community life throughout America, and reflects a larger fear that the way we Americans currently conduct business is ultimately unsustainable. So what would it take to make Dixon, and its counterparts across the country, economically and culturally vigorous again? How might the application of sustainable principles improve communities like Dixon in the twenty-first century?

A Growing Global Problem

Conditions in the developing world are much more troubling. Fifty-six percent of that portion of the planet live on less than two dollars a day—the official international poverty benchmark. Ten million Third World children under the age of five die each year simply from lack of essential resources.[26] While a global economic recession might contribute to such conditions, they were allowed to persist in an era of burgeoning production and low inflation, when more goods and commodities were available than at any other time in history. We have seen better than a sixfold increase in global economic output since 1950, but only a fifth of that new wealth has found its way into the hands of four-fifths of the world's people. Had the distribution been more equitable, economist David Korten observes, "poverty would now be history, democracy would be secure, and war would be but a distant memory."[27]

Even former Federal Reserve Chairman Alan Greenspan, that Ayn Randian individualist and perennial defender of an untrammeled free market, now concedes that a rising tide not only has failed to lift, but has caused too many fragile boats to founder: "The income gap between the rich and the rest of the population has become so wide, and is growing so fast, that it might eventually threaten the stability of democratic capitalism itself."[28]

Unfortunately, Mr. Greenspan's ominous forecast has not been accompanied by any list of appropriate remedies. I suspect the former Fed chairman knows as well as anyone else what a deep hole we have dug for ourselves. Too much natural and human capital has already been recklessly consumed. Yes, technology and the unleashed power of free enterprise have helped to produce a century-long upsurge in our species' material well-being. But Western civilization's astounding economic growth has been driven by unsustainable, extractive practices that have rapidly drawn down the planet's vast resources, leaving inhabitants of regions previously rich in natural capital powerless and penniless.

Its successes notwithstanding, our profligate production and development systems could not have rapidly produced a civilization so rich without that civilization discounting—and deceiving itself about—many of the social and environmental costs. "Our economic system," Boston College sociologist Charles Derber bleakly concludes, "is at war with nature"[29]—an assessment in keeping with anthropologist Loren Eiseley's 1970 description of human beings as "world eaters."[30]

Our current ways of conducting business have not been kind to either the "unbuilt" or the "built" environment. In 2005, the American Society of Civil Engineers issued its report card on the U.S. infrastructure, giving the nation's airports, roads, school buildings, and drinking water all a grade of D and its bridges and rail system a mediocre C.[31] Clearly, the current system is due for an overhaul, and the four keys of sustainability promise a fresh approach to the pressing social and economic problems we face.

According to Curtis White, what we are now witnessing is a contest of competing world views. This is not the "clash of civilizations" famously depicted by Samuel P. Huntington, which pits medieval Muslim jihadists against progressive-minded modernists. In White's view, one camp "sees nature and humanity as a culture of *life*," while a second "sees nature and humanity instrumentally, as *things* to be manipulated rationally and technically in a culture of *profit*."[32]

According to its advocates (of whom there is no shortage), it is *precisely* the "culture of profit" that provides the proper incentive for ordinary men and women to become efficient producers and dependable consumers. Free enterprise capitalism has secured for us the many comforts and amenities that define modern middle-class life. The principles that inform and support this system have become central to our self-understanding and to our core belief about how the world ought to work. The culture of profit receives strong and steady sanction from the highest authorities.

One of the primary reasons people haven't been able to grasp, embrace, and apply sustainable principles is that these principles are often difficult to reconcile with the rules that currently govern the marketplace. Sustainability emerges from and is accountable to the culture of life. It is not antithetical to profit, but does not treat it as a categorical imperative.

Adam Smith Would Disapprove

Capitalism has been around, in one form or another, for a very long time. There are indications of a thriving market economy in eastern India during the Axial Age.[33] The prophet Muhammad himself married into a family of successful traders, and the Italian city-states of Venice and Florence owed their early prominence to a particularly resourceful class of entrepreneurs and investors. Still, for most of human history, business and trade were viewed as necessary but not particularly admirable activities. In other words, a true culture of profit did not really exist. Free enterprise capitalism's star began to rise only in the eighteenth century when Adam Smith produced a novel theory based on personal observations of economic activity in his native Scotland.

Champions of the free market venerate Smith almost as much as Christians do the Holy Ghost. John Mackey, founder and CEO of Whole Foods, praises the noble Scotsman with phrases that resemble those of the disciples at Pentecost: "He is one of the greatest thinkers of all time. ... I have seen the invisible hand, and it is beautiful indeed!"[34]

Ironically, Adam Smith would no more condone capitalism as it is currently practiced than would Jesus approve the direction Christianity has taken in the centuries since the Gospels were composed. Many of Smith's observations have become irrelevant in a global economy dominated by multinational corporations and financial institutions whose purpose seems solely to maximize their return on investment.

Adam Smith developed his theories with much smaller, geographically restricted economies in mind. He was fundamentally opposed to absentee ownership, believing that capitalists could be held accountable only if they lived in the communities where they conducted business. The father of free enterprise always presumed that responsible (and successful) entrepreneurs would contribute by their activities to the aesthetic, educational, and spiritual uplift of the community. For Smith, profit making was a private means designed to secure a positive public outcome.

Were he alive today, Smith would find little to commend in the world's growing "wealth gap" and in the wholesale subjugation of labor to capital. He would have been scandalized by the measures modern businesses take to externalize their costs, thus imposing excessive burdens on future generations in order to fill the coffers of the privileged few. Smith was always a Christian moralist first and an economic theorist second. He fervently believed that, managed properly, a free market would be a boon to society.

The fact is, free market capitalism as practiced today owes more to late nineteenth-century social Darwinism than to the morally informed arguments of Adam Smith. The latter described acquisitiveness as a "necessary vice," but for many an aspiring MBA, it has become a virtue to be assiduously cultivated.

In *The Devil's Dictionary*, Ambrose Bierce described the corporation as an "ingenious device for obtaining individual profit without individual responsibility"—a definition that seems as applicable today as it was in Bierce's own Gilded Age. Cutthroat competition (or price-fixing collusion) is the economic rule of thumb, and "fair practice" is considered a fool's game. The objective is to maximize profit by whatever means necessary. Sadly, philosopher Robert Solomon points out, such behavior is deemed eminently sensible. "The real test of rationality . . . is maximizing one's own interests," Solomon complains. "It is the ability to get what you want, and this is stated not as an interpretation but as an inescapable insight into human nature."[35]

If free enterprise capitalism really operated as Smith believed it should, our world would look much different than it does, and the lion's share of the benefits would not be scooped up by such a small proportion of the population. He insisted that healthy communities are composed of multiple stakeholders, all of whose interests are taken into consideration. Diversity is the name of the game in economies as well as ecosystems. But unless savvy consumers and attentive regulators require it, the interests of "stakeholders" are routinely ignored by today's large corporations. Indicative of this is the less-than-stellar record compiled by the *Fortune* 500 companies with respect to sustainable practices designed to protect the environment and the local community. According to Joel Makower of GreenBiz.com, in spite of the concept's growing popularity only a dozen of the country's largest firms have made sustainability a corporate priority.[36]

A Better Way of Doing Business

Capitalism can be practiced in a variety of ways, and those who play the game conscientiously and fairly should be commended rather than castigated. We are right, the authors of *Good Capitalism, Bad Capitalism, and the Economics of Growth and Prosperity* concede, to be troubled by an oligarchic system in which the bulk of wealth and power belongs to a well-positioned elite. They agree that attempts by powerful business lobbies to control public policy must be thwarted. Still, responsible entrepreneurial investors should be provided sufficient incentive to take risks because "the engine of growth is innovation." If this means that some will become richer than others, it also means that society as a whole is likely to experience an increase of well-being.[37]

A few examples of capitalist activity consonant with both profitability and sustainability have already been provided: the Joie de Vivre Hotels and Sonoma Mountain Village. To that list I would add the six Wisconsin microbreweries that recently entered into partnership with local farmers to produce organic barley and hops for their premium beers. "This helps farmers who are my neighbors," one brewmaster notes, while another points out that today people are paying attention to where a product's ingredients come from and prefer that they be local.[38]

On a larger scale, the Business Alliance for Local Living Economies (BALLE), an association of fifty-one independently operated business networks representing more than fiteen thousand businesses and community organizations, reflects a promising trend. Its mission states that BALLE "is committed to prosperity through local business ownership, economic justice, cultural diversity, and environmental stewardship." BALLE's executive director reports that its members share a commitment "to adopt as many sustainable practices as we can."[39]

In my own state of Wisconsin, a twenty-year-old state-sponsored program to revitalize stagnant downtown districts is gathering momentum. Keeping central shopping districts competitive with outlying malls and big-box developments is one of the keys to assuring that more wealth is recycled through the local economy and greater economic diversity is maintained. This in turn gives residents of these communities more incentive to stick around and make a real commitment to where they live. Wisconsin's Main Street program works with cities as large as Milwaukee and as small as Tigerton (population 764).[40] This is capitalism more in keeping with Adam Smith's vision—a model in which sustainable values are factored in.

Kinks in the Current System

Moving from generalities to more specific issues, four prominent features of free market capitalism as it is typically practiced constrain further movement in a positive and life-affirming direction:

- The habit of short-term thinking
- A fixation with individual property rights
- A tendency to put a price tag on too much of the world
- Competition that just won't quit

A Talent for the Quick Killing

The primary definition of the word *consume*, as *New Internationalist* coeditor Jess Worth reminds us, is "to do away with completely: *destroy*." A secondary meaning is "to spend wastefully: *to squander*." Technically, "a consumer is one who squanders, uses up, and destroys," which is precisely what our widely heralded consumer culture has managed to accomplish in less time than it took for some of Europe's great cathedrals to be completed.[41] In our headlong pursuit of short-term profit and disposable products, we have systematically exhausted the sources from which we draw sustenance while simultaneously subverting the purpose for which certain important institutions were designed.

Consider the newspaper industry. Apart from the impact that web-based information sources have had on print media, newspapers have been undermined by the consortiums that in recent years have purchased them—investors with a fine nose for profit but not for news. Despite the fact that the profit margin for large newspapers has historically far surpassed that of most other businesses, the owners and business managers of many of the nation's dailies have attempted at every turn to cut operating costs. Staffing in newsrooms across the country was slashed, which prompted the principled resignation of more than one managing editor. John Carroll, formerly of the *Baltimore Sun* and the *Los Angeles Times,* was among them. While acknowledging that the old family-owned newspapers were far from perfect, Carroll argues that they did understand that for them to remain viable, solid journalistic practices had to be maintained. When "newspapers shed personnel and shrink the news hole [the space devoted to news]," profits may grow but "readers get less," and that is an unsustainable proposition, Carroll concludes.[42]

When a major newspaper's ability to provide thorough coverage and cogent commentary is compromised, culture is diminished, communications are disrupted, and democracy itself is endangered. For some, this may seem like an exaggeration; after all, there is always the Internet. But as Michael Massing points out, the daily newspaper is still the main collector and distributor of news in America. All our electronic outlets—television, radio, Internet—depend on the investigative and reporting staffs of newspapers for reliable, up-to-date information.[43] The cost to society of a mandatory high quarterly return on investment is incalculable.

This is an instance of what John Bogle characterizes as "manager's capitalism," which he defines as "a system of rules, practices, and standards of behavior designed to bring quick and sure rewards to a few at long term cost to many."[44] It could also be called "take the money and run," a practice with which I am personally familiar.

Facing the prospect of sending three children to college in the late 1960s, my parents sold our family farm in the upper Midwest and invested the proceeds in a Holiday Inn franchise in Naples, Florida. My father managed as well as owned the Inn, and my mother and I both had roles in the supporting cast.

The lower Sun Coast was still relatively undeveloped at the time, but as Naples' reputation grew, business picked up; soon we were expanding the operation. Every year saw improvements and upgrades, and a consistent effort was made to keep the facility clean and well maintained. As a result, we received kudos from our customers and commendations from Holiday Inns International as well as from the local business community.

After a few profitable years of operation, my parents received an attractive lease offer from a nonlocal leisure corporation. It was an overture they readily accepted, particularly since the lease contained provisions designed to prevent abuse of the property. Unfortunately, once the papers had been signed and control ceded to the new absentee operator, wholesale violations of both the letter and spirit of the agreement ensued. Threats of legal action accomplished little (the corporation commanded resources far greater than our own). Hospitality and housekeeping awards and positive customer reviews ceased, but these meant nothing to the lessee anyway. Minimize expenses in order to maximize profit—that was the name of the game.

Property Reigns Supreme

Since the nation's founding, Americans have been staunch supporters of the individual right to own and exercise sovereign control over private property. "Government is instituted to protect property of every sort," James Madison wrote. "This being the end of government, that alone is a *just* government which *impartially* secures to every man whatever is his *own*."[45]

Visiting the United States from abroad, Alexis de Tocqueville confirmed that Americans who seemed indifferent to some other rights were positively obsessed with this one. "In no country is the love of property more active and more anxious," he wrote in 1840.[46] Precisely here is where a second economic impediment to the development of a more sustainable economic system comes into play.

Capitalism, as Bill McKibben notes, tends to be individualistically rather than communally oriented. Accordingly, those who own property are to be given discretion to use (or abuse) it as they like. Property rights ensure that owners will be able to pursue their self-interest with minimal concern for the manner in which others in the proximate area are affected. Despite zoning laws, "smart-growth" initiatives, and environmental regulations, individual property owners have routinely been able to defend their prerogatives in the face of spirited public opposition.

Three-quarters of a century ago, Aldo Leopold expressed frustration with Americans' stubborn unwillingness to compromise on this issue even when serious conservation issues were at stake. "Individual thinkers since the days of Ezekiel and Isaiah have asserted that the despoliation of land is not only inexpedient, but wrong. Society, however, has not yet affirmed their belief," Leopold wrote.[47]

The ability of adversely affected citizens to prevent a private development plan from being approved and put in place is often very limited. Consequently, industrial feedlots mar and pollute the countryside, chemical plants are constructed in critical water-sheds, biologically and hydrologically important wetlands are drained for agriculture or residential housing, and auto-dependent big-box developments with acres of impermeable surface parking are not only permitted but enabled with tax-incremental financing. The problem that Leopold highlighted has not gone away and may grow more severe as the nation's courts increasingly side with those who complain that onerous environmental restrictions and regional growth plans violate their property rights.

A Price for Everything and Everything for a Price

"Everything and everyone has its price" is an axiom Robert Redford was determined to prove in his role as a love-starved business mogul in the movie *Indecent Proposal*. Free market capitalism exhibits an ineluctable tendency to reduce every artifact, every animate being, and every cultural activity to the status of a commodity. The notion that certain aspects of existence or portions of the planet possess intrinsic rather than instrumental value is largely absent from today's economic calculus.

The manner in which health and medical care is apportioned in the United States demonstrates how commodification subverts certain basic, noneconomic interests. Our system is "the only one in the world based on avoiding sick people," Marcia Angell of the Harvard Medical School complains. "Care in this country is distributed on the ability to pay, not according to medical need."[48]

Medical services cost substantially more in the United States than in any other developed (or developing) nation, cover fewer people every year, generate significant profits for the various players within the system (e.g., hospitals, clinics, insurers, physicians), but yield poorer outcomes with respect to most measures of wellness.[49] Until recently, few political leaders of stature have been willing to confront the problem head-on and state unequivocally that medical treatment is a human right, not an economic commodity. A more egalitarian and sustainable system won't be forthcoming until greater support for this proposition is forthcoming.

Commodification has given rise to the science of "cost-benefit analysis," which claims to provide an objective means for determining the value of an old-growth forest, the life of a Sudanese child, or a regulatory statute. Apologists for this approach to societal problem solving argue that the most economical (or profitable) choice is always preferable. For those who rigorously apply this methodology, very little, if anything, possesses intrinsic value.

In recent years, cost-benefit analysis has even been used to justify illegal or unethical corporate behavior. If "doing the right thing" would be more expensive than paying fines and penalties for breaking the law, it makes perfect sense to be a bad citizen. Or if manufacturing "enhancement" and "lifestyle" drugs for the privileged few is better for the bottom line than providing vaccines to combat the life-threatening diseases that afflict ninety percent of the world's people, cost-benefit makes the choice both easy and eminently defensible.[50]

A Contested Life

In case you hadn't noticed, Americans are a highly competitive people. A bumper sticker on one minivan proudly announces that an honor student belongs to the family, while another car sports a bumper sticker proclaiming that the owner's Irish setter is smarter than any honor student. Our children learn the lesson early: they compete not only in sports, but in spelling and geography bees, math Olympics, and art and poetry contests. Competition for the classiest car, the most capacious condominium, the BlackBerry with the most features, and even the prettiest preadolescent (remember JonBenet Ramsey?) consumes the attention of adults. "America," George Soros writes, "has cultivated competition and carried it to unsustainable extremes."[51]

Competitiveness is a built-in attribute that in an earlier era may have helped ensure the survival of Homo sapiens. While it's true that some archeologists have argued, based on excavations, that Neolithic human communities were more collaborative than competitive in nature, for as long as written records have been kept competition has occupied a prominent place in the repertoire of human behavior.[52]

As the principles and practice of free enterprise capitalism have spread, competition has crept into practically every nook and

cranny of our lives—too often with corrosive effect. The "suc-
ceed-at-all-costs" philosophy has diminished the credibility of venerable sporting events like the Tour de France and horse racing's
Triple Crown. Motorists' incautious and discourteous behavior on
the street is due as much to competitiveness as to impatience.
Pulling into traffic produces an automatic reassessment: harried
fellow commuters like ourselves toward whom we should exhibit
sympathy become competitors for scarce road surface.

Similarly, for the last fifty years the trend in new and remod-
eled single-family housing has been toward ever-larger residences.
Homes built in the 1950s averaged less than a thousand square
feet, but a half century later the *average* new home was 150 percent larger.[53] Fueled by cheap credit and the competitive spirit,
McMansions seemed for a while to be springing up everywhere.
Thousands of families succumbed to economist Thorstein Veblen's
"invidious comparison"—they just *had* to have that state-of-the-
art media room and three-car garage like their friends the Joneses
had. Many of those purchases were less than prudent, and the
occupants now face foreclosure.

In moderation and conditioned by other values, competition is
not a bad thing. In fact, it has played a prominent and positive role
in my own life. For many years I ran competitively as an individual
and as a member of a road-racing team. I relish competitive card
games and believe that a modicum of collegial competition keeps a
professional sharp and motivated. On the other hand, I have also
witnessed the deleterious effect that a culture steeped in competition can have on those of a milder temperament.

I sometimes wonder whether the current epidemic of childhood obesity and the disinclination of many children to exercise
aren't in part responses to competitive excess. Many inactive children may feel intimidated and simply choose to opt out. They
retire to the family entertainment center or to sedentary computer games where players are able to participate under a cloak of
anonymity.

Carried to the extremes we see in our own capitalist culture,
competition compromises our efforts to instill a sustainable ethos.

Competition is about winning, not thriving. We need to understand that the two don't necessarily complement each other. Having been taught that a successful economy requires spirited competition, we don't recognize the alternative systems that have worked reasonably well for centuries.

Take the peoples of Taos, Acoma, Zuni, and Hopiland, for example. Descendants of the sophisticated Anasazi culture that dominated the Southwest a thousand years ago, the Pueblans have worked, played, and thrived in the same well-integrated communities for centuries, having discovered how to live in harmony with the high desert landscape. Despite outside oppression and the introduction of catastrophic diseases, they have maintained their ancestral mores and collaborative economic pursuits.

Whether they will be able to resist the steady, encroaching pressure of American consumerism remains to be seen, but it is quite likely that collaboration rather than competition has enabled the survival of these remote tribes thus far. It may well be that the forces discussed above—short-term profit taking, property rights, commodification, and competition—have helped create the most materially successful civilization in recorded history. Will that civilization prove to be as sustainable as that of the Pueblos? Perhaps. But without significant modifications, I suspect it won't be.

Again, the foregoing should not be construed as a generalized indictment of entrepreneurs, business owners, and others who embrace capitalist values. The problem is one not of kind, but of degree. The British statesman Lord Acton once warned that civilizations typically fail from the excess application of a "first principle." It is no secret that for quite some time now the first principle of *our* society has been profit making. If we do not succeed in putting it in its proper place, our civilization will also eventually fail. "What is called for," Curtis White writes, "is an enormous project of translations ... that will transform capitalism from a state of nature to an ethical system that must defend its values in ... a competing market of values."[54]

The Broken Promise of Technology

Although it may seem counterintuitive, technology has become a powerful impediment to the development of a sustainable culture and lifestyle.

Clearly, many modern inventions have proved amazingly beneficial. They represent appropriate technologies because they respond to a real need without creating a host of new problems. The bicycle, which Eric Sorensen describes as "a masterpiece of physics," is one such device. He points out that a human being on a bicycle is more efficient (in terms of calories expended per mile) than one riding in a train or airplane, not to mention an automobile, boat, or tractor-trailer. And that's not all. "Pound for pound," Sorensen adds, "a person riding a bike can go farther on a calorie of food than a gazelle can running, a salmon swimming, or an eagle flying."[55]

Concentrated solar power (CSP) affords a second example of appropriate, sustainable technology. First used by the Chinese almost three thousand years ago, CSP was seen as a promised means of producing power in this country until cheap oil was discovered in the Middle East. At the most basic level, inexpensive CSP ovens can be used by families in poor countries to cook meals and purify water. No need to cut down scarce trees, pollute the air, or pay for imported power. At a much greater order of magnitude, CSP generating plants located in desert regions may be capable of producing inexpensive, pollution-free electricity for tens of millions of households.[56]

The Power to Move Mountains

Regrettably, some familiar tools aren't as appropriate as they should be and don't support the principle and practice of sustainability—particularly when used imprudently and in the wrong places.

For example, several years ago my wife Trina and I traveled with our son to Florida for a week's vacation in the Panhandle. In the late 1970s Trina and I had done graduate work at Florida State University in Tallahassee, and we both retained fond memories of weekend excursions along the aptly named Lost Coast extending from St. Mark's inlet to Pensacola. A quarter of a century ago, this sunny stretch of stunning white sand beaches and vast salt marshes so vital to the upper Gulf Coast's marine ecology had yet to be developed. Ramshackle oyster bars, streams running clear beneath the live oak canopy, and mile upon mile of pine and palmetto forest preserved a legacy that the peninsula's Gold and Sun Coasts had sacrificed decades earlier. Only Panama City, a kitschy resort community known for its inexpensive motels and working-class clientele, interrupted the overall serenity of the scene.

Although road signs and brochures still refer to this area as the Lost Coast, the name no longer applies. As we drove west from Apalachicola, we were astonished by the new resorts and housing projects that had sprung up along the waterfront and further inland. By 2001 so much of the coastline had been privatized that we often found it difficult to gain access to or even catch a glimpse of the glistening Gulf of Mexico. Judging from the vast sweep of pine and palmetto forest that had already been cleared for future development and the constant din created by phalanxes of earth-moving equipment, the Panhandle's transformation was still a work in progress. After a few days of disappointing exploration, it became obvious that the Lost Coast was indeed "lost," but in a far different sense than it had been previously.

Having lived for a number of years on the lower Gulf Coast, I wasn't surprised that the Panhandle, with its mild climate and clean waters, had finally succumbed to the same relentless development pressures that had altered so much of Florida's real estate. Most of the state's unprotected, accessible coastline had already been claimed. What *did* startle me was the speed and rashness with which the transformation to the west was taking place.

One morning I sat sipping coffee on the veranda of our historic Apalachicola hotel, watching as a rather formidable earthmoving machine across the street scoured a football-field-size piece of real estate. Having spent my early life amid large pieces of farm equipment, I was familiar with such implements, but it had been years since I'd closely observed a bulldozer at work. It was astounding to see what a new generation of human "tools" is capable of doing, and it didn't take much imagination to appreciate the effect they must have on Amazonia, rural China, and numerous other landscapes throughout the planet. "The bulldozer," as Philip Shabecoff has observed, "and not the atom bomb may turn out to be the most destructive invention of the twentieth century."[57] The venerable Robert Aitken, founder of the Buddhist Diamond Sangha in Hawaii, may not have been too far off the mark when he said "there is just one thing new, and that's *technology*." A compelling ideology, a captivating vision, or an elaborate economic model can only produce as much change as a culture's available tools permit. Since the industrial revolution, humankind's technological abilities have increased exponentially, breaking or straining every bond of cultural, social, and ecological restraint. As Aitken notes:

> We human beings can now devise better ways to slaughter people and create slaves and despoil the land than we could earlier because our weapons and our communications and our machines are more efficient. That's all. That's really all.[58]

A Truly Mixed Blessing

Some, of course, will strenuously object to such an assessment. On balance, they would argue, technology has been overwhelmingly advantageous to our species. Medicine has extended the human life span and prevented countless premature deaths from preventable maladies. Tech-savvy Bill Gates has poured hundreds of millions of dollars into programs to eliminate AIDS and malaria in underdeveloped nations, and he would surely argue that the key to human health and happiness is technology.

Technology has also led to vast improvements in both the quantity and quality of basic human necessities—clothing, shelter, food. At least a billion people now enjoy amenities that even the kings and cardinals of three hundred years ago could never have imagined. A genuine sense of global community now exists, thanks to mass communication and rapid transportation.

It is pointless to deny the many benefits that advanced technology has conferred on humankind. The problem, as I see it, is more fundamental: our lives and life in general are held hostage by a technological imperative. Like capitalism, technology has achieved a cult-like status. Most people's understanding of it is superficial at best, so we hold technology in awe and largely forfeit our right to challenge it. With its aura of mystery, its panoply of specially trained high priests and glib promises of redemption, the Church of Technology commands the fealty of billions.

To question the wisdom of our technocrats is to risk being labeled a technophobe or a Luddite. Technology aspires to omni-competence and asserts it has (or will have) an answer for every-thing. Even the unwanted side effects it has spawned can be readily resolved with yet another dose of the same medicine, we are told. If habitat loss has led to an alarming decrease in biodiver-sity, technology's response is to clone new representatives of endangered species. Lewis Mumford, the twentieth-century's pre-mier historian of science and technology, recognized the shadow side of this development:

> Western Society has accepted as unquestionable a techno-logical imperative that is quite as arbitrary as the most primi-tive taboo: not merely the duty to foster invention and constantly to create technological novelties, but equally the duty to surrender to these novelties unconditionally, just because they are offered, without respect to their ... conse-quences.[59]

The planetary scorecard isn't easy to calculate. Modern farm-ing methods have enabled us to produce far more food than ever before, but intensive, chemically dependent agriculture has also seriously depleted or poisoned local water supplies, reduced soil fertility, and weakened or wiped out numerous traditional cultures that had practiced sustainable, subsistence-level farming for cen-turies. Animal abuse is a fixture of factory farming and seriously challenges our moral sensibilities.

A new generation of "super-seeds" has helped feed a burgeon-ing world population, but has also led to a dramatic decline in genetic food-grain diversity. Traditional plant food varieties used for millennia are becoming extinct. "The very success of plant breeders' efforts," John Seabrook writes, "is eliminating the raw material that made their work possible."[60] Moreover, the past fifty years have seen a noticeable decline in the food value of many common garden crops—apples, tomatoes, potatoes, to name just a few. Technological innovations that permit farmers to grow fruits and vegetables that ship easily, look pretty, and enjoy a longer shelf life have often produced varieties with fewer nutrients and less palatability than those that preceded them.[61]

Fortunately, alternatives do exist. A method of crop production known as "Grow Bio-intensive" promises to be far more sustainable than the industrial system we currently employ. It actually "gives more back to the earth than it takes," and requires a fraction of the energy, water, and chemical inputs needed by conventional agriculture to produce a comparable yield.[62] Wes Jackson's Salina Institute has developed an equally prudent, scientifically sound agricultural system of "perennial polycropping" that marries agriculture to the ecology of the Midwest's native tall-grass prairies. Jules Pretty, an English agronomist, has studied these and similar small-scale, low-tech projects throughout the world and is encouraged by what they have achieved: an average increase of ninety-three percent in per-hectare food production.[63]

However impressive these results might seem to some, they are not sufficient to persuade the world's major agricultural players to support a shift to low-tech production. Corporate giants like Archer Daniels Midland and Cargill and machinery manufacturers such as John Deere, Caterpillar, and Kubota dominate the industry, and their interests are best served by the current system. Spokesmen for the agricultural industry have managed to convince most people that, despite its drawbacks, the industrial approach affords humankind the best chance to feed itself. As Jason Epstein put it recently, "Sustainable farming is not sustainable on a national scale any more than Alice Waters can cook for the entire United States."[64]

Technological innovations have caused problems in a number of other areas. Spectacular developments in electronic communications have often been lauded for their ability to bring the world closer together, bridge cultural differences, and increase commerce.

The flip side is that networked computer systems and new software packages allow supervisors to monitor employees' every keystroke in the workplace. An invasive program appropriately dubbed "The Investigator" not only permits the minute tracking of the computer operator's performance, but automatically blows the whistle when certain subversive words (e.g., *union, boss*) appear. The unreflective and automatic substitution of un-nuanced e-mail for phone or face-to-face communication, as the authors of *Send: Why People Email So Badly and How to Do It Better* point out, has multiplied misunderstandings and sullied many relationships.[65]

More seriously still, the ability to transfer vast sums of money electronically has made the lives of workers throughout the world far less secure. Through mass media, Western consumer culture has penetrated the far reaches of the planet, instilling new desires, uprooting old customs, disrupting traditional cultures, and causing mass migrations. Popular democracy has also suffered from a media of sufficient power and sophistication to literally "manufacture consent."

When it comes to our everyday lives, high-tech entertainment, like genetically modified food, doesn't necessarily produce greater satisfaction. A few years ago I had the opportunity to watch a 2005 World Series game between the Chicago White Sox and Houston Astros on a huge, wall-mounted digital TV at the home of an old friend. It was, in its own way, pretty impressive. But I also have fond memories of spending childhood evenings in bed listening to the play-by-play of my beloved White Sox with a small transistor radio hugged to my ear so as not to disturb my indifferent, sleeping brother. A comment made by the retired minister John Ames in Marilynne Robinson's award-winning novel *Gilead* reflects my own experience: "We have television now, a gift from the congregation with the specific intent of letting me watch baseball, and I will. But it seems two-dimensional beside radio."[66]

Radio, as John Ames suggests, leaves more to the imagination and demands one's full attention in a way that television simply does not. For some of us, this produces a richer, deeper pleasure than much-ballyhooed high-definition TV.

I wonder, too, how many people are as irritated as I am by the ubiquity of television in public places—airports, restaurants, waiting rooms, fitness centers—where they inhibit conversation and make reading or serious thinking practically impossible. I also worry that today's "plugged-in" generations will fail to develop strong, protective feelings for the natural world when their primary experience of it is vicarious and often badly distorted by ratings-driven programs like *Survivor* or *The Great Race*.

Marvels and Monsters

A familiar entity in Jewish folklore is the *golem*—an artificial being created by magically gifted rabbis to serve as an ally and servant. The golem, however, is something of a wild card. Normally he follows his master's instructions, but in a few famous legends he becomes uncontrollable and ultimately destructive.

Like Mary Shelley's great gothic novel *Frankenstein*, these rabbinical stories were meant to serve a cautionary purpose. "The golem," Luke Mitchell observes, "... turns on us not because we know too much, but because we know too little. We are punished not by the gods or by fate but by our own willful stupidity."[67]

The preceding observations remind us how important it is to pay closer attention, exercise patience, and apply greater prudence as we select technologies to reshape or restore our world. It is not a question of repudiating toolmaking, but simply drawing back a bit so that we can recognize how rapidly and indiscriminately we have been "burning through entire galaxies of other life ... amputating ourselves from the rest of creation," as Edward Hoagland soulfully laments.[68]

And having placed ourselves in a position where we can see the complete picture more clearly, perhaps we will also come to agree with a point Buckminster Fuller tried to impress upon us many years ago: that it's time "for our technology to do more with less."[69]

Are We Ready for a Shift?

Although they often have a hard time fathoming just where the problems lie, increasing numbers of people are coming to see the hazards of continuing with business as usual. A study commissioned in 1995 by the Merck Family Fund showed that a substantial majority of Americans—nearly ninety percent, in fact—feared that the country was headed in the wrong direction even then. Respondents blamed materialism, greed, and selfishness for weakening the bonds of family and community and compromising our sense of responsibility to and for others. The Merck survey revealed a growing awareness of the negative social and cultural consequences of America's materialistic orientation, and it registered deep concern about what the future might hold.[70]

A more recent poll conducted in April 2008 showed similar results, indicating that more Americans than ever before believe the United States is headed in the wrong direction. Significantly for the issue of sustainability, less than half predicted that their children would enjoy the same material advantages and opportunities as they did, and only a third believed the next generation would be better off than their own.[71] Whether a regime change in Washington will decisively affect people's perceptions and make them more hopeful remains to be seen. The Obama presidency faces impressive challenges, not all of which are amenable to political solutions. At some point, more of us must make a concerted effort to take charge of our own destiny by setting new goals and adopting sound practices. This may not be easy. Most of those who participated in the Merck survey saw little if any connection between their own lifestyles and the trends that concerned them.

But perhaps people will adjust if they recognize that meaningful and attractive alternatives are available. I believe that once individuals develop an appreciation for sustainability and its potential, they will have greater confidence in the future and feel more empowered themselves. The four keys highlighted in the chapters that follow are meant to engage individuals, families, and communities in creating and maintaining the good life for themselves, regardless of who happens to occupy the Oval Office.

Part Two

The Four Keys

Chapter 3

Pay Attention

Living on Long Island, the eastern tip of New York, in 1985, anthropologist David Abram rode out a strong hurricane that littered roadways with fallen trees, cut power lines, and interrupted telephone service. For several days, he remembers, the people in his town were forced to abandon their automobiles and, if the distance wasn't prohibitive, walk to their workplace or to the store.

This was, on the one hand, surely a time of inconvenience and frustration. But on the other hand, a rare natural disaster afforded the residents of the community a unique opportunity to reconnect both with each other and with the surrounding environment. Abram remembers that without the incessant din of internal combustion engines:

> The rhythms of the crickets and birdsong became clearly audible. Flocks were migrating south for the winter, and many of us found ourselves simply listening, with new and childlike curiosity, to the ripples of song in the still-standing trees and the fields.
>
> And at night the sky was studded with stars! Many children, their eyes no longer blocked by the glare of houselights and streetlamps, saw the Milky Way for the first time, and were astonished. For those few days and nights our town

became a community aware of its place in an encompassing cosmos. Even our noses seemed to come awake, the fresh smells from the ocean somehow more vibrant and salty.

The breakdown of our technologies had forced a return to our senses and ... we suddenly found ourselves inhabiting a sensuous world that had been waiting, for years, at the very fringe of our awareness—an intimate terrain infused by birdsong, salt spray, and the light of the distant stars.[1]

Abram carried away from this experience a conviction that a sustainable future for the planet and its imperiled ecosystems requires precisely the sort of sensorial reengagement accidentally triggered by that hurricane. Logical arguments, empirical evidence, and a stern environmental ethic simply won't suffice to create the passions necessary for people to alter well-worn habits of wastefulness and indifference.

The perspective of geologist Marcia Bjornerud is similar. Having spent the past several centuries "mastering" the forces of nature and positioning ourselves as creation's dominant species, we suddenly discover to our chagrin that we have been literally leeching the life out of the planet with our technological exuberance. Because our inborn animal sensitivity to the natural world has been knocked out of commission, it's hard for us to understand where we went wrong and what might be required to get back on the right track. "But if we *just stop to look,*" Bjornerud writes, "we can glimpse infinity again, in every grain of sand and living cell on this old Earth—a planet that is at once ... comprehensible and complex, predictable and chaotic, robust and fragile."[2]

Among the perceptual skills Western culture tries to teach, attentiveness isn't emphasized nearly enough. Most of us remember being admonished in school to stop fidgeting or whispering and "pay attention." But how much sustained effort was made to *inculcate* that basic skill or to make it part of the core curriculum?

A Famous Piece of Advice: *Look!*

What could be more important than teaching young people to attend? As Robert Fulghum remarks in his famous, semi-serious essay "All I Ever Really Needed to Know I Learned in Kindergarten," the word *look* that figured so prominently in those old Dick and Jane elementary readers is indisputably the biggest word of all. "Everything you need to know is in there somewhere," Fulghum insists, "the Golden Rule and love and basic sanitation, ecology and politics, and sane living."[3]

The word *look* in Fulghum's analysis is the practical and moral equivalent of *paying attention*. Its importance cannot be overstated, and without it, sustainable or even sane living is impossible. When attention is absent, the consequences become almost immediately apparent: Opportunities to experience wonder are lost; the quality of our work suffers, as do our relationships; caregiving becomes mechanical and perfunctory rather than empathetic and considerate. Generations of philosophers, psychologists, and spiritual masters have pointed to the close relationship between attention and the positive, life-enhancing sentiments of appreciation, equanimity, empathy, and enthusiasm. If our wish is to be fully and joyfully engaged in life, the ability to better attend is simply indispensable.

People hunger for attention and suffer emotionally and spiritually when it is not forthcoming. Today's Yellow Pages lists scores of personal helpers: therapists, life and fitness coaches, financial planners, paid companions. These paraprofessionals exist to satisfy an increasing demand for a kind of quality contact that seems to be in chronically short supply. We live in a society that is always in a hurry and that makes too many demands for us to pause long enough simply to "look" more closely and caringly at one another.

Those who market personal services of this kind are savvy enough to have recognized an emerging need and have found profitable ways to meet it. While each offers a somewhat different product, a critical part of the package is always "attention." This new class of service providers promises to observe, listen to, and draw out the client in order to offer customized advice and instruction. While you have to salute the enterprise and imagination of those who created this new vocational niche, it does cause you to wonder whether such highly specialized roles would be necessary if friends, relatives, and neighbors were more attentive to our needs. Does today's rapidly expanding field of "coaching" and "companionship" betoken a general decline in people's willingness to be present for one another? What if more of us could learn to empty our faculties and listen with our whole being, in keeping with Chuang Tzu's advice?

The good news is that attentiveness can be taught; it is a skill we can practice and improve. Hope College English professor Heather Sellers, in a tribute to one of her former teachers, writes that the most important professional and life lesson he taught her was how to "pay attention." The teacher, Jerry Stern, was a member of the English faculty at Florida State University, and for him, "art was life, attended to, revised, and perfected." He constantly implored his students to "look" and then report, accurately and precisely, on what they had observed. Her professor possessed remarkable powers of observation, Sellers remembers. To him, everything was interesting, everything potentially a subject for further reflection and commentary. The invariable first rule for writing well was to catch and hold your subject with whole, undivided attention.[4]

Watching Jerry Stern, Sellers came to realize that in order to receive the full benefit of her vocation, she would need to do something much more basic than read the right books, write the obligatory research papers, and feed her students information. If she could teach her mind to attend, a meaningful, joyful, and sustainable career could be hers.

Jerry Stern taught by example, but mindfulness exercises like meditation and tai chi can powerfully assist the process. Pursued with due diligence, such disciplines produce a calm and centered awareness that gradually alters one's whole demeanor, enriching one's work and personal life in the process. Over time, and without attaining "enlightenment" or entering some exalted state of imperturbability, one does begin to notice real improvement in the quality of one's attention. Slowly but steadily it becomes a customary rather than an occasional way of relating to the world.

In trying to convey more clearly the importance of mindfulness, ancient Chinese sages contrasted it with its opposite—inattentiveness and distraction. The latter they described as "killing life." When not fully present, we are literally deadening our sensations and cutting ourselves off from everything that lends savor to existence.[5] Every instant offers a singular encounter with an environment that is constantly changing, continually generating new surprises, creating fresh impressions. One who has learned truly to attend will never be bored, never be jaded, and never feel cheated by life.

But *attention* can be a tricky word. What's being described here should not be confused with *hypervigilance*—the kind of nervous alertness that one experiences when faced with real or imagined danger. Mindfulness is quite the opposite: relaxed, open, and nonanxious. Vigilance performs a valuable protective function, but it is typically accompanied by apprehension and requires more concentrated energy than paying attention. Mindfulness is more composed, more curious about, than frightened by, the world.

Michael Nagler, a retired UC, Berkeley classics professor, has been meditating for almost forty years and understands the difference. "We lose a lot of our vital capacity because we're anxious about the future," he writes, "… and that means that part of our energy is not there." In other words, if the way in which we contemplate the world leaves us feeling drained or depleted, we are probably practicing the wrong way. Though sharp and focused, our awareness is contaminated with fear.

Attending to Ourselves: Health, Wellness, and Fitness

It's hard to imagine a facet of life that a better ability to pay attention wouldn't improve. Take, for instance, the problem of maintaining health, wellness, and personal fitness. One can easily make the case that inattention is a significant contributor to more than a few of our physical and emotional complaints—especially those that originate with poor lifestyle choices.

Poor nutrition compromises our immune system and can make us sick. If it does not contribute directly to the onset of cancer, heart disease, or diabetes, it may well exacerbate the condition, particularly in those with a hereditary predisposition.[6] Eating well isn't easy. Only recently has ours become a sedentary civilization, and our food habits have yet to catch up with the shift away from a lifestyle characterized by strenuous manual labor—one that required the ingestion of many more calories. Moreover, very early on, members of our species developed the ability to store fat as a hedge against periodic scarcity. We're not used to living in a state of near-constant abundance where the need to produce extra adipose tissue is less urgent.

The challenge of eating prudently is compounded by highly suggestive advertisements for food—often of the worst kind—that constantly bombard us. Nothing gets the saliva glands flowing quite like the high-definition image of a steaming stuffed-crust pizza or a burger festooned with bacon and cheese. How many ads for carrots or cantaloupe have you seen on TV lately?

Fast-food aside, staples once believed to be balanced and nutritious have in recent years been degraded by the overuse of refined flour, high-fructose corn syrup, fat substitutes, sodium, and a host of unpronounceable and potentially unsafe flavor and freshness enhancers. Eating too much, as well as eating food of questionable quality, makes us miserable and ill—often for quite some time. "Medical advances mean that it takes a long time to kill us," British food writer Bee Wilson observes, "so we keep on eating."[7]

Here, then, are two problems that paying attention can help resolve: the propensity to overeat and a tendency to eat the wrong things.

Overeating has reached epidemic proportions. As of 2006 it was estimated that worldwide 800 million human beings were hungry and that about a billion were overfed. Ironically, in formerly underfed societies like India and China, obesity has suddenly become a major public health concern. Indians and Chinese who can afford more calories are routinely consuming too many.

With respect to our diets, paying attention simply means being cognizant of *what* we are eating and *when* we are eating it. Of the two, "what" may be the easiest to solve. Most products in the supermarket label ingredients and bear nutritional labels. More and more restaurant menus identify heart-healthy and low-fat options. If we need a basic rule of thumb, Michael Pollan provides one in his book *In Defense of Food*: "Eat food, not too much, mostly plants." Attention, flavored with a dash of determination, is the recipe I've followed for years to good and lasting effect.

But for many people, what they consume at breakfast, lunch, and dinner is only one side of the problem. So much more food is available throughout the day than there ever was before, and this, Stephen Shapin argues, is where many of us get into real trouble. It is the snacking, the noshing, the grazing, and the nibbling that slowly and insidiously elevate the blood pressure and add the extra pounds. Occasionally physicians will advise patients to eat multiple small meals rather than two or three hearty ones, but for most of us this behavior is either unconscious or compulsive; it is certainly not mindful. "We've become an eat-on-the-run, absent-minded feeding, cup-holding culture," Shapin concludes, and that's why paying attention is so important.[8]

The Cost of Inattention

It's not unlike another propensity many of us exhibit: whipping out that credit card for every purchase from a cup of coffee to a new car because doing so is the ultimate in convenience. But however incrementally, those charges all add up, which is why we get socked at the end of the month with a bill too big to pay off. Individuals mired in debt are routinely advised to take the following steps: use cash instead of credit, keep an expense log, balance the checkbook on a regular basis, set a reasonable limit on discretionary spending, resist the temptation to buy on impulse. In short, to place ourselves on a firm financial footing, we must begin keeping track—faithfully paying attention to our daily spending. The rules for diet are much the same, as anyone who's participated successfully in a Weight Watchers program will tell you.

The quest for vitality and better health is never ending and involves more than what goes into our mouths. To thrive, we need to be alert not just to what the stomach, but to what the whole human organism, is trying to tell us. Will Johnson, director of the Institute for Embodiment Training in British Columbia, is convinced from his work with human subjects that the average person is aware of only five to fifteen percent of his or her bodily sensations. Most of what the physical self is sensing and experiencing doesn't register; we are to a startling degree "numb." The source of the problem, Johnson maintains, lies "upstairs" in our minds. People spend so much time ruminating, daydreaming, problem solving, speculating, that they literally become alienated from their own body and thereby are rendered largely oblivious to its complaints, not to mention its pleasures.[9]

Worries, fears, and frustration have a cumulative effect on our systems, disrupting digestion, blood pressure, and a host of other metabolic functions. Unacknowledged emotions cause tensions to accumulate in our musculature, Johnson observes, "which over time produces yet more insensitivity." Gradually, we lose touch with ourselves, with consequences that are twofold. On the one hand, we become inured to the life-enhancing overtures of the surrounding sentient world. More gravely, perhaps, physical numbness and insensitivity prevent us from noticing the onset of illness and increase the likelihood of serious accident.

The need for greater mindfulness increases as we age. Younger bodies can tolerate more abuse than older ones; and if we wish to live well past retirement, "paying attention" is critical. Harvard University's Atul Gawande stresses the importance of increased vigilance as one ages and becomes more sensitive to and dependent upon medications, special food items, and different living arrangements. Greater attention must be given to the body and its alterations. It is prudent, Gawande suggests, "to contemplate the course of our decline, in order to make the small changes that can reshape it."[10]

Even those who are relatively young and fit are wise to develop a keener awareness of their bodies' physical and emotional status. My own career as both a serious and casual runner has lasted for thirty-five years largely because long ago I learned to pay attention to seemingly insignificant signs of discomfort. The secret to a sustained exercise regime is knowing when to slack off, switch temporarily to another form of training, or simply stop.

This is where mindfulness practices like tai chi and qigong are invaluable, for by sharpening awareness of the physical self, they bring underlying issues to the forefront. Even simple, conscious breathing exercises can help us safely process a troubling emotion or provide relief for minor discomfort.

Enhancing Our Work Experience

I give credit to "attention" for helping me enjoy a long and fruitful tenure in parish ministry. Most notably, it has enabled me to retain my enthusiasm for this work and to rectify mistakes that hampered my effectiveness.

For many years, preaching was my highest priority and the activity to which I devoted the lion's share of my energy. For ministers, particularly those with large congregations, the pulpit serves as the primary source of public acclaim and professional pride. On weeks when I was free from that duty—when I didn't write and deliver a sermon—I would typically feel mildly deflated and unfulfilled. During the early stage of my career, vocational satisfaction was mostly a matter of having given a good performance and (hopefully) said something that made a difference to my listeners.

I still enjoy the process of preparing for and presenting worship, and I continue to invest considerable time in research and writing. But gradually my appreciation for the more mundane aspects of parish work has increased. Activities that used to frustrate or bore me—business meetings, staff discussions, stewardship activities, coffee-hour conversation—have become personally rewarding. The single best explanation I can give for this is the long-term cultivation of "attention."

Mindfulness practice has delivered unexpected dividends in my professional life. From taking the time each day to bring my full attention to bear on a yoga pose, the tai chi form, or my own breathing, I have gained the ability to focus more intentionally and closely on other tasks—to apply the same quality of mindfulness to the daily routines of ministry. It is the equivalent of "chopping wood and carrying water," as the Zen Buddhists would say.

I'm in the human relations business, and I've learned that a faithful spiritual practice can improve the tone and tenor of one's relationships. The experience of an accomplished Insight Meditation teacher, as related by her colleague Jack Kornfield, resembles mine. After thirty years of contemplative practice, she really didn't feel all that different about herself, and yet long-time friends said they could see a big change in her demeanor. "I guess it's just the fruit of being present over and over," she concluded. "It's that simple."[11]

For me, what this shift has meant is that I am now routinely able to bring my best self, and not an impatient and preoccupied version, to each ministerial assignment. Oh, I still come into some meetings tired, and there are occasions when I lose focus and, more rarely, my composure. But I now find it easier to bring myself up short, see what's going on inside, and make an attitudinal adjustment. The moments when I'm most mindful are the ones in which I feel most fulfilled. The nature of the task—any task—has become less important than the quality of my attention.

The late Tibetan teacher Chogyam Trungpa observed that "for the [spiritual] warrior, every moment is a challenge to be genuine, and each challenge is delightful." To be genuine, in the sense that Trungpa intended, means to be fully conscious, fully aware, and fully present in every phase of life's journey.[12]

The Awakening of Compassion

Compassion is also largely a function of refined attention. The ability to bracket one's own concerns in order to observe closely and listen carefully to someone else's pain and frustration is characteristic of the caring individual. People know when they have our full and undivided attention and are typically more willing to open up and be vulnerable under such circumstances. It is precisely here that genuine ministry, in the broadest sense, takes place. Indeed, attention lends to our encounters with humans and other sentient beings that sacred quality described so beautifully by Martin Buber in his classic book, *I and Thou*.

Philip Simmons, who spent the final years of his life contending with the progressive symptoms of ALS, or Lou Gehrig's disease, gradually learned to make the most of each moment. It's downright foolish, he realized, to always be "thinking, worrying, doubting, self-congratulating, planning, regretting," fretting over past mistakes, and mentally preparing for life's next appointment. "The truly good man is always present to himself as simply doing," Simmons ultimately concluded.[13]

Setting Better Priorities

Paying attention is also important if one wishes to set boundaries, impose limits, and establish priorities. While some people take life easy, others accept assignments or assume responsibilities far beyond their ability to fulfill them. Well intended, they don't face up to their limitations and end up being a disappointment both to themselves and to others.

Sometimes we're flattered by a request for our services. Accepting an invitation to sit on a particular panel or draft an important paper confirms our value as a key player. It takes a while to learn that saying yes too often is just as irresponsible as opting out by reflexively saying no. We cannot possibly bring our best self to every cause, and each new endeavor subtracts time and energy from an existing one. To maintain a schedule that maximizes our effectiveness, we need to pay attention.

If burning the candle at both ends is causing us to suffer, it's important to restrict our activities to those that can truly benefit from our participation. Initially, turning down requests produces pangs of guilt and regret, but it also can provide a valuable lesson in humility. None of us is indispensable. Eventually it became clear to me that my presence and input weren't always necessary. There's a good chance yours isn't either.

Those with whom I work have benefited significantly from my efforts to attend to what really matters and let the rest go. By moving out of the limelight, other capable individuals have had the opportunity to step forward and to shine. In recent years I've watched coworkers develop new skills and gain greater confidence. As they have blossomed, I've become more comfortable delegating responsibility. As a result, our spiritual community has been better served, and our relationship as a staff has become more mutually gratifying. The assumption that you are the "go-to" person may tickle the ego, but it can also produce an unsustainable work pattern that disempowers others even as it erodes the quality of your own performance.

Establishing More Satisfying Relationships

In *Ethics for a New Millennium*, the Dalai Lama remarks that happiness is a condition that human beings everywhere naturally and legitimately strive for. Agreeing with the authors of the American Declaration of Independence, the Tibetan assures us that there is nothing self-indulgent about the pursuit of happiness; it is both an inalienable right and an appropriate priority.

What constitutes true happiness isn't always obvious, however. Problems arise when we misidentify the sources of our happiness or misconstrue its meaning. Material possessions, professional accomplishments, and visceral pleasure can all be gratifying and yet leave us with a gnawing sense of discontent. Those who live securely and comfortably in the modern West are so accustomed to connecting happiness with an ever-rising standard of living that they frequently neglect a point that the Dalai Lama has repeatedly emphasized: "Most happiness arises in the context of our relationships with others."[14]

Truth be told, there is no substitute for close, caring relationships. Investigators have repeatedly shown that people who live alone or who self-isolate are prone to far more physical and emotional ailments than those who belong to a reliable network of mutual aid and obligation. One study of heart attack sufferers indicates that patients with even a single good friend are only half as likely to have a second attack within the same year as those who lack a close human connection.[15]

As a general rule, American culture has tended to discount the importance of relationships in favor of individual autonomy and rugged self-reliance. "It is a common belief in this country," family counselor Mary Pipher writes, "that to be free of one's family is to be mentally healthy." Pipher contrasts this outlook with that of traditional peoples whose sense of identity and security hinges on their familial and clan associations.[16] Or as an African tribal aphorism puts it: "A person is a person through other people."

Sociologist Judith Wallerstein shares Pipher's perspective and argues that a "democratic ethos" that elevates the rights of the individual above the rights of the group, and that "stresses the needs of the individual over those of the family," is at least partially responsible for this country's high divorce rate.[17] Happiness is not about reaching some personal pinnacle after a long and arduous climb—although such an achievement might well produce transient feelings of accomplishment that resemble happiness. *Sustained* happiness has mostly to do with our relationships. It is about the quality of our experience with those who are willing to accompany us through the valley as well as to the top of the mountain. "Life's greatest blessing," the Buddhist text Sutta Nipata tells us, "is to support one's father and mother, cherish spouse and children, and follow a peaceful calling."

Forces That Pull Us Apart

It pays, then, not to take for granted but to give an extra measure of attention to our closest companions (animal or human)—which is not easy to do in today's plugged-in world. Two of the most powerful forces pulling families apart, psychologist and family therapist Bill Doherty observes, are electronic technology and the growing number of age- and gender-segregated outside activities. Distracted by television, computers, video games, portable music players, and cell phones, members of families are less inclined and often less able to pay attention to one another.[18]

These technologies are so affordable and readily available that they have become fixtures in most of our lives. They are also incredibly seductive. I know of a marriage that almost ended because of one partner's addiction to Nintendo, and another that was severely stressed by a BlackBerry. In recent years, concerns about online chat rooms or role-play games that monopolize family members' time have been brought to me. Furthermore, despite its clear advantages, online commuting can cause work to spill over into the domestic sphere and make it more difficult to maintain healthy boundaries.

The statistics are sobering: on average, fifteen minutes is the amount of time spouses spend in face-to-face conversation each day; less than a third of families regularly sit down to eat one daily meal together; the typical American spends four to six hours in front of the TV each day. As a family's bonds weaken, someone in the house may attempt to "pull the plug" on the electronics. Be warned: Such measures are likely to be greeted with sullenness and resentment by those still in the clutches of a tele-addiction.

The Tragedy of Inattention

"Strong families," Mary Pipher writes, "feature appreciation, open communication, time together, a commitment to promoting happiness and welfare, spiritual wellness, and ways to cope effectively with stress."[19] But none of this is really possible unless family members are paying attention and willing to be fully present for each other. Coping with domestic stress requires that we recognize its signs, but few families are equipped to do so. Society offers few supports or safeguards in this respect and does much to subvert intimacy and sever our connections. Too often a household has to reach the breaking point before its members wake up and begin to grapple with their problems.

The tragic massacre of a dozen students and a teacher at Columbine High School in Littleton, Colorado, on April 20, 1999 produced startling evidence of inattention in what appeared to be affluent, outwardly well-adjusted suburban families. The perpetrators were two disaffected students who, unbeknown to their parents, had bought and stockpiled expensive automatic weapons and built crude bombs in their own homes. Not only were other family members unaware of the deadly plot being devised under their very noses, they also seemed insensitive to the estrangement Dylan Klebold and Eric Harris felt from their teenage peers. The boys kept diaries and made home videos in which they freely expressed their resentments. But the truth is, no one at home or at school was paying sufficient attention.

As commentators scrambled for answers in the aftermath of Columbine, violent video games, movies like *The Matrix*, and certain rock groups were blamed for the boys' homicidal rage. Among the latter, Marilyn Manson was particularly singled out for scathing criticism. Surprisingly, Manson didn't respond defensively. In respect for the Columbine victims, he canceled three concerts;

and to the question "What would you have said to the killers?" he gave this cogent reply: "Nothing. I just would have listened, because no one else did."[20]

Adolescents, regardless of their social or economic status, are at high risk in our culture. The frequency with which they mishandle automobiles, abuse drugs and alcohol, cut and kill themselves, and commit acts of vandalism is deeply troubling; yet our typical response is to increase their medications or send them to prison. In that imaginary small town of Lake Wobegon, Garrison Keillor claims that all the children are "above average." If so, it is probably because parents and neighbors are paying attention.

But while the first key may be helpful in averting familial catastrophe, it's important for other reasons as well. Our own experience convinces Trina and me that it can enable family members to find and fulfill themselves.

The Payoff of Attention: A Nurturing Family

Almost from the time he could hold a crayon, we could see that our son, Kyle, was visually gifted. It took very little effort for him to earn good grades in school, but this is not where he normally chose to put his energy, and keeping him motivated was an ongoing challenge. Art—cartooning, painting, graphic design, installations, illustration—was his passion; and by his sophomore year of high school, Kyle's gifts were gaining him some recognition.

Wishing to encourage and nurture that interest, we signed Kyle up for classes at the local university and then for summer sessions at an art institute. Kyle ultimately decided to pursue a fine arts degree and has discovered a true sense of vocation.

Some of our friends thought we were irresponsible for "indulging" Kyle in this fashion. In a university town like Madison, bright children are supposed to load up on honors-level academic courses in pursuit of National Merit Scholarships and Ivy League acceptance letters. That's what "sensible" parents would insist upon. Trina and I went in a different direction because, after seventeen years of close observation, we thought that our assessment of Kyle's temperament and his talent was trustworthy and that he needed at least to attempt an art career.

Would it have been more appropriate to reprogram his spirit? Not according to the great spiritual educator Jiddu Krishnamurti. "If you dominate a child, compel him to fit into a pattern, however idealistic, will he be free at the end of it?" Krishnamurti believed that parents, teachers, and students ought to create a compact of freedom, supplying the appropriate means for an education without dictating the outcome. For society as a whole to move in this direction would, he thought, be truly revolutionary.[21]

Parenting and the demands of earning a livelihood can and often do cut into the time and attention couples are able to give each other. It is not uncommon for two people to complete the process of child rearing only to discover that their interests have diverged, and they are uncertain how to spend time pleasantly and profitably together. Reserving time each day for its members to recontact and attend to one another can help a family avoid that outcome.

Accordingly, while Kyle was still in high school, Trina and I formed a resolution: we would not allow the pressures of my profession or other commitments to pull us in opposite directions. Fortunately, we had established one unvarying rule years earlier: to share our evening meal together. Even rare exceptions to that unwritten family ordinance were frowned upon. But in the past few years we've taken other steps to strengthen our connection: a few minutes devoted each morning to sharing our dreams of the previous night; a twenty-minute mid-day walk with our cheerful papillon, Sasha; partnering on visits to local retirement communities to see parishioners. We regularly look for ways to collaborate rather than compete with each other when requests are made for our individual time and attention.

Trina and I agree that this alteration in our relational life has served us well as a couple and as individuals. Having set aside the model of the solitary spiritual seeker, we see ourselves as pilgrims, fellow travelers committed to supporting, nurturing, and helping to guide each other. In this role, we find that after forty years of partnership, we are not only growing closer together, but also growing in new directions. If today we feel renewed as a couple, it is because we make a more deliberate attempt to pay attention, to the effect that, as one well-known aphorism puts it, "When one cries, the other tastes salt."

Friends vs. Acquaintances

Important as they are, children and spouses cannot possibly meet all our emotional and intellectual needs. Friends and nonnuclear family members also play an important role, but these connections have also become more and more tenuous in a highly mobile, consumer-oriented culture. Most adult American men are unable to name a best friend; and of those who can, that person is often as not their marriage partner. Women establish and maintain friendships more readily than men, but, overall, the recent trend has been to forego friends in favor of low-maintenance "acquaintances." The latter, as Malcolm Gladwell notes, require minimal attention and no support. "They can be kept at arm's length. ... We don't need to send them birthday cards, share a meal, or visit them when they are sick,"—all of which fits right in with a population that's always in a hurry and always pressed for time.[22]

The problem is one with which I am quite familiar. For years, serving my parish, raising a family, and honoring commitments to the larger community were higher priorities than friendship. Even my relationship with my parents sat untended on the back burner. Physical distance didn't help matters. Our families of origin and friends from high school and college live hundreds and thousands of miles away. Attending to and nurturing those relationships seemed impractical. And since Trina and I had each other for mental and emotional sustenance, those outside the charmed circle of our immediate household were reduced to acquaintances.

In recent years we've both been making overtures to individuals whom we've long kept at arm's length. The positive response we've received has been encouraging and indicates that others are hungry for more contact, as well. My connection to my parents has grown stronger and become more personal with the weekly phone calls I began making a few years ago. Strengthening these bonds no longer feels burdensome and has become for us a blessing. Attending to our relational life isn't just a luxury. If the good life is our goal, it's one of the most practical things we can do.

The Attentive Volunteer

The events of September 11, 2001, temporarily reversed a long decline in the level of civic participation by U.S. citizens. Typically complacent consumers rose to the occasion when forcibly reminded that their own safety and the country's moral authority were threatened. During the autumn of 2001, volunteerism spiked, interfaith dialogue became the order of the day, and commentators remarked on the revival of a sense of civic duty and interpersonal responsibility among the American rank and file. Transcending their fears and shaking off indifference, citizens in record numbers sought out opportunities to help heal the country and forestall future attacks. The phrase "United We Stand" appeared on store window placards and automobile bumper stickers, reinforcing the conviction that if Americans pulled together, the country would recover from this unprecedented shock to its system.

But once the "attack on America" story had become a bit stale, the electronic media returned to its old habits of hawking merchandise and hyping trivia. The president did his part by encouraging Americans to return to the malls and max out their credit cards. Without question, the post-9/11 world economy really did need a boost, and renewed American consumer spending was a boon to struggling merchants. But little emphasis was placed on personal responsibility beyond the marketplace. TV programming which might have reflected, encouraged, or helped channel Americans' newfound instinct for altruism was almost nonexistent. As the weeks went by and the Christmas season approached, interest in "good works" abated, and by 2002 about all that remained was the "United We Stand" slogan. Once more, Americans had stopped paying attention to the needs of the surrounding community.

Historians tell us that the voluntary association is one of the more laudable elements of American "exceptionalism." Even before the revolution that freed the thirteen colonies from British rule, Committees of Correspondence and an array of clubs and societies were organized to advance the cause of independence. In subsequent years, an unprecedented number of organizations were established to address a wide variety of concerns. Together they helped create a dynamic civic culture unrivaled anywhere else in the world. Volunteerism, whether in a religious or a secular context, has always been as American as apple pie and has served as a necessary counterweight to our equally strong instinct for rugged individualism.

But voluntary service doesn't attract Americans as reliably as in the past. The membership rosters of traditional service clubs like the Elks, Lions, Masons, Odd Fellows, Kiwanis, and Optimists are increasingly geriatric, and aging has also affected the performance of once-powerful civic organizations like the League of Women Voters. With the rise of two-earner families, PTA participation has fallen off in many school districts. Research by Canadian political scientist Ronald Colman reveals that time devoted to volunteering fell by twelve percent in his country over the last decade, and he suggests that the trend is probably similar in the United States. "That's a real decline in community well-being," Colman writes, "but unfortunately it counts for nothing in our current measure of progress."[23]

It has also become more difficult to recruit and retain dependable volunteers in faith communities. Only a small percentage of those who offer their services are willing to make more than a minimal commitment, which is why churches increasingly rely on paid staff to function properly. People still have money to give, but unless a catastrophic event like 9/11 or Katrina occurs, they are chary about dedicating time and attention to "good causes."

If this trend continues, it will almost certainly lead to less awareness of, compassion for, and connection to those with whom we share our community. Voluntary organizations are vital because they direct our attention to issues and constituencies that would otherwise escape our notice or that, having noticed, we would just as soon ignore. Without a healthy and active civic culture, political and corporate elites become less accountable, the state grows less responsible, and our general sense of responsibility for the common good declines. To the degree that citizens mobilize in support of organizations that "pay attention," society's leaders can be held accountable and help can be provided to those who live on the margins.

Some say that Americans are being asked to do too much. Tsunamis in Indonesia, mudslides in Guatemala, an earthquake in Pakistan, wildfires in the Far West, and floods in the Midwest have exhausted our giving ability and caused "donor fatigue." It's time to turn our attention toward home and, as Voltaire would say, "tend our own garden."

One has to wonder how sympathetic a Mother Teresa, an Albert Schweitzer, or a Martin Luther King, Jr. would be to that position. Volunteerism can certainly be taken to extremes and end in burnout, but I doubt these great souls would support the notion that the world's most pampered people should stop attending to others' needs and get on with their private lives. Few activities are as intrinsically gratifying as those that enhance the health of the larger community. The effort a person makes doesn't have to be spectacular. Serving at a soup kitchen for an evening, devoting an afternoon to clearing the woods of invasive species, holding a house meeting to discuss a community problem—simple activities like these make a difference and help us all become better human beings.

Two decades ago a book entitled *The Good Society* by Robert Bellah and four coauthors was published. The concluding chapter was entitled "Democracy Means Paying Attention" and included lucid discussions of family, the economy, the community, as well as our political culture. Many of the problems that Bellah expressed concern about in the late 1980s haven't gone away. Some of them, in fact, have grown worse. To solve those problems, he suggested, we must begin with a basic change in our behavior. "A good society," Bellah admonished, "is one in which attention takes precedence over distraction." Perhaps the present generation will be able to heed what an earlier one failed to hear.[24]

Chapter 4

Stay Put

Americans are said to thrive on change and novelty. But do we? Are transient families more emotionally secure and financially stable than those who put down roots? Is a commercial district more successful when businesses turn over every few years? Is our spiritual nature well served by adopting a new practice every six months? Humans are curious creatures, and it's natural for us to want to explore new terrain. Nevertheless, a compelling case can be made for resisting this impulse. Thriving also has something to do with settling in.

The Happy Tale of a Small City Diner

The intersection adjacent to towering Camp Randall Stadium, home of the University of Wisconsin Badgers football team, is one of Madison's busiest. Several streets converge at that point, and a jumble of small businesses serves the area's burgeoning student population. One of the oldest and most easily recognized is an establishment called Mickey's Dairy Bar, a hole-in-the-wall diner a few doors up Monroe Street that has featured the same crimson-and-white Badger décor for a half-century.

Mickey's is open only on weekdays and caters to the breakfast and lunch crowds who routinely commend it as the best eating bargain in town. Staples include platter-size pancakes an inch thick, old-fashioned milkshakes, and sandwiches overflowing with fresh ingredients. Mickey's was for years our son's favorite place to chow down, and I cannot recall a single occasion when we didn't carry food away in a Styrofoam clamshell. "Nobody ever leaves Mickey's hungry," the present proprietor proudly boasts.

Mickey's did change hands a number of years ago. Payow Thongnuam, a Thai immigrant who studied culinary arts at the local community college and married a Wisconsin native, bought Mickey's in 1991. "Janet and I clicked with the owner," Payow remembers, "because we promised to keep it just the way it was." Indeed, the only real improvements the couple made were to replace the worn-out linoleum floor with one that was nearly identical and to update the menu with a few new items like liver and onions and chocolate chip pancakes. For the most part, Mickey's has remained the same and continues to pull in a stream of patrons from the campus and beyond.

Nevertheless, whether Mickey's will anchor the north end of Monroe Street and maintain its unique position in the Madison dining scene for much longer is an open question. Developers have been hungrily eyeing the block on which the restaurant is situated and have elicited promises to sell from neighboring property owners. Payow and Janet are stubbornly holding out, partly because Mickey's provides a secure livelihood for their large family, but also because they understand what this humble-yet-venerable business contributes to the local scene. Despite his Southeast Asian origins, Payow sums up the issue better than most Madison natives could when he observes that Mickey's longevity has made it "the grandfather of Monroe Street." He meets customers who once went to school in Madison and have made a point to visit the beloved diner on their return. In their minds, Mickey's will always be part of the Madison scene. "It makes me feel proud," Payow exclaims. "I won't sell, absolutely not. No way. I'm blessed to have a business like this."[1]

The Tale of Our Great Cities

In her landmark study of cities and neighborhoods that really function well for their residents, urban theorist Jane Jacobs challenged the mid-century advocates of urban renewal. Before engaging in massive redevelopment, reconsider the benefits conferred by existing "traditional" communities, Jacobs begged in *The Death and Life of Great American Cities*. Older residential areas that may appear to be in a state of decline from a bricks-and-mortar point of view create intangible assets that a complex of sleek high-rise apartments cannot match. For most of the 1960s and 1970s, hers was a voice crying in the wilderness, as "progressive" cities across the country repudiated the past in favor of partial or complete makeovers. Even a small city like Madison succumbed to the prevailing trend as the Greenbush—a quaint mixed-use, multiethnic enclave adjacent to the business district—was eliminated in favor of clusters of featureless housing units and a network of barren boulevards.

From her own research and personal observations, Jane Jacobs became convinced that safe, healthy, and interesting neighborhoods are largely a function of carefully cultivated social capital rather than physical "improvement." Such niches in our cityscapes, she wrote, "weave webs of public surveillance and thus protect strangers as well as residents; grow networks of small-scale everyday public life and thus generate trust and control." Whenever this capital is forfeited, the income from it disappears.[2]

Jacobs pointed to districts like Boston's North End and Manhattan's Greenwich Village as places that afforded a much higher quality of life for their residents than others that were newer and more in keeping with the modern Bauhaus aesthetic. The latter too often produced a monoculture, with families packed into near-identical living spaces, often surrounded by freeways and at one remove from the shops, schools, churches, restaurants, and taverns that have traditionally served as nodes of connection for urban dwellers. Ironically, by creating blocks of dense residential housing, urban renewal increased residents' sense of isolation and reduced their safety. All the mediating structures that help to create and maintain the spirit of community were missing.

And Jacobs pointed to another advantage of those traditional neighborhoods: their powers of retention. People tended to stick around, often for several generations, because this place provided a real home, not just a roof over their heads. Residents came to know their community well—its stories, traditions, unique heritage, and neighbors they could depend upon. In other words, the subculture encouraged and rewarded "stickers," and there was an unspoken consensus that "staying put" was a major contributor to sustainability.

What I Saw in Binghamton

Earlier in life, Trina and I lived for seven years a few streets away from such an area in Binghamton, New York—an old industrial town that had experienced several major shifts in its local economy. In the early twentieth century it became a center for the manufacture of shoes, and thousands of recent immigrants from Southern and Eastern Europe made their way up the Delaware River Gap to tan, cut, and stitch footwear in the Triple Cities (of which Binghamton is one—in case you are curious, the other two are Endicott and Johnson City). Many of these newcomers settled in Binghamton's first ward, occupying small, neat houses provided by paternalistic employers. Here they established ethnic funeral parlors, built great gold-dome Catholic and Eastern Orthodox churches, and introduced spiedies, pirogis, and kielbasa to the local food scene.

By the time we moved to the area in the early 1980s, the factories were all shuttered, as the shoemaking industry had long since moved overseas. But the descendants of the descendants of those Slavic and Italian immigrants soldiered on. Those modest first ward homes had grown a little shabby, the narrow sidewalks had heaved and buckled, and most of the working-class residents were now employed in some sector of the service economy. But in terms of social capital, the neighborhood still flourished, and residents seemed little inclined to "improve" their situation.

High-tech industries such as Singer-Link, Savin, and, most notably, IBM were the predominant players in the Triple Cities economy when we arrived. The professional and technical class that composed that workforce held a different perspective on "home" and "community" than their predecessors. Many regarded this as a temporary stop on their road to the top, a place to burnish their credentials before moving on to IBM's headquarters in White

Plains or to a more cosmopolitan environment. Despite its abundant natural beauty and general livability, few of the young professionals whom I queried planned to settle in the area (nor, for that matter, did we).

To be fair, sticking wasn't always a realistic option for people. Veteran IBMers wryly observed that the corporate acronym really stood for "I've Been Moved," since the likelihood of being transferred to another facility was rather high. An IBM engineer could no more expect a stable settlement than a Methodist minister fresh out of seminary. Regrettably, what was then considered somewhat unusual has become commonplace. The American job market has become increasingly unstable and unreliable largely because the global economy rewards companies that are the least loyal to workers or communities. In 1978 a middle-aged American could expect to remain with the same employer for eleven years; the average now is less than eight.[3]

The uncertainties that attended people's professional lives impacted the Triple Cities as a whole. Families tended to invest little in their neighborhoods, people were reluctant to forge friendships, and awareness of local issues was lacking. Apart from districts like the first ward, there was a widespread perception that this was essentially a city of strangers.

Trina and I felt these effects personally. After seven years in the same house and despite numerous attempts to connect, we were on familiar (speaking) terms with only one of our neighbors. Binghamtonians minded their own business and were unperturbed by the dearth of civic involvement. Fortunately, the local running club and the church I served provided a palpable and positive source of community, because the block on which we lived certainly did not.

Madison—A Most Livable City

Madison, Wisconsin, is, in this respect, rather different from many other cities—one in which neighborhoods have character and integrity and neighborliness is encouraged. The city has erected handsome signage to delineate its many neighborhoods and create a more distinct sense of identity. Neighborhood centers and associations abound; and in the summertime, streets are often closed to accommodate block parties, collective garage sales, and other locally organized events. Every year the student-centered Mifflin Street neighborhood sponsors a (sometimes raucous) block party that attracts hundreds of revelers.

Madison residents make a conscious and conscientious effort to patronize businesses in the immediate vicinity, which has helped limit the number of malls and big-box developments on the peripheries. As a result, a significant number of small, independent groceries, coffee shops, bookstores, taverns, and even pharmacies have remained in operation. Neighborhoods have been known to fight city hall and win. Not long ago, a local elementary school scheduled for closure was spared when residents rallied to its defense. In another section of the city, residents created a member-owned co-op to keep a struggling corner grocery alive.

Scott Russell Sanders is surely correct when he says, "None of us can live by wits alone." Both the person and the planet will be much better off if we make more effort to "settle in ... and make a durable home for ourselves, our fellow creatures and our descendants."[4] This "sticky" principle of sustainability is one that our family has tried to follow for the twenty-plus years we've lived in the same neighborhood—a place called Shorewood Hills, which is not technically part of Madison but is surrounded by it on three sides, with broad Lake Mendota lapping gently at its north boundary.

Shorewood Hills provides many small but meaningful incentives for staying put: a community swimming pool, sledding hill, and ice-skating rink (named for former residents and Olympic speed skaters Eric and Beth Heiden); a centrally located elementary school and village green; Fourth of July beer and bratwurst feeds and firework displays, Halloween parades, ballroom dances, and scouting programs; low-key winter basketball and summer baseball programs for kids; a garden club and community gardening program, a volunteer fire department, and a folksy and informative monthly newsletter. Together these create a real catalogue of inducements for those who might wish to join the dwindling ranks of the stickers, establish a *real* home, and pursue an alternative vision of the good life.

Viable communities like the Monroe Street neighborhood or Shorewood Hills can be sustained, Jane Jacobs points out, by a handful of people who "pay attention" and are willing to act in a purposeful fashion. Committed catalysts like Payow Thongnuam can raise public awareness and rally neighbors to protect their collective assets. Our own village directory lists the names of seven dozen residents who, as volunteers, work to enhance community life. However, strictly individual initiatives usually won't suffice. Communities need convenient venues where people can get to know and collaborate with one another. Our own neighborhood provides plenty of niches for activists to discuss problems, coordinate their efforts, and engage in serious, long-term planning. This leaves us in a much better position to resist undesirable or unwanted development and preserve the unique character of a place we all profess to love.

Staying Put Can Be a Challenge

In general, Americans do seem to recognize the value of being in community, which is why we still sing the praises of neighborhood schools and will frequently choose a faith community that's "in the neighborhood" rather than one that requires a long commute (for many mainline Protestants, I have found, the doctrinal position of a congregation matters less than its physical location and the friendliness of its culture). In other words, most of us would probably agree that a community is not just a place to live, but a place to live well—a context in which to thrive as well as subsist.

Unfortunately, our actions often misalign with our values. Americans are still all too willing to drive many miles to exercise at Gold's Gym, shop at Walmart, or feed the kids at a McDonald's Playland rather than patronize local sources of sustenance and satisfaction. With private automobiles always at our beck and call, the temptation "to raid and to run," as Wallace Stegner put it, is ever present. Higher fuel prices may make people reexamine their behavior ("The best way to conserve energy is to stay put," Frank Watson reminds us[5]), but fifty years of nonstop commuting has reduced many American neighborhoods to low-touch bedroom communities where people seldom take the time to practice neighborliness.

The speculative market in residential housing has transformed the way many American think about their living situation. "Only a couple of generations ago," Bill Perkins observes, "families chose a home and neighborhood because they would be nice places to live." As more and more Americans were persuaded by the real estate and mortgage industries to treat their houses primarily as an economic rather than a social asset, they undoubtedly became less willing to commit themselves emotionally to the people and place surrounding them. "Trading up became more important than liking our homes or our neighbors," Perkins writes.[6] If the market stays depressed, though, homeowners may be more inclined to settle in rather than to speculate, and that in turn might help to produce more cohesive neighborhoods.

I feel fortunate to live in a community which has a rich supply of social capital and where most residents have remained because they recognize and appreciate precisely this aspect of home ownership. After Trina was diagnosed with malignant melanoma ten years ago, our family was lovingly supported by goods-bearing, errand-running, well-wishing neighbors. On numerous occasions before and since, we have reached out to others in the same way. "In a changed world comfort will come less from ownership than from membership," Bill McKibben writes. To belong to a community is to feel more confident about our well-being, because the community can be relied upon to "meet at least some of our needs . . . for companionship, for entertainment, for succor."[7]

Reciprocity is one of human civilization's oldest, most useful, and most widely practiced ethical principles, but in an anonymous, disconnected society it is often given short shrift. In more cohesive communities the principle naturally and spontaneously expresses itself as people look after each other's children, arrange car pools, water plants and feed cats during family vacations, and perform other casual acts of give-and-take. This is the kind of cultural norm that induces residents to grow up and grow old in a community even when it might be more profitable or professionally advantageous to pick up and pull out.

What the Amish Know

One group of people—the Amish—is well known for the ability to maintain stable, sustainable communities. Although many Americans regard the Amish as severe, colorless, and technologically backward, the Amish know better than most how to take care of the land and each other. Once, at a conference, an Amish farmer named David Kline was asked for his definition of *community*. Eschewing generalities and abstractions, Kline offered a concrete example:

> When I and my sons are plowing in the spring, I can look around and see seventeen [horse] teams at work on neighboring farms. I know those teams, and the men driving them, and I know that if I was sick or hurt, those men and teams would be at work on my own farm.[8]

Apropos of that comment, Wendell Berry says that for a traditional Amish farmer like David Kline, the economy consists of more than a means of production and a charge of accounts. It is, he writes, a "loving economy based on the love of neighbors, of creatures, and of places." The *Great Economy* is how Berry describes this web of mutual aid and affection, and he contrasts it with the *Industrial Economy* "that is not comprehensive enough and thus tends to destroy that which it does not comprehend."[9]

Wendell Berry has long been an articulate and passionate advocate of sustainability, but his writing strikes some as elegiac and out of step with more recent economic and social trends. Still, few writers help us see so clearly what we've inadvertently sacrificed in the heedless pursuit of material gain, and much of what he finds troubling about the industrialization of rural culture is relevant to our urban neighborhoods, as well.

This is not to say that living in a closely knit community is invariably a bed of roses. Its members don't always know where familiarity stops and nosiness begins. The line between harmless information sharing and destructive gossip can be a fine one, and at times people will feel as if they were living in a glass house where the right of others to pry supersedes one's own right to privacy.

Staying Put Doesn't Mean Getting Stuck

The provincialism that has always figured prominently in borough and village life represents a social liability, not an asset. For all its advantages, *gemeinschaft* (as sociologists describe it) can be rife with prejudice, rigid mores, invasive practices, suspicion of outsiders, and knee-jerk resistance even to edifying change. A wholesale retreat to more parochial times when people hardly ever ventured far beyond the community in which they were born and raised is hardly desirable. Thanks to modern communications technology, in today's world we can have both: thriving local cultures *and* the kind of worldliness that opens minds and softens attitudes. That is the kind of sustainable community we should strive to create and in which the good life can be realized.

These arguments in favor of "settling in" and strengthening the bonds of community should not be construed as a criticism of those who love to broaden their horizons through travel or even temporary residence abroad. Trina and I take every available opportunity to venture out into the world and have spent appreciable time in 47 of the lower 48 states as well as in Canada and Europe.

Nevertheless, we have never been footloose and have always felt the tug of hearth and home. The "instinct for absolute freedom and mobility ... that drove America to the Pacific," described by essayist Joan Didion, has always been more subdued in us.[10] And generally speaking, it is probably not a healthy instinct. Even a peripatetic globe-trotter like travel writer Pico Iyer—a man who once proudly declared himself a citizen of the world equally at home in a Bangkok airport and a Los Angeles McDonald's—finally had to concede that such a lifestyle is not sustainable. "The unhappiest people I know these days," he writes in *The Global Soul*, "are often the ones in motion, encouraged to search for a utopia outside themselves."[11]

"Entanglement"

In an earlier era, the process of "entanglement"—of establishing a bona fide home—was assisted by storytelling and the informal sharing of local history and lore on the front porch, at church socials, over a beer at the local tavern, or with coffee and Danish at a family-run diner. For the most part, the traditions of oral transmission that made it possible for newcomers and each new generation to assimilate have disappeared, and that represents an intangible but significant loss. Without historical consciousness—which helps people develop a sense of belonging—it is more difficult to care about and to show proper consideration for a place.

Fortunately, we can to a remarkable degree compensate for the disappearance of the oral culture that oriented our grandparents. I get up and inspect the contents of my own bookshelves and note that among their several thousand volumes are many that helped me, a transplant, develop a deeper knowledge of and appreciation for Wisconsin. I espy a series of books about Frank Lloyd Wright, perhaps our most famous native son and the man who designed the National Landmark Unitarian Meeting House where I've served for over two decades. My personal collection also includes a well-thumbed copy of John Muir's youthful autobiography, as well as one by Blackhawk, the gallant Sauk Indian chief who, before being captured by U.S. troops after the battle of Wisconsin Heights, retreated through the boggy lake country where the city of Madison now stands. Personal narratives like these provide stimulating access to the local culture, helping the reader understand its character and the forces that contributed to its development.

Highly rewarding local and regional literature isn't hard to find. State and local historical societies are a good place to start, and popular periodicals like *Arizona Highways* and *The Wisconsin Magazine of History* provide excellent guidance for those who are curious about their surroundings. Resources like these have helped turn Trina and me into connoisseurs of our own state's quainter burgs and back roads. Over the years, we've visited most of Wisconsin's natural areas, tasted its local produce, and strolled many of its lovingly preserved main streets. We've learned patiently to pay attention and have been amply rewarded with an ever-deepening sense of familiarity and rootedness.

People quite rightfully want to live in a "nice" place—safe, sanitary, commodious, and reasonably attractive—but sustainable communities offer more and expect more. They are home to residents who maintain a lively interest in and have made a real effort to understand what makes it tick—people who want to get in touch with the genius of their place. From that interest comes the impetus to care and the intention to stay.

Naturalist Gary Ferguson tells the story of a group of eastern scholars who went on an anthropological expedition in the 1920s to meet with Northern California's Pit River (*Achumawi*) Indian tribe. During an exchange with a member of that band, one of the researchers asked what was the word in the Achumawi language for a recent arrival such as himself—a newcomer.

Reluctant to answer, the man to whom the question was put looked toward his elders for guidance. After the researcher repeated his question, an older Indian responded. The word is *inalladui*, he said softly. It means "tramp." The label was applied because the native people couldn't understand why whites traveled through a place without ever stopping long enough to learn something about it, without ever binding the land to their hearts. "We think a part of you must be dead inside," the old man said sympathetically.[12]

Do we want to have life and have it more abundantly? There is much to be said for sallying forth on an occasional adventure, but there can be no substitute for putting down some roots and pulling up sustenance from the native soil.

Vocation and Staying Put

The putative father of psychoanalysis, Sigmund Freud, is said to have identified *Leiben* (love) and *Arbeiten* (work) as the most important factors in the human quest for happiness and fulfillment. If he was correct, then few things could be more important than finding work that we love and love that works. The four keys of sustainability can be fruitfully applied in both departments.

When it comes to my own career, I have clearly proved myself a sticker. Having already served faith communities for over thirty years, barring some unexpected development I hope to continue in this role until retirement—not because it would be economically disadvantageous to do something else, but because the work continues to feel valuable and feeds my own spirit. I have chosen, as John Schuster would say, "significance over success."[13]

There was, however, an earlier time when I seriously doubted my vocational decision. At the age of twenty-five and with twenty years of academic preparation behind me, I left seminary ready and raring to go. It was high time, I thought, to do some real work and earn my own keep. Eagerly and without due deliberation, I accepted a call to a small church at the eastern edge of the Great Plains. It proved not to be a good fit.

I lasted less than three years in my first professional position and retreated to the academy to pursue further graduate studies and to reconsider my options. At the time, it seemed quite apparent that I'd misjudged my calling.

My next ambition was to earn a Ph.D. and settle into a college or university teaching career. Fortunately, in pursuing my doctorate it became financially necessary for me to instruct undergraduate students as a teaching assistant. Two years of attempting to instill a love for the humanities in a room full of nineteen- and twenty-year-old business and management majors soon disabused me of this new career goal. Teaching struck me as hard and thankless work. Although a few of my students were academically ambitious and intellectually curious enough to keep me mildly motivated, I could no longer picture myself competing for a tenure-track position at a comparable institution.

Sam Keene, a popular writer on philosophy and spirituality, faced a similar dilemma as a novice professor. For years Keene had imagined that earning a doctorate and commanding a classroom would provide both the social recognition and internal rewards he craved. But it was not to be. The pleasant flush of pride he felt when students addressed him as "Dr. Keene" quickly dissipated, and any pride he felt in his newfound status didn't compensate sufficiently for the daily drudgery of academic life. "The Kingdom of God became a drag," Keene confessed, "... papers to grade, committees, faculty meetings and endless talk, talk, talk. ... The future for which I had sacrificed arrived, but the promised satisfaction did not. ... I was in exile."[14]

Sam Keene didn't last much longer in the university than I did in my first parish. Following his instincts, he leaped boldly into the unknown and began to forge a fresh career as a professional writer and journalist—a calling in which he has thrived.

My own story turned out differently. The longer I taught, the more I found myself missing certain aspects of the ministry: interacting with people of all ages, creating and conducting meaningful rites of passage, presenting to audiences who came freely and curiously, not because they needed to fulfill a course requirement. Most of all, I missed the continuity of the parish—the repeated contact with individuals and families that helps create ties that bind. The studied objectivity and relational superficiality that are not the rule but definitely the norm in universities just wasn't doing it for me.

And so having earned my doctorate, I decided to take another stab at the parish—but without real conviction or a great deal of confidence. It took a number of years before I was able to develop a real feel for the work and the ability to perform reasonably well. I was tempted to walk away on more than one occasion, but unwilling to fail a second time, and with encouragement from a few older colleagues, I kept plugging away. To my surprise, the longer I persevered, the more comfortable my responsibilities became. "Might there yet be potential here for a career?" I asked myself.

Many of my friends in ministry have told me that they heard their "call" well before enrolling in seminary. They usually give me a funny look when I admit that the message wasn't delivered to me until I'd been practicing for nine years! In my case, it was a matter of staying put until I could grow into a role that initially seemed unsuited to my temperament. The same might be said for people in other careers that did not seem promising at first but in which a good fit developed over time. Like them, I'm glad I didn't throw in the towel too soon.

Coincidentally, recent studies have shown that raw talent and native ability may be less important factors in vocational success than regularity—commitment to developing one's repertoire of skills and abilities over a period of time. In his book *Outliers*, Malcolm Gladwell introduces the 10,000 Hour Rule. If aspiring individuals put twenty hours a week into their "calling" over the course of ten years, they will more than likely meet their expectations.[15]

Success: A Double-Edged Sword

To what extent does a sustainable career require one to be successful? While pleasant and meaningful work is a critically important component of the good life, what is it *about* our work that makes it "good"? Is it the public approbation, the admiration of one's peers, institutional growth, or something more subtle and less measurable? Success can come in many forms, not all of which are conducive to emotional and mental well-being.

Management consultant and business guru John R. O'Neil has studied and interviewed many of America's most outwardly successful men and women and noticed how many of them were arrogant and uptight and exhibited little real happiness. More than a few reached the pinnacle of their career only to crash and burn. Rick Chollet, the smart, handsome founder of Brookstone, committed suicide after struggling privately and unsuccessfully with feelings of inadequacy and depression. Work, Chollet's wife reported, was the trigger for his mood swings. "He constantly feared letting people down," she said.

Individuals who are willing to work sacrificially in order to achieve specific, short-term success do so at the cost of overall wholeness. O'Neil emphasizes the importance of adjusting our expectations and finding the right formula to become "long-distance winners." The people he's met who fit that description "know that the pleasures that come with success, as well as those that don't depend on it, are as valuable as the success itself."[16] This is not an easy lesson to learn, and I doubt that many people who have experienced significant "success" are receptive to it.

What counts is fulfillment—the settled feeling that one's work is being done well, that it is useful and relevant, interesting and challenging, and that it leaves one with a sense of "proper pride" upon its accomplishment. In *Zen and the Art of Motorcycle Maintenance*, Robert Pirsig reintroduces the ancient Greek concept of "quality." He argues that if those who are dedicated to it understand what quality looks like and have discovered in quality a reliable source of spiritual sustenance, they will have found their true vocation.

By contrast, success as it is typically understood conforms to some societal and cultural standard outside the self that is only tenuously connected to quality. We know we are "succeeding" when others tell us so or when certain official benchmarks have been met. Many widely admired and ostensibly successful men and women live false and troubled lives because the work they perform is inconsistent with their core values, with their code of professional practice, or with their own internal standard of excellence. "I was in my mid-thirties when I began to wake up to questions about my vocation," Parker Palmer remembers. "By all appearances, things were going well, but the soul doesn't put much stock in appearances.... I had started to understand that it is indeed possible to live a life other than one's own."[17]

I, too, experienced a day of reckoning during the headiest stage of my own career. Having served a congregation in upstate New York long enough to complete the process of ministerial formation and, at last, find my true vocation, I accepted an offer from the First Unitarian Society of Madison. This was a congregation with a surplus of latent energy waiting to be tapped, ready to take on new initiatives. And at the relatively young age of thirty-six, I was anxious to burnish my own professional credentials.

Within ten years the Society's adult membership had doubled, a new religious education wing had been built, major repairs had been made to the fragile Frank Lloyd Wright Meeting House, and a host of new programs had been solidly established. The local newspapers took note of our success, and the Unitarian Universalist Association recognized ours as the fastest-growing church in the movement.

Good things were happening, and the congregation was exceeding all expectations. I felt proud of our accomplishments but wasn't feeling as much internal satisfaction as one in my position should have expected. The problem was a classic one. As successes mounted, so did the pressure to maintain momentum and push on to yet higher levels of achievement. Eventually even the compensatory measures I'd always taken to maintain balance and wholeness—running, healthy diet, meditation—proved insufficient. I had reached the end of my tether.

And so one Sunday morning in the mid 1990s, I stood before my congregation and delivered a sermon entitled "Too Much of a Good Thing Can Be Wearisome" in which I confessed to having invested so much in my work that I now felt more oppressed than enlivened by it. Some listeners construed those remarks as a prelude to a formal letter of resignation, but the truth is, I was just venting—a self-indulgent strategy I do not recommend to similarly afflicted colleagues.

Although I probably shouldn't have shared it with an innocent audience, that sermon did turn out to be a valuable exercise in discernment. I had had a small epiphany: despite what our culture teaches us, a career that rests upon a foundation of success is probably not sustainable and is in fact inherently unstable. Writer Anne Lamott once found herself in a situation that led to comparable soul-searching:

> I wanted to be a writer my whole life. But when I finally made it, I felt like a greyhound catching the mechanical rabbit she'd been chasing for so long—discovering it was merely metal, wrapped up in a cloth. It wasn't alive. It had no spirit.[18]

My own awakening didn't produce instant results. I'd created over the course of a decade a professional identity that promised limitless energy and instant availability. Disassembling that identity and replacing it with one more in keeping with O'Neil's "long-distance winner" proved to be a formidable challenge and was not accomplished quickly. Looking back, I find it ironic that my first vocational crisis occurred because I felt ill-suited for and unable to perform the requisite tasks of ministry, but increased competence and excessive commitment to my calling created the second.

The Sustainable Career
Sustainability in a career is largely a function of internal fulfillment, and when we sacrifice or choose to forego those inner rewards, we experience frustration and world-weariness. Pay attention to such feelings, for they are the spirit's way of telling us we have

strayed away from the "path with heart." I can offer no single rule of thumb for the sustainable career because people's temperaments and their tolerance for work vary widely. One person's workaholism may well be another person's life passion. That being the case, adopting a regular discipline of self-discernment is critically important.

In this respect, Larry Morgan, the narrator in Wallace Stegner's novel *Crossing to Safety*, provides a useful counterpoint. As a young married professor at the University of Wisconsin, Larry pursued vocational success with grim necessity. He let nothing stand in his way and described himself as "your basic overachiever, a pathological beaver of a boy who chewed continually because his teeth kept growing." Larry admits that he "overdid" and in the process punished his wife, Sally, and himself. "Eventually I learned my limitations," he says, but then Larry deftly defends his behavior:

> Ambition is a path ... leading through *Pilgrim's Progress* regions of motivation, hard work, persistence, stubbornness, and resilience under disappointment. Unconsidered, merely indulged, ambition becomes a vice; it can turn a man into a machine that knows nothing but how to run. Considered, it can be something else—pathway to the stars, maybe. I suspect that what makes hedonists so angry when they think about overachievers is that the overachievers, without drugs or orgies, have more fun.[19]

So, yes, overachievers *can* find real fulfillment provided their ambitions are "considered"—reflected upon and periodically revised. Thus, staying put also implies paying attention to the way our career aligns with our values and to the aliveness we experience in its pursuit. In this respect, Larry Morgan may be more fortunate than most. He clearly loved what he was doing, enjoyed wonderful collegiality, and gained significant professional recognition.

Rick Dale is Morgan's real-life counterpart. Hardly an academic, Dale grows blueberries and raspberries on a farm near Lake Superior, on the Bayfield Peninsula. A college student who worked for him one summer came away impressed with this man whose "passion for life and love of work was contagious and his fusion of the two admirable."

Although he has put years of hard work into his modest farm, Rick Dale has never made much money raising berries. On the other hand, he confesses that he doesn't know what he would buy if he had more money. For him and his wife, the work they do and the lifestyle they've developed are their own reward. "Often when people talk about the good life," he says, "somehow it gets equated with being laid back." Dale thinks otherwise—fulfillment is a function of industry and intention.[20]

An Important Caveat: The Unhappy Workplace

Regrettably, a significant portion of the American workforce is in a less advantageous position than Dale. For those who work in the low-paying service sector, as well as for those in high-paid technical professions or with civil service positions, *Arbeiten* isn't meaningful and doesn't produce a great deal of happiness. Juliet Schorr, Barbara Ehrenreich, and others have amply documented the onerous conditions under which many people work and the dissatisfaction they profess.[21] Low wages and declining benefits are only the tip of the iceberg, as the difficulties many face in their employment run much deeper "Even in our postmodern age," Corey Robin observes, "the workplace remains a regime of old-world constraint in which an almost childlike subservience is routinely expected and disobedience is quelled by fear and coercion." Many of the rights we take for granted elsewhere—privacy, free speech, due process—are withheld in the typical workplace.[22]

Hired "at will" and unprotected by unions, guilds, or professional associations of any sort, some American wage earners endure feudal conditions that workers in other developed nations would find intolerable. Discernment and internal satisfaction aside, many in the workforce would gladly settle for greater security, decent health insurance, and a less repressive atmosphere. "At least sixty percent of America is working class," and these workers have little if any voice with respect to the conditions and nature of their employment, journalist Joe Bageant writes. "You do not control when you work, how much you get paid, how fast you work, or whether you will be cut loose from your job at the first shiver on Wall Street."[23]

Apart from the income they provide, some jobs just aren't worth having and don't qualify as a calling. Those of us who have careers we really care about and at which we excel are truly fortunate, and it behooves us to take the necessary steps to sustain them.

Staying Put in Personal Life

Most people appear to understand that they have to assume some degree of personal responsibility for their own future happiness, which is why books on diet, exercise, spiritual practice, intimacy, career building, and similar self-help topics frequently end up on the bestseller list. Experts willing and able to pull us up short and point us in the right direction—toward better health and spiritual and emotional wholeness—are in ample supply. Much of what they suggest is based on sound reasoning, and yet it frequently fails to upgrade the lives of those who try to apply it. What's missing here? Perhaps it's the willingness and ability to persevere.

I often hear people complain that contemporary culture offers too many choices and that there is too much emphasis on novelty. Taste the latest flavor; try on a new fashion; take up rock climbing, Pilates, or whatever the exercise du jour might be. Possibilities for greater pleasure and personal growth pour forth in a never-ending stream, and this makes it difficult for us to feel confident that the path we are on is the right one.

"Today we seem to have lost our belief in constancy, the unwavering good sense to follow a single path in life," Christopher Kimball, the editor of Cook's Illustrated, writes. Recalling how much pleasure he derives from the seasonal ritual of rabbit hunting with Tom, a local friend, Kimball expresses his admiration for a man who found reliable pleasure in scouting for rabbits with his dogs. Even when his children asked him what he wanted to do on Father's Day, this was his choice. "It is the consistency of the pursuit . . . that gives you the constancy, that gives you the encouragement, that gives you the way to understand . . . why it is important for you to do what you can do," Kimball concludes.[24]

An endless array of "new and improved" practices and products pass before and try to seduce us. However, life's real dividends are earned when commitment, consistency, and steady focus are maintained.

Hobbies and Avocations

As we grow older and wiser, we may, like Christopher Kimball, begin to recognize the importance of maintaining traditions that provide emotional comfort, personal disciplines that keep us mentally sharp and physically capable, and associations that are reliable sources of succor and support. Take, for example, the ability to read a score and play an instrument. Many of us were required to study music as children; and if you were like me, you hated the imposed discipline, were disinclined to practice, and abandoned the enterprise at the earliest opportunity—a decision I, for one, would later rue.

For you see, few activities provide as much sustained pleasure as playing a musical instrument. Whatever dissatisfaction one might feel toward a job or relationship, music always offers a reliable and satisfying diversion. It is a great redeemer, as the slaves who composed America's spirituals knew very well. Throughout life, music can serve as a social lubricant as we find or create opportunities to play with others at parties or at family gatherings. The older adult who can perform even passably well on the piano, guitar, flute, or fiddle is often in demand in retirement communities or at reunions. The good news is, practically anyone can learn to play an instrument, but relatively few are prescient or persistent enough to develop real competence.

"If I had known I'd live this long, I'd have taken better care of myself" is a regretful comment most of us have heard or even made ourselves. But "taking care of ourselves" implies more than maintaining physical and mental fitness. When the ability to speak a foreign language is allowed to erode, or a close friendship isn't nurtured, or ties to our spiritual community are severed, we are just as guilty of self-neglect as someone who refuses to exercise. Persistence is one of the keys to sustaining the good life and experiencing happiness in our later years.

It was in practicing tai chi under the supervision of a highly regarded teacher that I became convinced that the general population suffers from a perseverance deficit. Four semesters of study are typically required to memorize the Taiwanese version of the classic Yang-style form I use, and it takes three more semesters to develop a fair degree of proficiency. But because it is a mindfulness practice and not merely an exercise, tai chi is never perfected. There is always room for further growth, for refinement and deeper understanding of the form's meaning and purpose.

After four years of faithfully attending classes and review sessions, tai chi became a lifestyle activity that I continue to pursue. But I know of hardly anyone else who enrolled with me in that first class who still practices. In fact, by the end of the first year of study, three-quarters had dropped out. Was the form too complicated and physically demanding? Were the classes too expensive or the requirements too rigorous? Was the "excitement factor" missing in tai chi's slow, deliberate motions? Whatever the reasons, according to my teacher, only ten percent of those who begin the study of tai chi successfully learn the whole form. It's a good guess that even fewer continue to execute it on their own. The statistics are probably the same for other meditative and martial disciplines—lots of initiates and relatively few long-distance winners.

Don't Throw in the Towel Too Soon

It's never been easy for human beings to stick with a spiritual practice and other personal regimens. Over 2,500 years ago, the Buddha himself identified "restlessness" as one of the five most powerful hindrances to the pursuit of enlightenment. Thousands of people dabble with meditation, yoga, tai chi, or centering prayer but are unable to sustain that effort for more than a few weeks or months. Expecting to see rapid results, or at least clear evidence of progress, they become frustrated with a simple, repetitive routine and prematurely conclude that "it isn't working." The benefits of practices such as these are often quite subtle, but they are also cumulative and, given sufficient time, will noticeably improve the tone and tenor of one's entire life.

George Leonard, a noted philosopher of education and a master of the Japanese martial art of aikido, has analyzed the process by which expertise in any skill—whether it be music, meditation, or tennis—develops. The typical student will advance rather quickly at first and feel encouraged. But then the learning curve begins to flatten, and the practitioner will feel stuck, unable to make further progress. This is the "plateau" where motivation wanes and practice becomes a matter of keeping faith, exercising will power and paying closer attention. Plateaus must be accepted as a natural and inevitable part of the mastery process and not become a reason for discouragement. To the impatient and untrained eye, the plateau presents a seemingly barren landscape, and the persistent student must learn to love its subtleties.[25]

Our consumer-oriented culture attempts at every turn to discourage the pursuit of a single discipline long enough for the individual to understand the value of the process and to approach mastery. Watch the TV commercials and action shows, or faux sporting events like *American Gladiator*, and what do you see? "An endless series of climactic moments," Leonard writes. "Climax is piled upon climax. *There's no plateau.*"[26]

Why is that? Part of it has to do with an all-too-common conflation of excitement with fulfillment, which causes us to forfeit deep satisfaction for the sake of simply "having fun." But that's not the whole story. Without this constant vacillating, the acquired habit of careening from one health and wellness practice to another, most of America's opulent gyms, its promoters of fad diets, and its personal trainers and suppliers of athletic gear would be filing for bankruptcy. The market counts on people's fickleness and their willingness to spend their way to wellness without ever making a firm commitment to constancy. How many people do you know who haven't darkened their health club's door in ages but continue to pay the monthly fees? The inventory of tennis rackets, cross-country skis, fancy bicycles, roller blades, mitts and balls, ice skates, and healthy-eating cookbooks collecting dust tells a similar story: lots of good intentions and cash investment, but not enough persistence.

The Rewards of Constancy

If we could mount some resistance to the smorgasbord of options the health and fitness industry tempts us with, we might be in a better position to recognize that staying put has some real advantages.

Aspiring athletes are most prone to injury when they are attempting to get in shape and push unconditioned muscles, joints, and cardiovascular systems beyond their limits. This is one of the principal reasons people *stop* exercising: they sustain an injury, are forced to lay off, and lose their resolve. The best way to avoid injury and achieve constancy is to *pay attention* to the body's signals until conditioning is achieved and the regimen begins to feel comfortable. This is the formula I've followed for over forty years, and it generally does work.

Constancy delivers mental and emotional benefits as well. Whether it's the proverbial "runner's high," the experience of "flow" that University of Chicago psychologist Mihaly Csikszentmihayli describes in his book by the same name, or the relaxation response elicited by tai chi and sitting meditation, long-distance winners often enjoy an enhanced inner life.

No doubt, a person can live productively, successfully, and lovingly without ever getting in touch with such gratifying feelings. They could be thought of as a bonus, but perhaps they should be regarded as our natural birthright, part and parcel of the good life. All that's required are a familiarity with the pattern by which mastery develops and a willingness to persevere. "Staying with the sorrow or the pain [of meditation] is not ... an immediately gratifying process," the Buddhist teacher Pema Chodron writes. "But over time ... something begins to shift, [and] ... we begin to feel lighter and more courageous."[27]

The key to maintaining optimal body weight and wellness is much the same. In that UCLA study of thirty-one diets mentioned in an earlier chapter, participants in almost every case experienced initial weight loss. In other words, every approach could be shown to work. However, a majority of the subjects then faltered and regained most if not all of that lost weight. The small minority for whom the results proved permanent shared two characteristics: they conscientiously ate less and exercised religiously. "People who follow this [simple] regimen," science and health journalist Paul Raeburn writes, "report that their quality of life is higher, life is better than it was before. They get to the point with physical activity where they don't say that they love it, but they say that 'it's a part of my life.'"[28]

The well-known nutritionist Marion Nestle agrees that eating for health and fitness isn't complicated: eat less, move more, avoid junk food. "Ironically," she says, "this advice hasn't changed in years."[29]

Staying Put in Our Relationships

"Loyalty and commitment are archetypes in our human structure," Jungian psychologist Robert Johnson reminds us. "They are as necessary to us as food and air." Unfortunately, loyalty and commitment aren't salable, and their market value is negligible. So what have we been conditioned to strive for instead? "Passion," Johnson writes. That's what generates consumer interest and earns the entertainment industry and marketing firms money. Steamy affairs and families disrupted by stormy generational differences have become standard media fare—so much so that one could easily construe them as the cultural norm. "Passion has become unconsciously defined as our highest good," Johnson says, "… and all other values are commonly sacrificed for it."[30]

Remaining in place and honoring one's commitments to family and friends are real challenges in a culture as transient, constantly churning, and addicted to excitement as our own. The traditional virtues of loyalty and fidelity are commended from political rostrums and the nation's pulpits but are routinely disregarded as people seek to increase their personal autonomy and reduce their relational encumbrances. "Fidelity holds steadily to the people and institutions it loves and thereby provides more fickle souls with a sense of stability and security," former Anglican bishop and seminary professor Richard Holloway writes, but statistics would suggest that many people prefer being footloose and fancy-free.[31] Friendship is down, and acquaintanceship is up; for companies, loyalty is contraindicated if it reduces the bottom line; young adults are less than half as likely to belong to clubs and voluntary associations as their grandparents; and as noted in a previous chapter, the percentage of married couples who successfully reach their twenty-fifth wedding anniversaries is declining.[32]

Activities that settled domestic and community life require and that often prove to be deeply satisfying at the personal level are thought to lack pizzazz "Housework, fundraising, and teaching children to read ... are not of sufficient interest [for the media] to document," family counselor Mary Pipher complains, and yet these are precisely the sort of activities in which we must engage if a culture is to thrive and love is to last.[33]

Passion aside, committed partnerships may be more difficult to maintain than in the past simply because the average life span is now so much longer. Both my own parents and my in-laws recently celebrated their sixtieth anniversaries—a milestone that was practically unheard of even a half century ago. Until fairly recently "'til death do us part" typically meant twenty or thirty nuptial years together. Periods of wedlock longer than that demand adjustments that our forebears weren't usually required to make. If people understood what a modern marriage really committed them to, at least some would undoubtedly be a bit hesitant to make the leap. Novelist Jane Smiley's observations are enough to give anyone pause:

> You know what getting married is? It's agreeing to take this person who right now is at the top of his form, full of hopes and ideas, feeling good, looking good, wildly interested in you because you're the same way, and sticking with him while he slowly disintegrates. And he does the same for you. You're his responsibility now, and he is yours. If no one else will take care of him, you will. If everyone else rejects him, you won't. What do you think love is—going to bed all the time?[34]

Trina and I were both twenty-two when we exchanged vows, jumped in her car, and, with a U-Haul in tow, traveled from southwest Florida to the San Francisco Bay Area to set up housekeeping, enroll in seminary, and settle into our marriage. We had already rented a basement apartment sight unseen that several previous seminary couples had occupied. We were soon informed that all these couples had parted company before their degrees had been conferred or the lease had expired. At the time, it seems, a "culture of divorce" prevailed at the school, which made two newlyweds more than a little uneasy.

Trina and I broke the jinx, and now, thirty-five years later, we have learned that the benefits of staying put are significant. We revel in the review of shared memories, welcome the ease and comfort we feel with each other, and appreciate the absence of any need for posturing or pretense. Being the same age, we have similar tastes and preferences and trust that whatever adjustments might need to be made in one or the other of our lives, our core values are likely to remain in alignment.

In today's complicated and unstable social environment, couples often find it difficult to negotiate career changes and other major life transitions. If we aspire to a marriage for the long haul, then it is advisable to cultivate a flexible spirit and resist the temptation to stubbornly hang onto the person to whom, years earlier, we said "I do." What *is* important is that we each know, deep in our hearts, that we will continue to be at each other's side through all the changes of our days.

Trina and I have put a premium on sustainable relationships—not just our own but with our son, Kyle, and with the communities with which we are involved.

Keeping the Generations Connected

One of the saddest features of contemporary culture, in my opinion, is the dearth of casual contact between youth and adults. Apart from the mandated time that kids spend with adults in school or in structured activities like Scouts and soccer, the generations more and more inhabit separate universes. Connections even in families are tenuous, respect grudging, miscommunication and misunderstandings common. As parents and elders, our first responsibility to our children is simply to keep the connection alive and to *pay closer attention* when we begin to notice too much slack in the system. This means being available, reaching out, drawing in by showing genuine interest or concern—not in a pushy way, but firmly and persistently.

In our own family, connections were regularly renewed at mealtimes. Before Kyle departed for college, we belonged to the endangered domestic tribe that requires its members to sit down together at both breakfast and dinner. Trina established this cardinal family rule soon after Kyle was born, and it faithfully ensured that we saw and interacted with each other at least twice a day. Family came first in this department. Committees, councils, and parish leaders were all made aware that supper for the Schulers was a sacrament, to be sacrificed only in the gravest of circumstances.

With the dissolution of the extended family, the rise of the two-earner household, and the creation of a youth culture that often seems bent on making a clean break with its elders, the customary bridges between the generations have fallen into disrepair. Few grandparents live with or have regular contact with their grandchildren, as mine did. Fewer adults greet their children when they come home from school, inquire about their classroom experiences, or invite them to share in the performance of common household tasks and chores.

All of this exacts a heavy toll on the basic building blocks of family life: traditions are neglected, ancestries forgotten, important stories lost, values not reinforced, rules of reciprocity and basic hospitality left untaught. In former times, Mary Pipher observes, children present at family gatherings often sat with their elders during conversation, listening to the tales, the jokes, and the joys and regrets of parents, grandparents, and aunts and uncles. "Thus they learned the rich and idiosyncratic use of language that occurs in families, heard their cautionary tales and moral fables. Such talk is familial cement."[35]

Today, Pipher laments, when grandparents or close friends come calling, the kids are sent to the recreation room with a video or Nintendo game—a convenience that keeps youthful energy contained but that cedes to the media the responsibility for succoring and socializing the upcoming generation.

Bill Doherty, director of the Marriage and Family Therapy Program at the University of Minnesota, identifies excessive amounts of time spent away from home as another contributor to familial entropy. Too many outside commitments consume the energy we need to maintain bonds of intimacy and ensure that our families will remain committed to one another even when the nest empties. Doherty stresses the importance of establishing household "rituals" that regularly put everyone in the same room at the same time for a common purpose.[36] It doesn't make much difference *what* children, youth, adults, and elders do during their time together. The idea is simply to establish points of connection to keep the centrifugal forces at work in the larger culture from pulling us apart. Everyone has to eat, so taking meals together at the family table (with or without a formal blessing) is as good a place as any to start.

In an era where so many demands are placed on families, it is also advisable to settle into a neighborhood or faith community that can supply an extra measure of support. When Trina and I agreed in the late 1980s to leave upstate New York for Madison, our decision had less to do with my own professional aspirations than with our conviction that this new city was ideally suited for family living. We both hoped to find a place where we would be content to stay for the duration of Kyle's upbringing.

We've not been disappointed with our decision. As an only child, Kyle enjoyed the steady company of several "adopted" siblings—youngsters in the immediate area with whom he played and studied for sixteen years and to whom he still feels close. And with no blood relations in the vicinity, long-term friendships have provided us with a caring and conscientious support system.

Ours is a common story. American families often find themselves isolated and forced back upon their own resources. The problem escalates the more often they choose to relocate.

Hopefully, the preceding observations underscore the difference between a "house" and a "home." The former, a physical structure, satisfies our most immediate need for physical safety and comfort. But for a house to become a bona fide *home*, the occupants must be embedded in a larger community that provides companionship, occasions for mourning and celebration, and the promise of mutual care. Houses are more or less interchangeable, but homes are not. "Merely change houses and you will be disoriented," Scott Russell Sanders writes. "Change homes and you will bleed."[37]

Investing in a Faith Community

Another important locus of support for individuals and families is the faith community. A church, synagogue, mosque, or sangha is one of our best hedges against experiencing isolation and generational segregation as we grow older. A high-functioning faith community is one of the few places where casual interchanges between young and old can take place, where familiarity breeds appreciation rather than contempt. Moreover, faith communities keep us aware of and in conversation about our core values as we move through life and struggle with what it means each day to live with courage, generosity, and grace. Finally, few voluntary organizations offer succor and support as reliably in difficult times.

Here, however, is another instance where Van Rensselaer Potter's "fatal flaw" reappears. Once their kids have completed the religious education curriculum, parents often set them free and stop attending services themselves. Younger families "church-shop"; they skitter from place to place looking for a community that "fits their needs" and doesn't interfere too much with soccer games and shopping trips. Not many religious seekers take the long view, recognizing that the social and spiritual benefits of belonging to a faith community only accrue with prolonged, active affiliation. "We are constantly . . . tearing up the cultural environment and refashioning it every generation," Richard Holloway observes, which is why it is so important to develop a "network of social and religious institutions that will be a bulwark against our addiction to change."[38]

When we pay attention to and persistently pursue activities that really matter and that reliably produce satisfaction—activities that have little to do with marketplace values—we will feel better about ourselves and more secure amid the truculence and turbulence of the modern world. Sustainable relationships, a sustainable sense of vocation, routines designed to sustain mental, physical, and spiritual fitness, a sustainable and positive perspective on life— these are objectives well worth striving for.

Chapter 5

Exercise Patience

A well-known Zen Buddhist teaching story highlights the need to "practice patience" if one intends to make the most of his or her abilities, gain insight, and achieve happiness.

A young man approached the venerable master, seeking guidance. "If I meditate eight hours a day and study the Sutras four hours every night," he asked, "how long will it take for me to gain enlightenment?"

"Ten years," the master replied.

The novice was taken aback. "*That* long?" he gasped. "Well, then, what if I practice for ten hours a day and study for six? How long then?"

"Twenty years," said the master.

"But how can that be?" the incredulous novice wondered aloud.

The master shook his head and sighed, "For someone who is in such a hurry, enlightenment does not come easily."

The master knows very well that spirituality doesn't operate on a timetable. It requires aspirants to *exercise patience* through those long plateaus during which enthusiasm wanes and hope falters. The process cannot be hurried, and impatience is antithetical to the whole enterprise. The breathless inquiry—how long will it take—

135

suggests to the master that this young novice is easily discouraged. Stop thinking about the future, the master advises. Just settle into your practice and learn to enjoy the subtle yet considerable rewards of being fully present for each new and original moment.

This brief story could certainly serve as a guiding metaphor for modern American life. While most of us are not as eager for enlightenment as that young novice, we seem to be in a big hurry to fulfill whatever aspirations and ambitions we do have. One reason for this, Oxford University economic historian Avner Offer argues, is the relatively high level of material well-being most Americans enjoy. For all the benefits it confers, a successful free enterprise system "breeds impatience." More modest degrees of wealth, on the other hand, "foster reciprocity and commitment." As an example, Offer cites the declining number of people who are willing to make a long-term investment in their marriages. For some people these relationships are like products purchased at a mall: turn them in if they don't work out.[1]

Sustainability isn't about the quick fix or the cheap solution. Generally it means making a commitment and trying, as best we can, to honor it. In any worthwhile enterprise, from protecting the environment to preserving a relationship, we are going to encounter difficulties. The good life is not a problem-free life. In point of fact, the process of overcoming adversity often produces some of the most rewarding experiences we will ever have. Human beings need to be challenged to "test their mettle," as it were. Throwing in the towel at the first sign of trouble or small inkling of distress may be the easy thing to do, but it doesn't help our self-concept. Most of life's troubles can be overcome *if* we are willing to work through them with patience.

Cultivating a New Attitude

Patience—an attribute the Dalai Lama once likened to a muscle— is the key to a committed and meaningful life. Like any muscle, he points out, it can be significantly strengthened through exercise. If your ambition is to acquire tranquility and calmness, an enhanced ability to face adversity, and greater tolerance and acceptance of others, "Put the practice of patience at the heart of your daily life," the Dalai Lama urges.[2]

As a dedicated distance runner with a long-standing spiritual practice, I've come to appreciate the importance of patience and have felt the benefits of these activities begin to spill over into my labor, my loving, and my service to others. In other words, I've tried consistently to exercise this "muscle" in order to gain greater fitness.

But even a personal "patience practice" won't deliver the goods unless a shift of attitude accompanies it. Has there ever been a civilization so obsessed with *doing* and so uneasy about simple *being*? In order to cram as much productive and consumptive activity as possible into every waking moment, we've steadily reduced the time allotted for discernment and quiet reflection. Hard-charging professionals brag about being able to subsist on six or fewer hours of sleep, largely unaware of the irritability and crankiness it causes.

In his semi-whimsical book *The Tao of Pooh*, Benjamin Hoff recalls one of A. A. Milne's original stories in which Rabbit comes to call on Christopher Robin only to find him gone, a misspelled note tacked to his front door: "Bisy Backson" (busy, back soon), it says. Rabbit misconstrues the message and imagines that Christopher is referring to a person and not to his own absence. Reflecting on this episode, Hoff suggests that our Western world is literally crawling with Bisy Backsons—people who are always out, always on an errand. Convinced that they are saving time by doing as much as they possibly can, they fail to recognize that compulsive busyness strips their experiences and their relationships of much of their savor.

> Let's put it this way; if you want to be healthy, relaxed, and contented, just watch what a Bisy Backson does and then do the opposite. There's one now, pacing back and forth, jingling the loose change in his pocket, nervously glancing at his watch. He makes you feel tired just looking at him. The chronic Backson always seems to have to be going somewhere, at least on a superficial, physical level. He doesn't go out for a walk, though; he doesn't have time.[3]

Americans (and the billions who imitate us) have established

an unhealthy and unsustainable standard. Nothing is more important than increasing our productivity and living life to the hilt.
Ignoring natural circadian rhythms, society operates "24/7"—col-
loquial shorthand for a population that abhors the whole notion of
downtime. Exciting as it might seem always to be on the go, the
consequences of such a lifestyle are less than salutary. The
ancients knew this better than we. Idleness is a prerequisite for
deep reflection and philosophizing, Socrates insisted, and his Far
Eastern contemporaries reached a similar conclusion. In Chinese,
the pictograph for *busy* is composed of two characters: *heart* and
killing. Daily life in traditional societies may have afforded fewer
modern amenities, but lack of leisure was not generally one of its
drawbacks. Busyness was regarded as a form of oppression that
dulled humans' ability to feel and to care.[4]

People's career expectations are conditioned by a civilization that's
in perpetual overdrive. It is assumed that one must move up the ladder quickly, in emulation of the well-dressed, perfectly coiffed attor-
neys and business types portrayed in the media and who one
presumes are representative of that class. Even members of the clergy
are susceptible to such messages. I was once accosted by a young colleague at a ministers' retreat—a man who had recently been ordained
and hadn't yet completed a year of service at his first church. He
wanted to know how long he'd have to work before he could compete
for a congregation as large as mine. I wanted to reply that parishioners
aren't stepping-stones and that ministerial success isn't measured that
way. That man has since moved into another field.

A half-century-long spell of hyperactivity has made many of
America's major metropolises less desirable places to live. Freeway
gridlock, sprawling developments, derelict inner-city neighborhoods, overburdened infrastructure, and a surfeit of cheaply constructed architectural eyesores are the order of the day. Much of
this mess is the consequence of rapid, underregulated development
that hasn't given residents or their elected representatives a chance
to see the big picture and come up with better long-term
approaches to the growth process. Sadly, any attempt to slow
things down long enough to anticipate and resolve problems associated with urban growth is routinely characterized as "antibusiness."

No Speed Limits (on Anything)

Those who would throw caution to the winds and forge ahead offer the typical, tempting incentives: more jobs for residents, greater tax revenues to support government services, and lower prices for consumers. In light of such tangible benefits, waiving environmental rules and granting zoning variances seem a small price to pay. Alas, such promises have often proved illusory. Creating extra slack in the regulatory system has destabilized rather than strengthened many American communities and contributed little to people's quality of life.

Nevertheless, circumspection is frowned upon. The prevailing sentiment is to eliminate as many hindrances as possible so that business may be conducted in a cheap and expeditious manner. While serving as secretary of the Treasury under President Clinton, Lawrence Summers spelled out the formula to be followed: This administration, he announced, "cannot and will not accept any 'speed limit' on American economic growth."[5]

According to philosopher Mark Kingwell, "Speed is our preeminent trope of control and domination." What we are just beginning to realize is that ever-greater speed and the constant pressure applied on people to hurry and hustle place a tremendous strain on everyone. We are, Kingwell warns, "always speeding up to a standstill, a spasm of useless speed that masks the coercion of contemporary society as it undergoes a simultaneous acceleration and terminal shutdown."[6]

People's hopes and expectations with respect to their own economic future reflect this general tendency. Eager to get rich quick, millions of Americans invested heavily in Internet-related corporations during the 1990s, expecting to see the price of these hot new stocks soar quickly into the stratosphere. News of successful IPOs dominated the business pages, but then the dot-com bubble burst, the NASDAQ lost two-thirds of its value, and millions of retirement nest eggs disappeared in a matter of months. Not to be deterred, middle-class investors turned next to real estate in their quest for a fast fortune. Alas, "irrational exuberance" led once again to tens of thousands of imprudent investments. After reaching historic highs in late 2007, stocks again took a nosedive, with the Dow Jones losing nearly fifty percent of its value in the space of just a few months. For too many Americans, the slow, sustainable route to financial security through saving money and living within one's means holds little appeal. We invest the same way we spend: impulsively and impatiently.

The 2003 invasion of Iraq by the "coalition of the willing" followed the same pattern. Despite the repeated efforts of close allies, foreign policy experts, and U.N. inspectors to forestall military action against Saddam Hussein, the White House was adamant. Iraqi WMDs pose a clear and present danger to the world community and must be eradicated immediately, we were warned. To underscore the urgency of the situation, Condoleezza Rice invoked the specter of nuclear holocaust: "We don't want the smoking gun to be a mushroom cloud," she said ominously. Those who questioned this assessment were likened to the appeasers who underestimated the ruthlessly ambitious Adolph Hitler prior to World War II. Impatient and mendacious, the Bush administration chose to remove Saddam by force, British journalist Jonathan Freedland writes, "rather than ... do the long, gradual laborious work of nurturing democratic and liberal elements in the Arab and Muslim world." How was Soviet power ultimately neutralized, he asks? Not by a hasty invasion of an Eastern satellite but by encouraging the internal forces of dissent over several decades.[7]

Freedland reminds us that sustainable, free, and democratic societies are not normally or reliably created by fiat. A conquering force can install a puppet government, but ultimately the impetus to tear down a Berlin Wall or topple a colonial regime must come from within a nation. The Vietnamese Buddhist teacher Thich Nhat Hanh offers an appropriate metaphor for our own country's recent behavior: A man is riding a horse that is galloping very quickly. Another man, standing alongside the road, sees him and yells, "Where are you going?" The man on the horse yells back, "I don't know. Ask the horse."

"I think that is our situation," Thich Nhat Hanh explains. "We are riding many horses that we cannot seem to control."[8]

How Impatience Sullies Everyday Life

Impatience and inattention reduce the quality of our personal lives as well. Having been conditioned to spend most of our waking hours in the fast lane—desiring to do, see, and achieve as much as possible in the shortest time permissible—we deprive ourselves of rich pleasures that have served and sustained human beings for centuries. "Between friends," an ancient Chinese aphorism states, "the fifth cup of tea is the best," but today who has time for even the second cup?

Reading is a remarkably fulfilling activity that loses its luster in an impatient world. Although for a number of years book sales steadily increased as major chains like Border's and Barnes & Noble expanded and Amazon.com made ordering books cheap and easy, the average person actually spent *less* time reading and did so with less comprehension.[9] Reading requires powers of sustained attention and the patient, uncluttered quality of mind that fewer people seem to possess these days. "Readers aren't viewers," novelist Ursula Le Guin observes:

> They recognize their pleasure as different from being entertained. Once you've pressed the ON button, the TV goes on, and on, and on, and all you have to do is sit and stare. But reading is active, an act of attention, of absorbed alertness ....
> In its silence, a book is a challenge. It can't lull you with surging music ... and it won't move your eyes for you the way images on a screen do. It won't move your mind unless you give it your mind, or your heart unless you put your heart in it. ... No wonder not everyone is up to it.[10]

Events that in the past drew families and friends together for celebration, sympathy, and support have also been compromised. Invited to a wedding, people skip the ceremony and attend the reception. Even more impolite is an increasingly common behavior I've witnessed at end-of-life celebrations. It would have been practically inconceivable fifty years ago for someone to walk out of a funeral service before it had concluded, but such irreverence no longer even raises an eyebrow. Whenever I conduct a service that stretches beyond an hour—which often happens when an assortment of friends, family, and colleagues deliver tributes—I notice people beginning to stir and consult their watches, and a few of them quietly rise to make a not-so-discreet exit.

A certain percentage of mourners appear to have convinced themselves that by simply showing up, they've paid their respects in a proper manner. But what does it say about us when not even the deceased and his or her surviving family deserve more than an hour of our time? Better not to show up at all than to make a public spectacle of one's lack of patience.

And then there is the grief process itself. In former times, society sanctioned a lengthy, even indefinite period for loved ones to recover from loss and reorient their lives. The funeral or memorial service signaled the beginning, not the end, of a long, difficult inner journey. Today people are made to feel guilty if they mourn and mope for more than a few months. "Get over it and get on with life" is the not-so-subtle message our impatient civilization sends the bereaved.

This is a dangerous trend, for studies have shown that foreshortened mourning can gravely affect the individual's mental and emotional well-being. "Integrating loss into the depths of one's soul does not take place in sound bites," the noted grief counselor Alan Wolfelt warns. Professionals agree that the grief process cannot be rushed and that individuals should be allowed to do this work in their own way and without feeling pressured. Nevertheless, contemporary mental health practice has more and more fallen in line with managed care's emphasis on rapid treatment and recovery. Wolfelt's paraphrase of the Beatitudes captures the latter's mechanistic approach to grief work: "Blessed are those who mourn quickly and efficiently in response to abbreviated counseling techniques, for they shall meet our criteria for successful treatment."[11]

Impatient to Save the World

Volunteer activity that promotes the common good is another arena where people need to alter their expectations. Effective social witness requires more than a casual, occasional commitment, but people willing to make a sustained effort are in short supply. In my own experience, it has become increasingly difficult to find people willing to work on long-term projects or to serve a term or two on boards and committees.

To be sure, Americans remain eager to contribute, and they still embrace the idea that volunteerism is in everybody's interest and that it is a noble thing to do. There is widespread appreciation for the soup kitchens, free clinics, literacy councils, and Habitat for Humanity–style housing providers that fill the void when public, tax-supported services are lacking.

Nevertheless, we are impatient for change. We want rapid reassurance that the effort we have put forth has made a difference; and if evidence of that is lacking, we tend to become disillusioned. But endeavors to teach an illiterate adult to read, clean the detritus from a lake or stream, or lobby the public safety commission for a stoplight at a busy intersection take time, and the process isn't always straightforward and free of hindrances. Many of today's volunteers have a low threshold for frustration and throw in the towel too easily. Several days of exposure to Jun-San, a transplanted Japanese Buddhist nun who has inspired many people with her tenacity, humility, and boundless patience, might shift our perspective.

Since coming to the United States, this wisp of a woman has dedicated herself to peace and justice causes. Known as "Walks Far Woman" by the Lakota people with whom she has marched in solidarity, Jun-San has overseen the construction of Peace Pagodas across the country. At the end of a long day working on one such project in upstate New York, her coworkers found Jun-San sitting in a deep hole, excavating with a kitchen spoon. Startled, they asked her what she was doing. In her own evocative grammar, she replied: "I was tired using pick. I very always hitting stone. It hurt. I can sitting do something. Digging with spoon." [12]

It didn't bother Jun-San that her modest implement wasn't going to get the job done by noon tomorrow. She was contributing as best she could to a collective effort that reflected her deepest values, and that was all that mattered.

During the thirty years I've practiced professional ministry, many well-intentioned men and women have shared with me their desire to live more generously, responsibly, and caringly, knowing that the good life requires giving as well as taking. They come seeking advice about worthy organizations they might join or volunteer positions or social causes in which they could invest time and talent. I have always tried to support such sincerely expressed interest and to make appropriate recommendations.

But lately I've begun to feel less comfortable with these conversations. For too many of the men and women I meet, humanitarian service seems to be a fleeting impulse provoked by a twinge of guilt or a temporary swing outside the normal arc of middle-class ambition. The impetus to assist others or to bear social witness often follows hard upon disappointing election results, a devastating hurricane, or some comparable perturbation in the moral universe.

The problem is lack of patience and perseverance. Among those who hear the call to serve, relatively few respond in a consistent manner. Having made a commitment, people soon realize that to fulfill their responsibility, something else in life will have to give. Like a daily spiritual practice, service requires self-discipline: setting aside time, making space, removing mental and emotional obstacles, and interrupting habitual patterns. But also like a daily spiritual practice, a patient, persistent pattern of volunteer service can deliver long-term personal and social dividends: intellectual growth, a more open heart, collegiality with good and caring people, and an improved self-concept. One middle-aged volunteer reports that he feels fortunate to be able to put in time at the hospital. His motives are not altogether altruistic, because in the course of serving the sick, injured, and post-surgical, he gains perspective. "They help me realize that you can take things for granted until you get sick, and then you stop and think about what life really means."[13] To make the good life last, we should aspire to this level of maturity.

Unfortunately, work commitments, housekeeping responsibilities, media, and recreational allurements prevent many of us from making a serious commitment to a larger community. Last hired, our volunteer role is often the first to be fired when push comes to shove and busy schedules need to be pared down.

This problem is likely to persist as long as Americans keep piling so much onto their plates. In order to perform good works in a sustainable manner, some of the unnecessary and meaningless clutter must be eliminated. We're all familiar with the adage, "If you want something done, ask a busy person." Not necessarily. Volunteer tasks tend not to be fulfilling for the person who is already overburdened and are probably accomplished more effectively by someone who has some extra time to give.

Relatively few Americans are in a position to become dedicated full-time activists, but it is critically important to the long-term health of our society that we carve more time out of our workaday lives for the nonremunerative roles that originally shaped and have helped strengthen America's unique civic culture. The fact is, both our natural and social environments need far more attention than they are presently getting.

As the main character in an old British television series, Dr. Who was a science fiction hero whose quirky wisdom became a notable feature of this popular show. In one episode, his adversary challenged the virtuous doctor, "Do you really think your puny efforts can change the course of destiny?"

With a canny wink, Dr. Who replied, "No ... but I might just tamper with it a bit."

That's the outlook we need to adopt. The point is to do a little tweaking here and a little meddling there, faithfully expecting that with time the arrow of destiny will begin to curve a degree or two in a more humane and just direction.

Strengthening the Muscle of Patience at Mealtime

What steps might we take, as individuals and as a society, to strengthen the muscle of patience? An obvious place to begin is with eating—an act practically everyone has to perform on a daily basis. Despite a good deal of recent publicity about the "slow food" movement, the way most Americans eat—on the run—suggests that it hasn't made a very deep impression. In a "fast-food nation," MREs (meals ready to eat) aren't just for the military anymore. We expect our victuals to be dispensed and consumed in the twinkling of an eye, and if at all possible, while we're commuting or cruising the Internet. But mindless, impatient eating not only deprives us of one of the real pleasures in life; it can be downright dangerous. According to the National Highway Traffic Safety Administration, dining while driving (seventy percent of Americans admit to doing so) is a leading cause of automobile mishaps. Fender benders aside, people who wolf down their food typically consume more calories and are thus more susceptible to weight gain and are likely to join the growing ranks of the obese (a health hazard almost as significant as smoking).[14]

Slow, mindful eating is a practice many Eastern teachers emphasize—placing one's full attention on the sensations that accompany each simple gesture and each succulent bite. Feel, smell, and taste the section of a juicy tangerine before separating and popping the next one into your mouth. Stretch the process out, and allow the tranquil, appreciative feelings that mindful eating produces to filter into and inform your other daily activities.

Slow Down and Live a Little

Several passages in the *Tao Te Ching*, the ancient book of Chinese wisdom attributed to Lao Tzu, underscore the centrality of patience among the virtues of the sage. "I have just three things to teach: simplicity, patience, and compassion," Lao Tzu announces in chapter 67. Patience, he continues, "accords with the way things are" while impatience and impetuousness cut against the grain. "Forcing a project to completion, you ruin what is almost ripe," the sage warns.[15]

Whereas today's society extols speed just about every-where—on the highways, on the Internet, on the assembly line, and in the checkout lane—monastics and spiritual teachers have for centuries counseled just the opposite: be selective and be slow; do less but attend more closely to what you do. That, the wise say, is the surest formula for achieving satisfaction. Or as the cele-brated novelist Willa Cather wrote: "Men travel faster now, but I do not know if they go to better things."[16]

As a lifelong athlete and one-time avid competitor, I know something about the dangers of "going out too fast" and pushing up against my mental and physical limits. I have always had to remind myself that acquiring a competitive advantage in any single race is far less important than cultivating a *lifestyle activity* that can anchor my wellness up to and into old age. It took time, but eventually this muscle called patience became and to this day remains the cornerstone of my practice.

Amby Burfoot won the Boston Marathon in 1968 and has indulged his running habit for over forty years. He says that he's "never known a runner who had as much patience as he needed," which is why so many running careers end prematurely with injury or burnout. Eager to prove themselves, many novice competitors overestimate their abilities or underestimate how physically and mentally demanding a long race can be. As a result, they end up having a miserable (and quite often injury-plagued) experience. "Distance running requires you to take the long view," Burfoot writes. "It takes weeks and months to get in shape. Give yourself time. Don't make hasty and unnecessary mistakes. Remember: life is a marathon, not a sprint. Pace yourself accordingly."[17]

If we hope to sustain a relationship with an intimate partner, patience must again become a priority. "Love at first sight" prompts some couples to tie the knot too quickly, before those first powerful waves of libido and emotional attraction have had time to settle down and a better rounded and more realistic picture begins to emerge. Abbreviated courtships don't necessarily produce disappointment, but they do entail greater risk. From their very inception (when compatibility has yet to be determined) through the peaks and valleys (when elation and despair must both be dealt with) and across the long plateaus (when we must pay attention to love's more subtle rewards), domestic partnerships require patience. "It may take a lifetime to learn to make a relationship flourish, but that happens to be exactly how long we have," writes Robert Taylor, whose quarter century of marriage gives him some credibility.[18]

When we are patient and don't demand of loved ones and friends strong doses of supercharged stimulation, when we give ourselves more mindfully and less fretfully to the activities that constitute ninety percent of customary relational life—cooking, housekeeping chores, Scrabble games, strolling, biking, grocery shopping, or simply watching birds at the feeder—our chances of experiencing deep, abiding soul satisfaction increase accordingly. "Stirring the oatmeal love" is how Robert Johnson describes the sentiment that is "content to do many things that ego is bored with."[19]

Lessons from an Unlikely Subject

Patience can enhance the quality of our friendships as well. In this respect, that enduringly popular television series *Seinfeld,* despite its fictional, comedic nature, may give us something serious to think about.

Jerry Seinfeld's friends are a collection of odd ducks. There is George (insecure and manipulative), Kramer (impetuous and inept), Elaine (needy and clinging), and an assortment of other regulars with whom the level-headed, emotionally contained Jerry consorts. But despite the dramatic differences in their temperaments and the irritation and distress they occasionally feel toward each other, these characters stay connected. Time and time again, fences are mended with honest explanations, apologies, and simple acts of atonement. The members of Seinfeld's crew refuse to give up on each other. Why? Because the unquantifiable sustenance that friendship brings to their lives is well worth all the extra effort it requires.

Real friendships demand an investment of time and attention—more of both than many of us think we have to spare. Without them we don't have the necessary resources to work through the misunderstandings and misdemeanors that inevitably crop up in any relationship where there is a strong emotional attachment. *Seinfeld*'s characters have all made a tacit but mutually understood commitment "to be there when it's not convenient or easy" and to remain "steadfast in the face of change and crisis," as Mary Pipher puts it.[20]

Crows, Trees, and the Gift of Patience

In a poem entitled "About Crows," the late John Ciardi suggests that patience is a principle only those who are more advanced in years can appreciate. His words are worth quoting at length:

The old crow is getting slow
The young crow is not.
Of what the young crow does not know
The old crow knows a lot.
At knowing things the old crow is
still the young crow's master.
What does the slow old crow not know?
How to go faster.
The young crow flies above, below,
And rings around the slow old crow!
What does the fast young crow not know?
Where to go.

Even if young crows, young lions, and young Turks are more interested in sprinting than in slogging through a marathon, ways can be found to make them aware that patience and persistence have advantages and can both deepen our understanding and increase our pleasure. Like *paying attention*, this key can be taught—indirectly if not directly. Dena Wortzel of the Wisconsin Humanities Council recalls receiving a lesson in patience from her third grade Washington, D.C., science teacher. "She took my class out on the lawn in front of the school building and asked each of us to pick a tree," Wortzel recalls.

Kids dashed from tree to tree, looking for ... what? What were we searching for in the tree we would call "mine?" I wish I could remember. I know the teacher gave us some time and did not tell us how to choose. What she did tell us was that we would visit our tree regularly throughout the spring to watch and record the changes it went through.

Wortzel found her tree, which she did faithfully return to and closely observe throughout the year. In the process, she learned that "there is all the difference in the world between looking at something and living with it," as Joseph Wood Crutch once put it.[21] This was my first "love affair" with a tree, Wortzel writes, and equipped with patience and newfound powers of observation, she has "been acquiring such lovers ever since."[22]

This is a very different picture of the good life than our culture typically provides. Wortzel's teacher managed to instill in her and perhaps in a few other eight-year-olds an appreciation for the slow rhythms of arboreal life, and for at least one person the lesson stuck. If more of us could apply the same logic to the slow growth of the spirit and the gradual maturing of our relationships, the whole world might be far better off.

Closed on Sunday

How might patience become a societal as well as a personal virtue? Perhaps we would be wise to reconsider the practice of "Sunday closings" that most communities have abandoned as inconvenient and uneconomic. Could we not have one day a week when nonessential commerce ceased and people were encouraged to be nonproductive and to take their ease for at least twelve hours? To be sure, computers and the Internet will always pose a problem since they enable us to produce and consume continually and from the privacy of our homes. Still, a bona fide, culturally mandated day of rest would restore a positive and healthful precedent.

The measure could be presented not as a sacred obligation but rather as a way to safeguard our personal, public, and planetary health. Sunday closing would give everyone and everything an interval to recover, to reconnect, to reflect, and to savor. Shuttering stores, encouraging people to leave their cars in the garage, organizing neighborhood events, banning advertising for a single day— one can easily imagine how such simple measures would elevate the tone and tenor of our common life. In addition to the precious resources conserved, the net reduction of mental and emotional stress felt by the general population would, I predict, be noticeable.

This whole idea of a dedicated "day off" is of very ancient lineage. The fourth of Yahweh's Ten Commandments composed over 2,500 years ago enjoins the Hebrews to "remember the Sabbath day, to keep it holy." Scholars agree that of the Old Testament's many injunctions this was one of the most significant. The ancient Hebrews took it so seriously that they were reluctant to even defend themselves from attack on the day of rest.[23]

In ancient times, Sabbath observance entailed far more than attending worship services and fulfilling formal religious duties once a week. Nor was it equated with "leisure" in the way we think of it today—as a casual, "twiddling your thumbs" kind of interlude from labor. Sabbath provided an opportunity, as Wayne Muller suggests, "for other things—love, friendship, prayer, touch, singing ... to be born in the space created by our rest." A convention that our dour Puritan ancestors misconstrued as a day of privation and gloomy soul-searching possessed far more positive and life-affirming connotations in the beginning.[24]

By including Sabbath observance in the Decalogue, the ancient Hebrews wished to underscore that it was not merely customary to rest; it was in the very nature of things periodically to suspend all productive activity. According to the Genesis story, following six stupendous acts of creation even God rested—not out of weariness (for God is indefatigable) but because the Almighty is not a Bisy Backson who must always be up to something. At the culmination of creation, God stops. For now, the Deity has done enough. The new cosmos may not be perfect in all respects (after all, it contains wily serpents and suggestible Homo sapiens), but still it is good enough.

Whatever deference previous generations may have shown toward it, the Fourth Commandment is undoubtedly the one least honored and observed today. Not only secularists but the vast majority of Jews and Christians violate it with impunity. The pressure to treat Sunday (or Saturday, in the case of Jews and Sabbatarians) as nothing special is almost irresistible. A few years ago a nationwide chain of stores that sells Christian merchandise succumbed to the capitalist imperative and opened its doors for business on Sunday afternoons. Corporate officials disingenuously explained the shift as a "way of fulfilling its calling to provide ... Bibles, books, and other Christian resources to their customers." In response, *The Charlotte Observer*'s Ken Garfield acidly observed that it is "another sign of the culture turning Sunday into one more day in the rat race."[25] The commandment most in need of reexamination and renewed emphasis, then, could be the Fourth—not least because in failing to honor it we have surely made our world a less pleasant and more perilous place to be.

The concept was broadly inclusive and intended to benefit all creation. Ancient peoples knew very well that proper stewardship of the earth required periodic suspension of cultivation. Farming is a taxing enterprise, but it also requires patience. If the agriculturalist is too ambitious and does not allow the land to lie fallow—to rest—it will soon be exhausted. Sabbath law ensured that this important principle of stewardship would be taken with the utmost seriousness and that farmers would not be tempted to reap short-term gains at the expense of future generations. We discount such perennial (and now scientifically validated) wisdom at our own peril.

The Land Itself Grows Weary

North America boasts some of the most productive farmland on the planet, and a significant portion of humanity depends on the American soil to meet its food needs. Yet intensive industrial production of cereal grains has seriously degraded much of the continent's best and most arable acreage, while overgrazing threatens to reduce millions of acres of marginal grasslands to desert. With worldwide demand for animal protein and ethanol-based fuel rising, farmers eager to maximize profits are abandoning "best practices" by pulling acreage out of land banks and tilling areas highly susceptible to erosion.

The desire of farmers to make up for years of marginal existence is understandable. Those who grow the nation's crops have suffered from low commodity prices in recent decades, and many have been driven out of business or are barely hanging on. Nevertheless, the soil needs time to rest, and impatience with the natural rhythm of cultivation and recovery may in the end prove the surest road to ruin.

Creating or restoring fertility to the soil does take time. The process can be artificially hastened with chemical inputs, but there will come a point—as with performance drugs in the human body—at which crop yields dwindle and further transfusions make little difference.

Over the years the eco-poet Gary Snyder has learned a great deal about the forest ecosystems of Northern California, and he has adapted himself to nature's slow and patient rhythms. Fifty years is not a particularly long period for a forest to naturally reestablish itself after fire or logging, he writes, and if we try to hurry the process along with replanting or salvage operations, we are likely to sabotage the languorous forces that create a rich, healthy environment. "This is bold and visionary science and contains the hope that both the Forest Service and industry might *learn to slow down* and go more at the magisterial pace of the life of a forest," Snyder says. We are beginning to understand that maintenance of the soil and preservation of wildlife diversity are critical to a sustainable forest system and that these are not tasks that can be rushed.[26]

Patience and Community Improvement

Although they are often tempted to cut corners, farmers and foresters *do* understand better than most the fallowness principle and the importance of patience. Functionaries in the economic and political spheres have yet to learn that lesson.

What if, in the spirit of the Fourth Commandment, municipalities placed a complete moratorium on new development once every seven years? Such an interlude would give the entire community an opportunity to study and evaluate the achievements and the mistakes of a six-year cycle of activity. With time set aside for review and analysis, a county or city would be in a better position to resist the pressure that private interests bring to bear on public officials to "fast-track" proposals or risk losing their business.

This is not to say that most American communities, including my own, don't already engage in planning processes that include input from many stakeholders. Reports are generated and circulated, public feedback elicited, and guidelines established, all of which is commendable. Yet very few citizens participate in or even pay much attention to discussions that can have a major impact on the character of their community. Why? For pretty much the same reason we don't step into volunteer roles. The average American has so many

interests and commitments to juggle and is pulled in so many directions that assimilating and evaluating new and often technically challenging information is just more than they have time for.

A sustainable approach to community development would
create an appropriate interval for citizens to focus and to engage in
deeper reflection. In an earlier era, the town meeting afforded citizens this opportunity. That practice endures in hamlets and villages throughout Vermont, where, as Bill McKibben notes, "the
traditional meeting lasts all day. People take off from work, and
there is often a potluck supper. ... Town meetings can be dull ...
but they are a school for educating residents about public affairs;
for making them citizens."27

Due Deliberation

Bruce Ackerman and James Fishkin have sketched out a plan for a
Deliberation Day to precede every major national election, an
undertaking similar to the town meeting but on a much larger
scale. Creating a pre-election "holiday" with the proper incentives
for citizens to study and discuss candidates, party platforms, and
ballot initiatives would help counteract negative "hit-and-run"
advertising and those deceptive sound bites that erode citizen's
confidence in their representatives and in the entire electoral
process. Without due deliberation—the patient process of sifting
and winnowing opposing political claims—a society composed of
free, informed, and active citizens cannot be maintained.

Americans pay lip service to democracy and to the spread of
democracy abroad. Yet our own democratic traditions are perennially threatened by ignorance and apathy. It was encouraging that in
the 2008 elections more young people cast ballots than ever before
and turnout in many places set modern records. Still, too much of
our political information is delivered in sound bites and is bereft of
context. Deliberation Day would be a step in the right direction
because it aims to remind voters that "voting is not an occasion for
expressing consumer-like preferences, but a crucial moment in
which they are confiding ultimate coercive power to representatives who ... may determine the fate of billions of their fellow
inhabitants of the planet Earth."28

Patience is a hard sell because many people feel that there is already too much foot-dragging and deliberation. What kind of society bottles up important legislation for months and years at a time; leaves prisoners to languish on death row for over a decade before their appeals are exhausted; makes a person wait months for a comprehensive physical exam; permits young people to dilly-dally for years before finally finishing their college degree? Even a patient person can become indignant about the glacial pace at which some of our sectors seem to operate. Why can't more of the world's necessary business be expedited, we ask?

The scale and the increased complexity of our modern social, political, and judicial systems have undoubtedly slowed some processes down. The interests of many different parties must be considered, due diligence done, and necessary precautions taken. While it's important to strive for efficiency, delays will be inevitable and, often as not, prudent as institutions attempt to meet new contingencies and growing demand. Too often in recent years, an unwarranted sense of urgency has caused our leaders to cut corners—authorizing the invasion of another country and passing problematic legislation like the PATRIOT Act and a $700 billion financial bailout package without sufficient understanding of the risks.

How One President Made Patience Work

The passage of comprehensive civil rights legislation in the mid 1960s was one of the twentieth century's most notable political achievements, signaling the official end of almost a hundred years of discrimination reinforced by Jim Crow laws. The magnitude of that shift is demonstrated by the election, some forty years later, of a mixed-race United States president, Barack Obama. It seems appropriate to end this chapter by highlighting the role that our third key—patience—played in that historic process.

President Lyndon Johnson was a key player. Remembered and criticized as the American president who ratcheted up our entanglement in a war that cost America fifty thousand lives and left scars that still are visible today, Johnson often isn't given sufficient credit for helping secure the civil rights of American minorities or for ambitious social programs that cut the American poverty rate in half.

Johnson made some egregious mistakes, and none so serious as his desperate, dogged pursuit of victory in Vietnam. By failing to pay attention to what was really transpiring in Southeast Asia, Johnson was unable to adopt a more sensible approach to the region's problems. As a result, he remained wedded to an unsound policy for far too long. But with regard to civil rights, President Johnson presents a model of patience intelligently and effectively practiced.

As the campaign for voting rights was heating up in Alabama and violence in Selma had begun to capture the nation's attention, the president felt pressured to act formally and decisively to defuse the situation. Send in federal troops to neutralize the local police and prevent hostile whites from injuring nonviolent protesters, civil rights leaders begged him.

Johnson was himself a white southerner who previously had supported continued white dominance. But he knew that the days of Jim Crow were drawing to a close and that the rules of the game would have to change. Within a few months he would sign into law the landmark Voting Rights Act that successfully enfranchised millions of black citizens. At this critical juncture, however, he took a calculated risk and ignored calls for federal intervention. Johnson wasn't vacillating, and despite the appearance of indifference, the president knew very well what he was doing. According to Ronald Heifetz, by permitting the drama in Selma to play out a bit longer on national TV, "he prevented premature closure ... and waited to seize that moment when he could address the issue of racial justice rather than merely diffuse the dissonance."

Through deliberate inaction, in other words, Lyndon Johnson put the American people on the hook and made it impossible for them to ignore their own responsibility for the "harsh reality of black people being beaten for requesting an equal right to vote." Had he defused the situation prematurely, it would not have become the transformative event it subsequently proved to be.[29]

Patience is the key that enables us to sense, as Lyndon Johnson did in this instance, when "ripeness" occurs. Patient people appreciate the importance of timing and won't allow themselves to be pushed into a decision or an action against their better judgment.

Chapter 6

Practice Prudence

An Unhealthy Predilection

According to recent cognitive science research, "teenagers have a hard time foreseeing the consequences of their actions." In other words, they find it difficult to calculate the risks and anticipate the drawbacks of any particular decision they make.[1]

Actuarial experts understand this perfectly, which is why auto insurance rates for the typical young driver are three to four times greater than those an older person would pay. The phenomenon is also familiar to criminologists, educators, and millions of parents who have tried to forestall calamitous adolescent behavior by reciting sobering statistics and cautionary tales of young lives gone up in smoke.

"The young and the impetuous" are one thing, but as Rensselaer Van Potter observed, those under twenty-five have no monopoly on lack of foresight. No ... mature adults generally don't drive as carelessly or flout the rules as casually as their juniors, but that doesn't mean we are as circumspect as we need to be. Evidence of this is not hard to come by. How we treat our aging bodies, tend to our relationships, support our community, and treat the environment provides ample proof that the choices we've made and the habits we've maintained are not designed to serve humanity's (or our own) long-term best interests.

A sustainable civilization is also a sensible one, judicious in its judgments and willing to temper spontaneity and the spirit of adventure with a healthy dose of circumspection. No prescription for the good life would include the kind of penny-pinching parsimony that figures so prominently in *Poor Richard's Almanack*. Nor should it require us to identify and address every conceivable future contingency in order to prevent any and all negative outcomes. Caution should not be confused with cowardice. Prudence permits us to take reasonable risks, ones that we've at least had time to contemplate and to consider in light of other options.

Almost forty years ago David Brower, then the executive director of the Sierra Club, spent a number of days hiking in the northern Cascades with a party that included the dean of the Stanford University School of Earth Sciences, Charles Park. The two men engaged in a number of animated discussions on the trail and around the campfire, which often led to pointed disagreements. On the issue of exploiting the planet's mineral wealth, Park's position was clear: if today's growing economy requires mining even in pristine, protected areas like the Cascades, he was in favor.

"The future can take care of itself," he told Brower. "I don't condone waste, but I am not willing to penalize present people."

A staunch proponent of wilderness protection and the careful shepherding of natural resources, Brower replied, "I suppose I accept Nancy Newhall's definition: 'Conservation is humanity caring for the future.'"[2]

The dialogue between these two knowledgeable and well-meaning men reflects the quandary in which our culture now finds itself. Charles Park isn't interested in sustainability, how to make the good life last. His ambition is to make the good life even better for his contemporaries. It could be that Park is more inordinately optimistic than he is irresponsible. Like many humanistically oriented scientists of the middle twentieth century, he probably was counting heavily on human ingenuity to pull us through any future patch of trouble. We really don't need to worry about conserving nonrenewable resources because, when push comes to shove, there will be technological breakthroughs, and viable substitutes will become available to meet the needs of tomorrow.

David Brower, on the other hand, isn't willing to leave his successors out of the accounting. In keeping with the great law of the Iroquois ("in every deliberation we must consider the impact on the seventh generation"), he emphasizes the ethical responsibility of those presently alive to exercise sensible restraint. Unless we are supremely confident that proposed land and resource management practices will not prove deleterious in the long term, we should forego the temptation to employ them.

The good life is not meant to be morally neutral or bereft of responsibility. Most people experience a vast sense of relief knowing that they have made adequate provision for those loved ones who will come after them. A collective conscience is no different. How can a community feel good about itself when, as Bill Moyers said, it is guilty of robbing its children of their future? So whether it is drilling for oil off the California coast, driving an ATV through the Mojave, drilling corn into a seasonal wetland, or buying bottled water, our actions are bound to have consequences of which we are ethically obliged to make an honest assessment. "Because we don't think about future generations," Henrick Tikkanen warns, "they will never forget us."[3]

Those who inherit the earth will find themselves hard pressed if we choose to continue discounting their importance. To the extent that present patterns of production and consumption diminish their prospects and threaten to raise their level of insecurity, such practices may be described as ignorant, imprudent, and, as Matthew Fox suggested, morally repugnant. A sustainable approach to human problem solving seeks to maximize health and happiness in the present without needlessly putting those who follow at risk.

Not Too Late to Learn

Fortunately, Charles Park's cavalier attitude is less common than it once was—which is not to say that it has disappeared completely.

Many more people do understand the cumulative effect that a burgeoning, resource-hungry human population is having on our beleaguered planet. Far fewer are as blithely optimistic about technology's ability to control or reverse unwelcome developments like loss of biodiversity and climate change. But while more people are paying attention and awareness is increasing, behavioral changes come slowly. We still are not sure what it means to think and act more prudently.

Broadly speaking, a good place to start is with the Precautionary Principle—a statement drafted in the late 1990s by an international interdisciplinary team that met at Wisconsin's Wingspread Conference Center. This group hoped to refine and build upon earlier work performed by delegates to the 1992 U.N. Environmental Conference at Rio de Janeiro. Both these and subsequent efforts of a similar nature signal an increasing willingness by at least some prominent scientists and social planners to proceed with greater caution. Though lacking in specifics, Wingspread's Precautionary Principle—like the physician's first rule to "do no harm"—is an ideal to be pursued and points us in a more promising direction:

> While we realize that human activities may involve hazards, people must proceed more carefully than has been the case in recent history. Corporations, government entities, organizations, communities, scientists, and other individuals must adopt a precautionary approach to all human endeavors. [This means] when an activity raises threats of harm to human health or the environment, precautionary measures should be taken even if some cause-and-effect relationships are not fully established scientifically.[4]

Because this principle implies the need for certain curbs on economic and technological entrepreneurship, it is felt by some to be inexpedient. When profits are jeopardized, the Precautionary Principle is likely to encounter stiff resistance. So-called subprime mortgages are a recent case in point.

Chafing under federal regulations that had protected mortgage holders since the Great Depression, the nation's large investment banks lobbied Congress to loosen the rules and expand the home-loan playing field. In 1999 federal legislators obliged, and for a while business boomed and the banks' coffers swelled. The construction and real estate industries were swept along in a rising tide as millions of prospective homeowners were persuaded to take advantage of "innovative" mortgage offers. But for many, the dream of living in a McMansion or acquiring greater equity wasn't realistic because the whole setup was unsustainable. When real estate values plunged and time ran out on all those attractive "teaser" interest rates, hundreds of thousands of homes headed for foreclosure, and the avaricious institutions holding their paper begged Congress for a bailout. The Chairman of the Federal Reserve, Ben Bernanke, was shocked (shocked!) and belatedly admitted that "a more robust framework for the *prudential* [my emphasis] supervision of investment banks and other large security dealers" was needed.[5]

Because they are always seeking new ways to gain a competitive advantage, the Bear Stearns and Enrons of the world aren't particularly enamored of prudence. The key makes much more sense to Jeff and Shelly Schlender, a couple who practice sustainable forestry on a four hundred-acre parcel in Wisconsin's unique and ecologically fragile Baraboo Hills. Content to make a modest living rather than a killing, they harbor other ambitions than simply to maximize their profit.

A few years ago the Schlenders were approached by representatives of the Nature Conservancy, who apprised the family of the Conservancy's intention to protect for posterity as much of the area's natural heritage as possible. After careful thought, the couple signed off on a conservation easement for their entire property. The agreement restricts what the Schlenders and their heirs can do with the land—for example, residential and commercial development is prohibited—but it allows them to continue logging and farming in the same sustainable manner as before.

As the parents of two teenage girls, Shelly and Jeff were delighted with the new covenant. "We know this is a unique area," Shelly concedes, "and we feel a responsibility to take care of the land and give something back to this community."

"When we're gone," Jeff adds, "we hope one day that our girls will want to live here after us, though you can never be sure of that. But we'll take care of it like they were. We'd like to see this place stay together."[6]

The Schlenders, one might say, have applied their own version of the Precautionary Principle to this small but sensitive problem. They gladly agreed to limit their own economic opportunities in the interest of protecting aesthetically, environmentally, and agriculturally valuable terrain from the predations of future commercial developers. Whether or not his own family chooses to continue living on and working the land, Jeff Schlender feels confident that future generations will commend his preservationist ethic and his commitment to the health and well-being of the "Great Economy."

Low Prices and High Mortality

Imagine how different our communities might look and how profoundly our daily lives would be affected if the Schlenders' sensibility was more widely shared. What if global, big-box developers like Walmart and Target or fast-food operations like McDonald's and KFC were required to abide by some version of the Precautionary Principle? They would need to prove beyond a reasonable doubt that their presence in a community wouldn't produce long-term negative consequences for that culture and economy.

Much evidence now suggests that big-box discounters have wreaked economic havoc throughout the country, emptying historic business districts, depressing wages, drastically reducing economic diversity, and rapidly erasing the small-town aesthetic that our Christmas cards still depict. Every day, independent diners and supper clubs close their doors, victimized by the cheap food and saturation advertising of the national food franchises. Not only does the demise of these local businesses—which often paid a living wage—deal a heavy blow to local economies, but it has homogenized people's appetites and doomed many of our nation's distinctive regional cuisines to extinction.

A civilization dominated by large corporations bereft of loyalty either to people or to place and for whom return on investment is the sole measure of success has proved no kinder to human communities than to the natural ecology. Throughout America's midsection, as Thomas Frank observes, vacant storefronts, a scattering of thrift shops, and a tavern or two greet the occasional visitor to down-at-the-heels historic Main Street, while on the outskirts cars crowd the vast parking lots of Walmart and Farm & Fleet.[7]

Although my wife Trina and I very infrequently patronize national franchises of any sort and make it a point to buy local, on one trip to the Southwest we found ourselves in a bind. We were planning to visit a rustic resort that features warm mineral springs and had forgotten to pack any bath towels. After spending the night in a town with just over five thousand residents, we began searching for a store that carried linens. After several stops and inquiries, the situation became clear: Walmart was our only option.

We were incredulous, but as incomes have steadily declined in the midsection of the country, people have increasingly looked to "low-cost leaders" for their sustenance. Linens, like so many other consumer items, are not something an independent dry goods store can sell competitively any longer.

Unfortunately, the immediate advantage to the low-income consumer may be outweighed by the long-term cost to the community in which they live. Research performed at the University of Pennsylvania indicates that counties with a Walmart have grown poorer than surrounding counties and that the pace of decline increased as the number of Walmarts multiplied. The reasons are simple: the typical Walmart eliminates a job and a half for every job it creates and establishes a lower wage-and-benefit threshold that, in order to remain competitive, other businesses are forced to adopt. Moreover, while a locally owned, nonfranchise business returns on average forty-five cents of each dollar spent to the local economy, the typical big-box retailer recirculates only a third of that.[8] Walmart can offer those low prices, Bill McKibben observes, "precisely because of the damage it does to communities."[9]

In an attempt to protect their assets, some communities have passed ordinances banning big-box stores and franchise establishments entirely. Others are looking at somewhat milder restrictions. For instance, policy makers for the City of Los Angeles, alarmed over the growing number of obese residents, have developed plans to control the spread of fast-food restaurants—a tactic that could be called "health zoning." "The people don't want [these restaurants]" Councilwoman Jan Perry avers, "but when they don't have any other options, they gravitate to what's available."

Mark Vallianatos, director of the Center for Food and Justice at Occidental College, also believes the new proposal makes sense. This is "bringing health policy and environmental policy together with land-use planning," he said. "I think that's smart, and it's the wave of the future."[10]

We are just beginning to fathom how destructive millions of undifferentiated acres of genetically modified, chemically controlled cereal crops have been to plant and animal diversity and thus to the planet's ecosystems. Loss of diversity in the local marketplace produces similar social and economic consequences. Management consultant Larry J. Eriksson has studied this issue closely and concluded that when communities depend on a small number of retailers and one or two major industries or on a single commodity like corn, cattle, or cotton, they risk catastrophic harm if one of these props is removed. Echoing Jane Jacobs, Eriksson also argues that commercial enterprises of modest size embedded within the core community help weave together neighborhoods and create sustainable social capital. Despite their convenience and attractive pricing, national chain and megastores "cannot duplicate the personal service, connections to the community, and stability provided by main street stores," and as the latter disappear, we experience a decline in the richness of our lives.[11]

Focus on the Local

Keya Tehrani is one successful local entrepreneur who doesn't have to be convinced. Thirteen years ago he opened his first Coffee-X-Change in Tucson, and now several more shops operate under the same banner. Tehrani buys only fair-trade beans, produces a first-rate product, and understands how a business like his helps strengthen the city's infrastructure. He says:

> I support local businesses, and I want people to know that I'm a local businessman. It's very important to me. I think we should take care of Tucson and not send our money to national chains. If [coffee drinkers] send their dollars up to Seattle, potholes in Seattle will get fixed, and the things we need to get done here in Tucson won't get done.[12]

Tehrani tries to make coffee drinkers more aware of how their patronage subverts or supports their common life. In a small but significant way, where a person sips her latte affects the level of maintenance available for Tucson's broad avenues and the responsiveness of the local fire department. Prudent producers and consumers pay attention to such things and act accordingly.

But if this key strikes the reader as just a bit too sober and conservative, be assured that it can also lead to greater pleasure. I travel to Boston fairly often and have grown to love its cobblestone colonial ambience and unsurpassed seafood. What always disappoints me, however, is the quality of Boston coffee. You can find a Starbucks or Dunkin' Donuts on practically every street corner and at many subway stations, but I have yet to find a locally owned, independent coffee roaster anywhere from Boston University to Beacon Hill. The city's overhead may be just too high for small purveyors to be successful, but lack of choice means a less palatable cup of coffee. In Madison and Tucson, on the other hand, local coffee shops still challenge the national chains, with the result—as Adam Smith would have predicted—that quality is higher all around.

Judy Wicks, whose White Dog Café in Philadelphia has earned a national reputation for superb food and progressive business practices, possesses an even broader vision. She believes that for independent businesses to thrive, they must help to develop and maintain a sustainable economic system. Prudent proprietors realize that the long-term viability of their own business is directly related to the vitality of the community that supports them.

In keeping with this philosophy, Wicks seeks out local purvey-ors to supply the White Dog Café. She meets with farmers and has made low-interest loans to those who were willing to adopt sustainable practices and partner with her. Such initiatives have a multiplier effect because they help make family farming more fea-sible and thus more attractive to newcomers. According to Dan Barber, another successful restaurateur from New York, because of boosters like Wicks, smaller farms that employ sustainable methods and that grow food of superior quality have a better chance of succeeding.[13]

For Judy Wicks, further growth of her business in the usual sense of the word isn't part of the game plan. "Rather than start-ing a chain of White Dogs, I've tried to make our one restaurant a special place," she says. Based on her conviction that cooperation is just as vital to a sustainable economy as healthy competition, she freely shares the secrets of her own success with others in the industry and encourages them to do likewise. "There is no such thing as one sustainable household or business; it's about being part of a community ... and working together toward a common goal." If more people realized how much joy this creates, Wicks enthuses, they'd get on board.[14]

Often as not, at the root of local economic problems one finds less in the way of inordinate greed than simple lack of foresight. While there is much to be said for good old-fashioned rugged indi-vidualism—a curious phenomenon Alexis de Tocqueville first observed and commented upon during his U.S. travels in the 1830s—when carried to extremes and invoked to defend behavior that pushes other people down and pulls communities apart, it often produces catastrophic results. By failing to think like Judy Wicks in terms of sustainable systems and opting instead for short-term expediency, residents of many once-thriving American com-munities are now witnessing a steady decline in their quality of life.

Most of the world's great moral codes (as opposed to its busi-ness manuals) emphasize the importance of unselfish or at least collaborative behavior. A simple piece of commonsense logic rather than a divine revelation buttresses those codes. "Moral sentiments," science writer Matt Ridley writes, "are a way of settling the conflict between short-term expediency and long-term *prudence* in favor of the latter. To reap the long-term reward of cooperation may require you to forego the short-term temptation of self-interest."[15]

Ancient Wisdom for a New Age

In their book *For the Common Good,* economist Herman Daly and theologian John Cobb urge us to reexamine the assumptions upon which our current practice of economics is based and consider adopting a model similar to that advanced by Judy Wicks. These authors suggest that an approach advocated by the ancient Greeks might serve us better than one in which the pursuit of individual self-interest is given near-unqualified support.

Economics can be practiced in two ways, Aristotle observed. He used the word *chrematistics* to describe the "manipulation of property and wealth so as to maximize short-term monetary exchange value to the individual owner." The motivation behind chrematistics is the rapid accumulation of private wealth with little or no thought given to how the means of acquisition might affect others. According to Daly and Cobb, Wall Street and the corporate world are "dedicated to chrematistics of the purest kind," which is definitely bad news for anyone who cares about anything more than the bottom line.

But there is an alternative—*oikonomia*—from which, ironically, the English word *economics* derives. The purpose of *oikonomia*, Aristotle writes, is "management of the household so as to increase its use value to all members over the long run," which seems like a much more prudent and sustainable approach to the generation of wealth. Wendell Berry's contrasting descriptions of the Industrial Economy and the Great Economy are the modern equivalent of these two ancient concepts.[16]

Chrematistics—the industrial economy—is growth oriented and presumes that the only alternative to growth is stagnation. Growth means expansion: more production, more consumption, and a steadily rising GNP. If we wish to continue living well, orthodox economists maintain, a robust rate of growth must be maintained. Growth and the good life go together.

Unfortunately, such logic flies in the face of everything we know about organic, living systems—systems that human economic activity ultimately depends upon. Is it at all realistic to think that this one aspect of existence is free from the forces that constrain all others? Ecosystems change and reproduce themselves, Steven Stoll observes, but "they do not increase in extent or abundance year after year."[17]

According to *chrematistics* accounting methods, China qualifies as an unparalleled economic success. Its rate of growth over the past several decades has been nothing short of spectacular, making it a powerhouse on the world stage. *Oikonomia* would look deeper and, by factoring the social and environmental costs of growth into the equation, try to determine whether the entire Chinese "household" has been rendered healthier and is likely to continue in that direction. The jury is still out, but it appears that China's development policies may backfire in the long run. The "green" entrepreneur Paul Hawken helps clarify the issue with a simple but seldom-made distinction: "A growing economy," he writes, "is getting bigger; a *developing* economy is getting better."[18]

This has become an issue of global proportions. In a comprehensive study of the world's economies, Cambridge economist Partha Dasgupta found that, despite rising GNP, between 1965 and 1993 almost every nation experienced a net decline in real wealth when various natural and social assets were taken into consideration.[19] In other words, as of 1993 few if any of these economies could accurately be described as "sustainable."

Judy Wicks predicts that it might take a bona fide disaster to change some people's attitudes, but perhaps the mere threat of economic and environmental calamity would cause people to think and act more prudently. Few human societies have been as fiercely competitive and individualistic as our own, but it's a character trait we can no longer afford. Past civilizations owed their prosperity to a collaborative spirit that has largely deserted us. Perhaps they have something important to teach.

Necessity, the Mother of Invention

The ancient Anasazi of New Mexico were notable in this respect. These mysterious precursors of the Pueblo peoples were masterful engineers who built immense multistory "houses" in dry, desolate areas. The largest concentration of Anasazi structures is found in and around Chaco Canyon in northwest New Mexico. Archeological evidence suggests that the Anasazi lived comfortably and peaceably in this less-than-ideal environment for over four hundred years.

How did their civilization survive? Kendrick Frazier draws attention to the sophisticated system the Anasazi developed to capture and channel snowmelt and the region's infrequent rainfall. "The need for the water-control system may have helped shape the Chacoan society," Frazier suggests. By enlisting the entire community in the construction and ongoing maintenance of an elaborate system of canals, dams, and sluice gates, a highly collaborative way of life was created that not only ensured sufficient food but made it possible for residents to adjust to a changing environment.[20]

Frazier's theory makes perfect sense. In most situations, cooperation is more prudent than competition. People in traditional communities help build each other's houses, raise each other's barns, jointly till and harvest fields, and pull together to create and maintain schools and churches because they know how foolhardy it really is to remain independent and aloof. The Amish still maintain this way of life, and in most instances it has helped this "quaint" culture resist the destabilizing and atomizing forces of modernity. The Amish are not survivalists, and their way of life isn't a response to fears that modern civilization might founder. But should hard times come, they will be better able to preserve the key elements of the good life than the rest of us.

Canadian writer Margaret Atwood is hopeful that even as it creates discomfort, a prolonged economic downturn might serve to bring society back to its senses. Perhaps people will begin to realize that the most reliable sources of happiness—family, friends, good literature, home-cooked meals, communing with the natural world—mean so much more than the plethora of possessions we've acquired. And perhaps, Atwood writes, "'I' will be spoken less, 'we' will return, as people recognize that there is such a thing as the common good."[21]

Must citizens of the United States of America maintain their present level of material consumption in order to feel good about their lives? Not if recent studies of happiness have any merit. Research shows that once a fairly modest standard of living has been achieved, the happiness curve flattens out.[22] Further gains in possessions, opportunities, and income do little to inflate that feeling. Moreover, "most American consumption is wasteful and contributes little or nothing to our well-being," Jared Diamond says. Our overall quality of life wouldn't suffer a bit and might even improve if we learned to cut back. Western Europeans consume half the oil we do; yet statistics for life expectancy, health, infant mortality, access to medical care, financial security after retirement, vacation time, quality of public schools, and support for the arts all surpass ours.[23]

It is generally presumed that as a rule Americans aren't willing to sacrifice, which is why politicians are careful never to utter that word. We want to hold onto what we've got, even if that means turning our backs on the less fortunate and on those yet to be born. But what if America's much-ballyhooed "standard of living"—coupled with our anxiety about maintaining it—is what's really dragging us down? Prudence counsels that we scale back, but that needn't imply sacrifice. It may be our best chance to fend off the "hungry ghost" and get back in touch with the true wellsprings of human health and happiness so that they can flow freely into our lives again.

The Real Bottom Line Is Happiness

If Americans were truly satisfied with the present state of affairs, it would be one thing; but an increasing number of men and women admit to feelings of deep discontent. Not only is self-interested short-term thinking putting our communities and the economy at risk, but it's also making it harder for us to be happy. Immediately after World War II, the happiness quotient in the United States reached its highest level, driven perhaps by the sense of relief the public felt after years of military strife and economic hardship. The country had pulled together in an unprecedented fashion, and people understood the importance and the power of collaboration. But thirty years later, Americans professed to be less happy than the citizens of seven other developed nations. Since then, the mood of the country has fallen even further. Studies have shown steady decreases in the percentage of Americans who say they are happy in their marriage, are satisfied with their jobs, and like the place where they live.[24] Both at the personal and the collective level, we have failed to set a sustainable course for ourselves.

Several decades ago the leaders of the small Himalayan nation of Bhutan chose a development path decidedly different from our own. Rejecting advice from experts at the IMF and World Bank and ignoring *chrematistic* metrics like GNP, Bhutan formulated new goals based on a simple, straightforward proposition. "We want to see an increase in our nation's gross national happiness," the country's hereditary monarch, Jigme Singye Wangchuck, proclaimed.

In pursuit of this dream, Bhutan's leaders promised they would take steps to reduce economic inequality and ensure that all citizens benefited from the nation's increasing prosperity. Furthermore, economic development would not be allowed to undermine Bhutan's unique cultural assets or degrade the natural world. "We have to think of human well-being in broader terms," Home Minister Lyonpo Jigmi Thinley insisted. "Material well-being is only one component, and it doesn't ensure that you're at peace with your environment and in harmony with each other."

By Western standards, Bhutan is still a poor nation and has not become a twenty-first-century Shangri-La. Still, progress has been made, and that has prompted a few other nations to reappraise their own development indicators. In Canada, for example, a group of government-appointed economists under Hans Messinger have been working on that country's first national index of well-being. "A sound economy," Messinger believes, "is not an end in itself, but should serve . . . to improve society."[25]

Sometimes Religion Gets It Right

On a much smaller scale, something similar to what its leaders are trying to accomplish in Bhutan occurs with some frequency in

American faith communities. This is one of the few places where *chrematistics* doesn't dictate terms.

It is a source of great personal satisfaction to have served a congregation with a legacy of unselfish, collective action to its credit. The names of our "Stonehaulers" are still invoked at the First Unitarian Society of Madison, and newcomers in our midst are often regaled with tales of their exploits. Their story is worth repeating.

In 1946 a small, dubious community of Unitarians was persuaded by their young minister, Kenneth Patton, to hire one of their members—the eccentric and irascible Frank Lloyd Wright—to design for them a new home. Wright proved agreeable to the proposal and assured the building committee that it was possible to erect a serviceable and architecturally notable building within the assigned budget. But as was often the case with Wright's clever and demanding designs, costs soon spiraled skyward, and the congregation faced a crisis. The contractor, having cashed in his own insurance policy to stay solvent, was tapped out. Additional fundraising was out of the question. It became clear that the Unitarian Meeting House—now a registered national landmark—would not be completed unless members of the congregation pitched in to finish the project.

And so for more than two years, young and old hauled thousands of heavy blocks of limestone from a local quarry, applied sheetrock and lathing, wove draperies, caulked windows, painted walls, planted bushes, sewed pew cushions, treated cuts and bruises, and prepared meals for one another. These untutored, amateur builders were instrumental to the creation of an architectural masterpiece, but their efforts produced something else less tangible but no less significant: a lifelong commitment to one another and to the community itself.

By the time the new Meeting House was dedicated, the congregation was weary and indebted, but the members had experienced a marked increase in "gross congregational happiness." The Stonehaulers had put their individual short-term interests aside to work on an edifice that would strengthen and sustain their own community and serve as a source of pride and inspiration to future congregants.

It would be a pity if faith communities were the only place people could have an experience like this. Peter Block, one of the country's most respected authorities on management issues, agrees. Block argues that businesses are missing the boat if they do not inculcate a comparable culture of stewardship from top to bottom. "We were born into an age of anxiety and become adults in the age of self-interest," he writes, but if we allow ourselves to be defined by the spirit of our age, we are unlikely to find the fulfillment we crave as individuals, and our institutions will suffer from a lack of commitment and a dearth of community. Pay is important to an employee, but so is partnership, Block insists. "Anyone who says they work just for the money has given up hope that anything more is possible." People really want to be part of an enterprise that succeeds because it addresses an important need or serves some higher, socially valid purpose. When it does, esprit de corps develops naturally.[26]

Unfit for Life: Prudence and Personal Choices

As a behavioral key, prudence has profound implications at the personal as well as the social level. What is it that gives men and women their greatest sense of inner satisfaction and overall well-being? Do our objectives make sense, and are we putting sufficient thought and energy into areas that matter the most?

The results of one open-ended British questionnaire suggest that when it comes to happiness, good physical and mental health and dependable, supportive relationships mean more than income.[27] Perhaps, then, the good life eludes us because we lack proper regard for the basics: we eat too much of the wrong things, aren't very conscientious about exercise, and take our loved ones for granted. In order to thrive, this is where we ought to be making a greater investment.

Everyone has to eat, and while diet may not be the most significant factor in staying fit, it has to be taken seriously. Quantity isn't the problem. Industrial agriculture has successfully met the challenge of feeding a burgeoning world population, albeit with a few rather undesirable side effects. If some people in some regions are still going hungry, it isn't because food isn't available but because for one political or logistical reason or another, access to it has been denied.

Hypothetically, everyone on the planet could be fed with the resources presently available. But probably not *well* fed. Being unusually adaptable, human beings can subsist quite well on a large variety of foods—including worms, grasshoppers, termites, and a host of other gastronomical oddities. We are, as Michael Pollan suggests, true omnivores. But as previously mentioned, the highly refined sugars and carbohydrates derived from hybrid fruits and grains of low nutritional quality and the inordinate amount of fat in the average meal are stealthily undermining our health. The modern Western diet may be one to which our systems simply can't adjust.[28]

Upwardly mobile families in developing nations aren't the only ones feeling the effects of the global shift away from traditional fare. Diabetes has reached near-epidemic proportions on many Native American reservations, a development directly related to the substitution of modern convenience foods for ones Indians have eaten for centuries. A study of health problems among the Australian Aborigines reached an unsurprising conclusion: that many of their maladies could be successfully treated simply by resurrecting old eating habits.[29]

Relative to earlier times, food today is more affordable and requires much less preparation time. Unfortunately, abundance and convenience tempt people to eat too many products that our bodies can't process properly. Science and nutrition writer Barry Popkin warns that if spirited resistance isn't mounted against today's mass-marketed fare, we can expect most of the wellness and life-expectancy gains made in the last century to be forfeited.[30]

A Deceptively Simple Regimen

Trina and I changed our eating pattern in the early 1980s after she started doing nutritional research and I began to see a connection between diet and athletic performance. The steps we took were simple: the elimination of most fast-food and prepackaged fare, a significant decrease in fat and animal protein consumption, more water and far fewer soft drinks, and avoidance of food with additives and high levels of sodium. Lo and behold, within a few months of making the relatively painless alimentary adjustment, my times in races from five kilometers to the full marathon all dropped significantly. Although I stopped competing fifteen years ago, the eating regimen has remained in place and continues to serve both of us well.

I have never counted carbs or calories and do not monitor my weight (you won't find a scale in our house). We do not deny ourselves good food and do not forego the occasional indulgence. Ours are not hard and inflexible rules, but sensible guidelines. We eat responsibly, experimentally, and with considerable relish.

"A foolish consistency," Emerson once said, is the "hobgoblin of little minds," and that is especially true for eating. If we cling too tightly to a prescribed diet, it soon becomes boring and distasteful, and the temptation to abandon it completely will become irresistible. The "chemistry of pleasure" is an inescapable part of the human constitution, nutritionist Marc David tells us. The pleasure principle is built into our brains for a reason: to keep us aware of what the organism needs in order to stay healthy. That being the case:

> If you're the kind of person who believes you can control your appetite and therefore lose weight by denying yourself pleasure, I suggest you reevaluate immediately. I have yet to meet one person who has successfully lost weight and kept it off by overcoming his or her natural inborn drive to enjoy and celebrate food.[31]

A compulsive attitude toward eating can have interpersonal as well as personal drawbacks. Over the years I have witnessed family members and friends struggle to find "appropriate" nourishment at weddings, dinner parties, and business lunches and heard them lament the restrictions imposed by whatever diet they happened to be testing at the time (bona fide food sensitivities are, of course, a completely different matter). Some try to finesse the problem by carrying food with them, or they may choose to abstain. Both solutions can cause host and guest alike to feel awkward.

Trina and I follow the ninety percent rule. We try to eat prudently and properly nine meals out of ten, which allows us to be less discriminating when entertaining or enjoying a meal out. We both understand the importance of a healthy diet, but hospitality provides nourishment for the soul, and therefore we refuse to let food preferences impinge on our social life.

Eating prudently can have even broader implications. According to geophysicist Gidon Eshel, "The good of people's bodies and the good of the planet are more or less perfectly aligned." While nutritionists point to the physiological problems associated with the overconsumption of meat products, environmentalists warn that meat production is hazardous to the planet's health. Livestock production is responsible for one-fifth of all greenhouse gases and is a major contributor to the degradation of America's streams and rivers. Moreover, the processing, packaging, and distribution of nutritionally poor convenience foods consumes four times again as much energy as farming itself.[32]

A sustainable diet—one that does right by the person and the planet—is within most people's reach, and it will leave us feeling better. It's simply a matter of paying attention, doing our homework, and thinking carefully about the long-term consequences of our consumption. That's what it means to be prudent.

Balance, Not Burnout

What about exercise, the second important piece of the fitness puzzle? The important thing is to find a program that's personally appropriate and create a stable niche for it in one's daily existence.

During my own formative years, I tried quite a number of sports and fitness activities. I played football and wrestled, ran track, and even took up surfing when our family relocated to Florida. Later I learned to play tennis, struggled through a few rounds of golf, and horsed around the basketball court. All these forms of exercise proved to be passing fancies except for distance running, at which I achieved some real proficiency. I don't recommend it to everyone because for some people—my wife, for instance—running just isn't body-friendly. As with diet, choosing the wrong form of exercise sets us up to fail.

Because I still love to lace on my shoes and head out the door in the morning, I don't push the envelope, and I do everything I can to prolong my running career. Too many of the men and women with whom I used to train are hobbled today with blown-out knees, sore hips, plantar fasciitis, or some other chronic affliction. Their running days are over, and at least part of the reason is that they failed to make the sensible adjustments that aging bodies and shifting roles demand.

One of the simplest routes to sustainable fitness is cross-training, which ensures that conditioning is balanced and that the entire body, not just a portion of it, is toned and strengthened. For a runner, cross-training provides periodic relief from a high-impact exercise in favor of others that are less stressful. In recent years I've added yoga, tai chi, and biking to my own weekly regime, and I've been much less bothered by muscle soreness and joint discomfort.

It may also be necessary to bring a fresh approach to a familiar practice. Ultra-marathoner Danny Dreyer says that the "how" can be just as important as the "what." Many runners, he believes, develop knee, hip, and lower back problems because they overstride, repeatedly jarring the body more than is necessary. Dreyer recommends a shorter stride, a slight forward lean, and relaxed abdominal breathing. He calls this technique "chi running" because it mimics the relaxation and alignment principles applied in the practices of qigong and tai chi.[33] Dreyer's system is eminently sensible, and serious runners have always distinguished between "striders" and "shufflers." Whereas the former usually enjoy an advantage in terms of speed, shufflers (naturally gifted "chi" runners) tend to have greater stamina and staying power.

Swimmer Dara Torres, who at the unheard of age of forty-one set the American record in the fifty-meter freestyle and won an Olympic silver medal, has drawn attention to yet another secret of longevity: resistance training. According to Carl Foster, former president of the American College of Sports Medicine, for a competitor like Torres, resistance exercise works to strengthen core muscles in the abdomen and back, which gives the arms and legs a "better platform to work from." Most people exercise the peripherals, but physiologists believe the deep muscles of the torso are the key to sustainable strength and endurance.[34]

Of course, too much vigorous physical activity can be just as debilitating as too little. Another key component of resistance training is rest—to avoid over-training and to take time to warm up and to cool down. In pursuing fitness or competitive advantage, most people are tempted to push too hard. A prudent approach to conditioning emphasizes moderation, factors in time for recovery, and encourages us to be patient with ourselves.

"Anyone can hammer themselves all day, can train long and hard," Phil Peck, a former coach with the Olympic Nordic ski team sniffs. "But to get better requires restraint."[35]

Jack Kelly, a former Olympic rower, could have used Peck's advice. Following a typical workout—a couple of hours of rowing followed by a five-mile run—Kelly collapsed and expired from heart failure. A close friend and physician, Irving Dardik, vowed to investigate, hoping to answer the question, "What would cause a world-class athlete in prime physical condition to die so unexpectedly?" After close study of the case, Dardik concluded that his friend had, like the legendary John Henry, "driven so hard that it broke his poor heart." According to Dardik, the way some people exercise appears to cause heart failure. Many athletes just don't obey the body's natural rhythms, and they regularly fail to rest enough.

But it's not easy to enjoy a respite when you've been taught that real competitors play through pain and weariness and that the laurel goes to those who push the hardest. The most ambitious athletes, obsessive CEOs, and prolific scholars are the ones we praise—the very people whose lives reflect the least balance. The flip side of American hedonism is its vain workaholism. "Americans are queer people," the Canadian humorist Stephen Leacock has observed from across the border. "They cannot rest."

Here again we run into that "Bisy Backson" phenomenon, the reluctance to stop and give ourselves a break. As he was being escorted around New York City, a visiting Tibetan Buddhist monk was struck by this propensity. "If we do a complex subway switch at Grand Central," the monk's host proudly declared, "we'll save ten minutes." As the two men emerged from the underground station into Central Park, the monk saw a bench and sat down. "What's the matter?" the American asked anxiously. "Nothing at all," the monk replied. "I just thought we'd enjoy the extra ten minutes." Clearly, the option of simply sitting and savoring had never occurred to his ever-restless guide.

Kids, Careers, and Other Complexities

Family and calling are other aspects of personal life where prudence can play a beneficial role. When I was in my mid thirties, two watershed events occurred that caused me to reconsider my own priorities. First, a child, Kyle, was born to us. Shortly thereafter I accepted an offer to serve the First Unitarian Society of Madison, a much larger congregation with greater demands than the congregation I was presently serving. At that point it became clear that if I wished to function effectively as a father and parish minister, competitive running was an indulgence I could no longer afford. To repeat: a successful and sustainable lifestyle involves setting priorities and then paying attention and putting energy into what really matters.

Is One Really Enough?

Prudent parents don't fly by the seat of their pants. They look carefully at their resources—internal and external—and make decisions that will increase their prospects for success. They do not assume that repeating a nuptial vow or birthing a child will automatically strengthen their commitment or secure their future happiness. In other words, a prudent family is strategic.

For Trina and me this meant setting long-term educational and professional objectives and resisting societal pressure to begin parenting before we were ready. Although married when we were both twenty-two and debt-free, our first and only child didn't come into the world until thirteen more years had passed. Neither infertility nor a tepid desire for children caused the long delay. It was purely a matter of timing—doing first things first. Trina and I both wanted to feel reasonably confident about our financial future and clear about our vocational direction before venturing into the deeper waters of parenting. Having a child was too important, the lifestyle adjustments too significant, and the responsibilities too imposing to begin the process prematurely.

Our hesitancy wasn't always understood. As we moved into our thirties, parents and parishioners presumed we had chosen to be childless. But we were just biding our time. As Trina put it, "When we *do* have children, it will be for their sake, not for ours." In other words, our baby would be born only when he or she could be properly and attentively nurtured, and not before. Many couples, perhaps even most, won't choose to wait thirteen years before having children, but the point is to want them and be prepared for the many changes and increased responsibility that accompany parenthood.

Prudently limiting ourselves to a single child wasn't easy to do either. Friends and family predicted that Kyle would become lonely and narcissistic without a sibling. But as a special education teacher, Trina understood the dangers of late pregnancies for mother and child alike, and we decided to play it safe. Furthermore, we had chosen demanding, emotionally draining professions that didn't pay as well as some others. We understood that a second or third child would stretch our meager resources, and we wanted to do our best by the child we did have. By staying within our own emotional, physical, and financial limits, I am convinced we spared ourselves unnecessary hardship and disharmony. Prudence does not always dictate a limit of one or two children, but it does emphasize the need for parenting decisions to be made carefully and in full awareness of the time and resources required.

Trina's and my prospects for a sustainable partnership were improved by prudent family planning, and research suggests that our own stability as a couple has benefited society at large.

Family researcher Judith Wallerstein argues that the surrounding community suffers when it is forced to cope with too many failed marriages. By reinforcing an ethos of obligation and accountability, stable families have a positive effect on the entire culture.[36]

But has Kyle himself suffered as an only child? As previously mentioned, close friendships with peers in our neighborhood provided him with reliable companionship and protected him from feelings of isolation. To our knowledge, Kyle has never felt cheated or deprived in this respect, and today he is certainly as well adjusted as any of his peers. Bill McKibben, whose book *Maybe One* makes a cogent case for limiting one's offspring, would not be surprised. Authorities he cites disconfirm the popular notion that children with siblings are happier and better adjusted than only children. On all relevant measures of psychological well-being—self-esteem, autonomy, generosity, peer popularity, maturity—only children do as well as or better than their peers who have siblings.[37]

McKibben and his wife also have one child and felt strongly that their decision was prudent for environmental as well as personal reasons. Overpopulation and overconsumption will exact a heavy toll on future generations, McKibben points out. Why keep increasing the human species until the planet is thoroughly plundered and scarcely habitable? Why not guarantee a decent quality of life for a smaller human population rather than force a much larger one to cope with shortages and the need for rationing? "Overpopulation is an unpopular subject," Richard Heinberg says, "but in fact, it is bad for children today and in the future. Population control is motivated by a desire to see future generations enjoy their existence."[38]

For the Love of Labor
Labor lovingly and attentively performed is life affirming and delivers significant emotional dividends. According to the renowned research psychologist Mihaly Csikszentmihalyi, the best moments in our lives are not those in which we feel relaxed, unproductive, or disengaged. As important for health and wellness as "downtime" might be, human beings typically feel most vital and relevant when "their bodies and minds are stretched to their limits as they are making some supreme voluntary effort to achieve something."[39]

Even so, engaging, deeply gratifying work can be overindulged and become a means of escaping other responsibilities that pull us out of our comfort zone. It's not always easy to determine when a

legitimate passion for work has become an unhealthy preoccupa-
tion, but a prudent individual should always be aware that winning
at work may mean losing out in the domestic, spiritual, and social
spheres of existence.

The ancient Chinese sage Chuang Tzu recommended a work
ethic that few in the modern world have adopted, but his point of
view may be worth considering. It is probably not the sort of
advice someone eager to climb the ladder would accept, but it
should appeal to those who have come to recognize the ultimate
futility of the rat race and are seeking greater equanimity.

If the true men of old failed, no sorrow.
No self-congratulation in success. ...
Their entrance was without gladness, their exit, yonder,
    without resistance. ...
They did not forget where from, did not ask where to,
Nor drive grimly forward, fighting their way through life.[40]

Chuang Tzu would have us realize that moral, emotional, and
spiritual gains matter just as much as financial ones; that promotion
in the professional pecking order means nothing if it fails to promote our own and other people's happiness.

Challenging our culture's prevailing work-consumption ethic
requires, as Thich Nhat Hanh observed, an act of resistance. But if
we understand that what's at stake is our own precious, irreplace-
able life energy, we may well choose to do things differently. As voluntary simplicity advocates Joe Dominguez and Vicky Robin have
argued, it's the energy and not the money that ultimately matters.
If we pay attention to what really makes us feel healthy and happy
and are prudent with our resources, we can learn to get by rather
nicely on a very modest income. There's nothing wrong with having a job that pays well. But what's important, as Carlos Castaneda
insisted, is first to choose the path with heart.

Despite his acquired wisdom, the spiritual teacher Ram Dass
wasn't able to internalize this lesson until, in his early sixties, he
was felled by a life-threatening stroke. The episode left him
severely disabled and unable to pursue the writing and lecturing
that had brought him so much pleasure and prestige. Loyal friends

helped him survive the emotional and spiritual crisis that ensued, and eventually Ram Dass gained a new and more profound understanding of what "work" really means. "As we move along in years, the rigid notion of right and wrong, and of success in general, should be irrelevant to how we make our decisions," he remarks. If we approach it positively, it dawns on us that aging releases us from ingrained patterns and lifelong roles. Now we are "free ... to follow our hunches, experiment boldly, or *do nothing at all.*"[41]

These days, Ram Dass tells his admirers, "Whatever I'm doing now is my life's work, even if it's sitting by the window." Like this flexible spirit, we must be willing to adapt to imposed limitations and be eager to entertain new, life-affirming possibilities. The aging process will require all of us to adjust eventually, and if we hope to "work well" into and through retirement, our definition of vocation will have to broaden, together with our sense of what it means to be useful.

For example, making a greater investment in nonremunerative, benevolent activities would be quite prudent. Why? Because for many people the road to happiness is paved with good actions. The relationship between generosity and happiness is becoming clearer all the time. In studying charitable giving, researchers at the University of British Columbia found that "personal spending was unrelated to happiness ... but [giving to others] was associated with significantly greater happiness."

Lead researcher Elizabeth W. Dunn said she wasn't surprised that doing something for others made people happy. But she was struck by how big the effect was. And, she added, "there's nothing special about money"; giving time or special skills to help other people also enhances a person's feeling of well-being.[42]

The importance of pursuing activities aligned with heart values and not just with financial and personal ambition is confirmed by some of the twentieth century's most notable reformers. After examining the lives of Mohandas Gandhi, Alexander Solzhenitsyn, Martin Luther King, Jr., and Lech Walesa, Robert Inchausti concluded that in each case the individual had shifted from a desire to increase his or her own stature, or even to fulfill a moral duty, to a passion for "serving others out of gratitude."[43] Without that shift, Inchausti argues, these men would never have found the strength, the courage, and the time to surmount the obstacles and endure the setbacks such work imposes.

One hopes that the preceding argument and examples with respect to the fourth key have shown its relevance to sustainability and the good life. Prudence is not as bland or lacking in feeling—as at first we might have imagined. The genuinely prudent individual is just as concerned with what makes the heart sing as with careful planning and proper management of the purse strings. It's about discernment—making decisions whereby the whole person and the whole planet are well served and their futures ensured.

Conclusion

A Sustainable Code of the Soul

Consider the Spirit

As comprehensive as this discussion of sustainability and the good life has been thus far, one final piece deserves further elaboration. Already we've seen how crucial the four keys are to preserving the health and beauty of the planet, creating communities that thrive, maintaining a healthy lifestyle, and producing deeper satisfaction at home and on the job. What remains is to address a need common to all human beings that could loosely be described as spiritual.

The Jesuit philosopher and scientist Pierre Teilhard de Chardin once declared, "We are not human beings on a spiritual journey. We are spiritual beings on a human journey." His comment suggests that failure to recognize and attend to this unquantifiable aspect of existence betrays something fundamental to our nature. To reflect happiness, a person's life must be meaningful, purposeful, and inspirited, as well as satisfactory in the ways already mentioned.

It's not easy to mature spiritually and grapple successfully with the existential pressures that mount steadily as we age. How can I feel less alienated and more at home in the world? What is my ultimate responsibility to self and others? Is it possible to make sense of suffering? What must I do to face death unafraid? Questions such as these—quintessential spiritual questions—become increasingly pressing as our years increase.

Half-Hearted Spirituality

Although most Americans profess to be religious or spiritual in some sense of those words, they don't engage faithfully in activities that draw out and strengthen that quality. Too many of us pursue our spiritual interests in fits and starts. Something will turn us on to spiritual literature, and we lay aside our murder mysteries for a time in favor of the Dalai Lama's latest reflection on happiness or Rick Warren's handbook on purposeful living. Or being troubled by a vague but persistent sense of inner emptiness, we decide to go to church for a change—a resolve that lasts for a few Sundays until we realize that dynamic spiritual communities demand some degree of commitment and really don't have much to offer casual, self-absorbed consumers.

Our interest in spirituality might also have been piqued by reports of revelatory experiences some have had. We begin to crave such experiences ourselves and adopt a contemplative practice to induce them. In the beginning, sitting on our new meditation cushion and avidly following the instructor's directions, we feel strong and determined. But then, inevitably, we reach a plateau, and the road begins to look longer and the prospects less promising. Even though we've been cautioned about spiritual ambition and encouraged to settle peacefully into our daily practice, we become frustrated. Patience is not our strong suit.

Few people seem to devote sufficient time to processing important spiritual questions or making a spiritual inventory. When queried about their religious convictions, most Americans provide superficial answers. They profess belief in the Golden Rule and a personal God who hears their prayers and bestows rewards and punishments. They say it's important to be a "good person" as though it were self-evident what that means. They seldom consider the spiritual and ethical implications of our competitive capitalist economy or their own upwardly mobile ambitions. Without the supports and reassurances that a more stable, traditional culture might provide, such nonchalance about spiritual matters leaves us at the mercy of a kind of chronic, objectless anxiety that we often end up trying to quell with mood-altering medications or multiple distractions. Shopping and sedatives are the most commonly prescribed methods for taking the sting out of those troubling questions.

Obsessions and Idolatries

Before proceeding further, let me clarify what the term *religion* suggests to me. I agree with religious historian Karen Armstrong that it is "not about accepting twenty impossible propositions before breakfast." Nevertheless, misperceptions abound; and all too frequently, popular conceptions reduce religion to an unsophisticated assortment of stories and beliefs centered on the supernatural.

On the other hand, a growing number of Americans have grown skeptical of supernatural claims and profess not to be religious. These self-described secularists, naturalists, and scientific materialists support their own beliefs with empirical evidence and logical analysis. However, one often gets the impression that these contrarians are in no better position to confront the deep questions than the casually orthodox because they have been too eager to throw the baby out with the bathwater. They are no more aware of religion's true mission than those who uncritically accept the existence of angels.

Neither of these parties recognizes that history's great saints, saviors, and sages—individuals like Muhammad, Gautama Buddha, and Jesus—have proved to be enduringly significant because of their worldly rather than their other-worldly accomplishments. "Icons of fulfilled humanity," they teach by word and example that if we behave in a certain way, we too will be transformed. "The myths and laws of religion are not true because they conform to some metaphysical, scientific, or historical reality, but because they are life enhancing," Armstrong (a former nun) argues.[1]

As serious seekers, how, then, shall we proceed? A sustainable spirituality begins and ends with *attention*. That means, in the first place, attention to what's important, to what ultimately matters. "What we attend to is what we become." If one's primary focus is professional football, one is likely to become a rabid fan with expensive season tickets, a vanity license plate, a color-coordinated wardrobe, and an impressive collection of memorabilia.

Football junkies spend an inordinate amount of time poring over statistics, discussing players' performances, and obsessing over their chosen team's prospects. In so doing, they hope to capture the sort of self-transcending experience that religion promises to others. Indeed, professional and collegiate spectator sports occupy a quasi-religious position in today's modern, media-driven culture, and many men in particular find them far more compelling than any other interest or activity. For the avid fan, no sanctuary holds the same appeal as a packed sports stadium. In America, throngs of the faithful live vicariously in and through "the team," thrilling over its victories and agonizing in the wake of defeat. Recognizing what they're up against, some faith communities have installed large-screen televisions in their lounges in order to entice men into church on game day.

Spectator sports are a significant but hardly the only surrogate for spirituality. Bird watching, gardening, photography, and antique collecting pull in devotees who pursue these activities with a passion and sustained interest that the uninitiated find quite remarkable. But fulfilling as such avocations might be at one level, they are ill equipped to address the deeper promptings of the spirit.

Hobbies and outside interests have a legitimate place in our lives. It is only when they are accorded a status incommensurate with their actual value that they become counterproductive and, from a theological standpoint, idolatrous.

However, recreational obsessions are peripheral to the main problem. The primary impediment to enjoying a sustainable spiritual life lies in the familiar realm of getting and spending, spending and getting. We work in order to consume, and then to support our overconsumption find ourselves obliged to work even harder. Debt accumulates as well as more "stuff" that must be managed and cared for. Before we know it, the tail is wagging the dog. Our toys have become us, commanding our attention and consuming the lion's share of our available energy.

While the aim in all this was to find happiness, for many people the heady march toward a material magic kingdom has proved profoundly frustrating. And yet after decades of importuning by sophisticated marketers, America's millions of "hungry ghosts" find it hard to envision any viable alternatives. The trend has to stop somewhere, of course. "A culture based on the universalizing of money and ever more possessions is unsustainable," Curtis White writes, "which is a euphemistic way of saying that it is a culture bent on making provision for its own death. We are always busily providing for our own defeat."[2]

In the absence of other life-affirming values, overconsumption produces not happiness but a pattern of habitual behavior that can land us not only in deep debt and bankruptcy, but in despair. Recent studies of consumer behavior are telling us something pretty scary about ourselves. For a growing number of shoppers, the "act of purchase" has quite literally become an end in itself. *Transaction utility* is how psychologists characterize this uniquely modern phenomenon. People now head for the mall not because they really *need* something, but because the act of purchase itself produces a biochemical reaction that is mildly stimulating. In other words, buying something—anything—provides a temporary fix that over time develops into a bona fide process addiction and a substitute for spirituality.

The late Walter Capps taught religious studies before he was elected to Congress and, in the former capacity, wrote and published a book on monasticism. While pursuing this subject, Capps kept asking himself whether cloistered monks led meaningful lives or were simply escapists who couldn't cope with the strain and stress of secular living. One day he was returning from an early-morning visit to a particular monastery and decided to stop at a department store for an item he needed. The store wasn't open when he arrived, but a crowd of women had already gathered outside. When the doors were unlocked, Capps was swept along in a mad race toward the lingerie department where a large array of items had been placed on sale. He watched bemusedly as scores of frenzied shoppers pawed through the piles of undergarments looking for bargains, and he came away from the store with a fresh and more pertinent question in his mind. Who were the escapists? The monks he had been investigating or the nation's consumers who "looked as if they were trying to assuage their spiritual emptiness" with their fevered patronage?[3]

The point is not to denigrate shopping per se. It, too, has a rightful place in our lives, and should the process prove pleasant, so much the better. But transaction utility is a poor substitute for activities that can reliably serve our long-term best interests. Whatever form it takes—sitting or movement meditation, journaling, contemplative or centering prayer, devotional exercise—spiritual practice leads to deeper insight and enhances our appreciation of and regard for the world around us. Some form of practice has always been central to the religious and ethical enterprise. It is the leaven that causes the heart to swell and consciousness to expand.

Without discounting the helpful role that books, teachers, and other learning tools can play in the process of spiritual growth, it is a mistake to rely too heavily on secondary sources. "If you've read every word the Buddha ever said but haven't practiced with it, it won't have much effect," Larry Rosenberg writes. "Intellectual understanding in itself doesn't have much transformative power . . . and has little to do with the reason the [Buddha's] words were uttered in the first place."[4]

No Substitute for Faithful Practice

Without sustained commitment to a time-tested spiritual discipline, any aspiration we might have to plumb the depths and touch the soft and sensitive seat of the soul isn't likely to be answered. Rather, we will continue to identify with and live through a culturally conditioned self whose manufactured desires don't reflect our deepest needs. Before we can become who we really are, the Trappist contemplative Thomas Merton wrote, we must realize that the person who we presently *think* we are is at best an imposter and a stranger. One of the principle purposes of religion, he suggests, is to "create a psychological environment hospitable to contemplation," which in turn enables the individual to achieve self-knowledge.[5]

Meditation and its allied disciplines are not a cure-all, and they will not preserve us from making mistakes and exercising poor judgment from time to time. The behavior of even history's most celebrated saints and sages was sometimes less than exemplary. But because of the insight it provides, spiritual practice can keep us from making quite so many life-distorting errors and help us learn and profit from the ones we do commit.

Moreover, meditation and its allied disciplines will help us develop more fully the four keys—*pay attention, stay put, exercise patience,* and *practice prudence*—advocated in this book. With the aid of a regular spiritual practice, theory becomes operational; abstract principles are primed for practical application. I, for one, have found life to be so much better when I am able to remain attentive and undistracted, control my restlessness, and savor that second or fifth cup of tea; when I am less reactive and more patient in difficult situations and able to be deliberative rather than impulsive in decision making. All of this is also implied by spirituality, for it has everything to do with the full flowering of our humanity.

Most Americans profess to be religiously active to a greater or lesser degree. But what does that mean? Very seldom does it include a daily discipline of any sort. Most people's prayers are discursive and petitionary in nature. In other words, they are requests for supernatural assistance that bear little resemblance to the prayer practices developed over the centuries in the great contemplative traditions. Real prayer, the devout Anglican poet W. H. Auden once declared, is a highly refined way of paying attention. Whatever we train our full and undivided attention upon, whether it be "a landscape or a poem or a geometrical problem or an idol or the True God" such that we "completely forget our own ego and [listen raptly] to what the other has to say to us, we are praying."[6]

Mastery in this department doesn't come easily. Commitment, consistency, and a healthy measure of self-possession are all required. The intellect and the ego will always offer stiff resistance to contemplative practice because, as Parker Palmer puts it, they are used to being in charge and will work overtime to keep us busy and distracted. "It is so much easier to deal with the external world, to spend our lives manipulating material and institutions and other people instead of dealing with our own souls."[7]

It takes time to develop the ability to sit patiently and consider quietly one's own inner life, noting the stirrings of the id and the machinations of the ego, observing the ebb and flow of one's fluctuating moods and impulses. But there are tremendous benefits to be had if we stay the course. Gradually we do learn to discriminate between needs and wants, to analyze our motives more objectively, to recognize our blind spots and our susceptibility to selfish and injurious impulses. And when we do veer off course, it is easier to acknowledge and atone for our mistakes rather than remain mired in guilt and remorse. The unreflective, impatient person "regards himself as harmless, and so adds stupidity to iniquity," Carl Jung once remarked.

A regular mindfulness routine gives us the ability to experience our impulses and emotions without giving them free rein to express themselves inappropriately. The steady, discerning self develops powers of restraint. Through mindfulness practice, the more rambunctious parts of the personality are gradually tamed and brought under conscious control. If we hope to be insightful and reasonably virtuous, it makes sense to cultivate a practice that points us in that direction.

Those who have had no experience with it and therefore can't appreciate its contributions often dismiss spiritual practice as self-indulgent. Like Walter Capps, it strikes them as socially disengaged, self-protective quietism—what a previous generation of skeptics called "navel-gazing." Perhaps in some cases contemplative activity does lead to an abdication of responsibility. But under proper guidance, the practitioner should become more rather than less aware of and responsive to the larger world. Some neuroscientists have suggested that the spiritual impulse may prove to be an adaptive mechanism whose purpose is to keep us sensitized to and concerned about that world. It is what "prompts us to live prudently and to care for one another as well as for the earth on which we live, if we want to survive and flourish," former Anglican bishop Richard Holloway writes. Human spirituality "reflects that greater harmony behind a life that is well-balanced, well-tempered, and well-intended."[8]

Spiritual practice will inevitably test our resolve, but the rewards of mindful living, though subtle, are worth the effort. The good news is that the process is deceptively simple and straightforward. All that's really necessary, Larry Rosenberg assures us, is a "lifetime of gentle and determined effort, falling asleep, and remembering to wake up again and again."[9]

It's important to remember that spiritual practice can take many different forms, and before settling on one, we are wise to engage in experimentation. For those who find it physically painful, sitting on a cushion for long periods of time may not be appropriate. Cross-training could be called for—my own routine includes yoga, tai chi, and numerous "minute meditations" spread throughout the day. For those of us who are accustomed to walking or jogging without the interference of an iPod or MP3 player, the results are similar to those produced by meditation. The "why" and the "how" are more important than the "what" and the "where."

But because even the most personally rewarding discipline will seem tedious at times, appreciation for the small and the subtle is important. Are we finding it easier to abide more calmly in stressful situations? Have we become more aware of modest incremental changes in ourselves and our surroundings? Are we affected more deeply by the beauty of the transitory? As our ability to patiently attend increases, hidden worlds spring into focus. "Wherever you turn your eyes the world can shine like transfiguration. You don't have to bring a thing to it except a little willingness to see," Marilynne Robinson writes.[10] That, in a nutshell, highlights the connection of spiritual practice to the good life.

Subtle but Substantial Rewards

In my own case, humble tasks have become much more pleasurable and intrinsically interesting because I am now able to approach them mindfully and without undue haste. Because spiritual practice has made me more spacious, I can take in more, which means that conversations have become richer and my relationships with family, community, and the natural environment more meaningful.

The relational element is especially important because, as previously noted, it is so closely correlated with human happiness. No life is really satisfying, no human fulfillment complete, without a kind and compassionate connection. Here, too, spiritual practice makes a significant difference. "Prayer," Parker Palmer writes, "means the practice of relatedness."

The mind immersed in prayer no longer thinks in order to divide and conquer, to manipulate and control. Now, thinking becomes a ... way of acknowledging our common bonds and assuming our rightful role in the created community.[11]

The Dalai Lama's view of spiritual practice is similar. Having been taught to think of ourselves as independent, autonomous beings, during most of our waking moments we feel only a tenuous connection to other people and the environment. As we go about our daily business, self-concern and self-interest reign. Although compassion and empathy are natural human endowments, our ability to feel and express them has been blunted.

While the *concept* of interdependence is widely understood and accepted, for many of us its existential truth hasn't really hit home. As a result, understanding hasn't produced the compassionate action our world needs. The Dalai Lama observes that for this to happen, a greater effort must be made to kindle loving kindness in the soul. "We must diligently apply the mental techniques necessary to bring about the desired effect," His Holiness has said. A steady friction, similar to rubbing two sticks together, should be maintained until the temperature is high enough to create the necessary internal spark. It is a process we must work at patiently and continuously.[12]

Without that heart connection established and nurtured by spiritual practice, maintaining a lifestyle consistent with the principles of social and environmental sustainability will be difficult. Even if we understand theoretically that it is in our own best, long-term interest to uphold sustainable standards, we still lack bedrock conviction and haven't developed sufficient inner resources to stay focused. When enough people are thoroughly convinced that their own and other people's interests are, in the end, inseparable, a sustainable future will be ensured.

A Matter of the Heart

A "human cannot for a moment live without consciously or unconsciously committing outward violence," Mahatma Gandhi conceded, but still it is incumbent upon us as moral beings to be mindful and try to minimize the suffering we cause. Gandhi adopted *ahimsa* (nonharm) as his own first principle. Hardly naïve, he fully understood the sacrifice of other lives that his own life required. Nevertheless, he did his best on a daily basis to soften the impact. He tried to treat the miraculous, multifarious world that supported him reverently and with the utmost consideration. Gandhi's motivation derived less from some abstract notion of "higher duty" than from a feeling of "rightness" that welled up from some deeper source. Parker Palmer would describe it as "soul-centered," for "the soul wants to give us life, and wants us to pass that gift along, to become life-givers in a world that deals too much with death."[13]

This, too, is an important spiritual consideration and a necessary component of the good life. Helping others—supporting a culture of life—can be, we've already discovered, a deeply satisfying experience. Trina and I have certainly found it to be so, and over the years our own spiritual practice has sensitized us to the intrinsic value of other sentient beings. It has practically become second nature to pay closer attention to the collateral damage our small decisions and casual gestures can and do inflict.

Although it might sound silly to some, for me it feels good to live-trap and release the mice that invade our domicile or, in the manner of Loren Eiseley's vigilant Star-Thrower, to move stranded earthworms from sidewalk to grass lest they shrivel and die beneath the noonday sun.[14] When purchasing provisions, Trina and I patiently look for commodities produced without herbicides and pesticides, and we try whenever possible to buy foods raised humanely and according to sustainable standards. We do our homework and patronize companies known for their progressive labor standards, clean environmental record, and fair-trade procurement practices. Soul work unearths little nuggets of satisfaction as we go about our daily business.

Unfortunately, despite their cumulative effect, little gestures such as these don't mean much to some people. They want to see the world, or at least their corner of it, noticeably transformed and sooner rather than later. Otherwise, what's the point?

Mahatma Gandhi achieved some amazingly big things, but like Albert Schweitzer, he also paid attention daily to the little things, the small random acts of consideration and kindness. Sustainable social witness demands a shift of attitude in this direction. To be sure, for every forest or prairie that is preserved, ten are cleared to make way for a new subdivision; and despite the support given by faith communities to the homeless and the hungry, their numbers continue inexorably to climb. Still, we must learn to be less concerned about results and make our efforts more a matter of the heart. "Anyone can become a great spirit," Martin Luther King, Jr. insisted, "because anyone can serve." Special expertise, broad knowledge, and public speaking ability are not prerequisites. "You need only a heart full of grace, a soul generated by love," King said.

Moderation, Not Martyrdom

To be transformative, however, love must be accompanied by prudence. Too great a commitment even to heart-centered service isn't sustainable, for it will eventually begin to feel onerous rather than joyful. According to tradition, the compassionate Buddha taught and served for half a century, and his career was undoubtedly prolonged by his commitment to the Middle Way and the avoidance of extremes. The Buddha and his disciples spent a significant portion of each year in retreat, for they regarded "rest as a spiritual act" (to borrow Anne Lamott's phrase). These early Buddhists enforced a Sabbath discipline as surely as did those who formulated the Fourth Commandment.

Without compassion for self, our service to others begins to look and feel like martyrdom. In his collection of interviews with contemporary spiritual celebrities, Bill Elliott describes a brief encounter with Mother Teresa and comments sadly on the deep fatigue and world-weariness of her demeanor. A woman whom many regard as the twentieth century's greatest saint, Mother Teresa looked overwhelmed. The strain of her servanthood had erased any trace of personal satisfaction she might have taken in her humanitarian activities.[15]

By contrast, several years ago the Madison congregation I serve had the honor of hosting a reception for the Dalai Lama—a man who has certainly seen his share of hardship and who has been unflagging in his support of the Tibetan people and of peace and justice causes more generally. Standing in our sanctuary after three long days of teaching before a large midwestern audience, His Holiness radiated energy, warmth, and humor. He had invited a beloved former teacher, Geshe Sopa, to share the spotlight with him, and the two men took such great pleasure in each other and the occasion that the mood of the whole room quickly shifted from reverent solemnity to playful appreciation.

Great spirits should not be evaluated solely by the degree of their sacrifice but by their prudence—the consistency with which they strive for balance in moral and spiritual development. If we aspire to care for others in a truly mindful and appropriate manner, we cannot neglect our own self-care, for if we routinely deny ourselves the rejuvenation that human beings need, we won't possess the requisite insight to serve others effectively. "Without the in-breath of self-care and reflection," Gail Straube writes, "we can't sustain our involvement with the suffering of the world, nor do we have the clarity of heart and mind required for the complex challenges we face."[16]

The Gospels are also quite clear on this score. Jesus may have died on the cross, but he wasn't willing to live on one, and at times allowed himself to be conspicuously attended to. He took advantage of opportunities to feast and relax in other people's homes and to be anointed with rich, aromatic oils. When he felt fearful and uncertain, Jesus requested emotional support from his closest associates. The quintessential minister, Jesus understood that it's as important to know how to gratefully receive as to generously give. Those who feel compelled to be always active and "on duty" may be driven more by guilt, ambition, or anxiety than true compassion.

Robert Gass, designer of the Rockwood Art of Leadership, has noted the propensity of many well-meaning, talented people to overfunction. He encourages those who attend his workshops to examine their motivations and the long-range implications of their behavior. Have we simply become "habituated, even addicted to a high level of urgency?" If so, our service is likely to be tainted by self-conceit and not as effective or enriching as it could be. "At Rockwood we work on 'load management'—learning what constitutes a sustainable workload," Gass reports.[17] To me, that sounds like a sensible, spiritual approach that begins with self-love and leaves time for self-care.

Toward a Graceful Exit

Fuller self-understanding, increased awareness of life's wonders, the genuine experience of loving kindness and its translation into helpfulness—these are a few important facets of an engaged, naturalistic spirituality. But to be sustainable, any spiritual orientation must also come to terms with the stubborn, unavoidable fact of death.

Conventional wisdom suggests that without firm religious faith—the kind characterized by belief in a benevolent deity possessing the power to grant everlasting life to those whom He has chosen—the prospect of "going down to dust and ashes" can't be tolerated. There are no atheists in foxholes, we are told. When faced with the certainty of their own demise, human beings desperately seek reassurance that the story won't end with the grave.

Religion is often said to have developed in response to human beings' death anxiety, its purpose being to provide us with the reassurances we need to cope with it socially and psychologically. Through the ages the grim reaper has been dealt with in many ways and billions of minds put at ease. But not all religions have been as hostile toward death and as enthusiastic about immortality as the ones with which we are most familiar. Some have jettisoned the afterlife altogether, while others simply dismiss the issue as irresolvable and a distraction from matters of more immediate concern.

Two ancient philosophic traditions, Epicureanism and Stoicism, maintained that the good life was attainable even if no prospect of a future life was apparent. These schools addressed existential questions of meaning, purpose, happiness, and morality, and in this respect they resembled and functioned as religions despite the fact that "they had remarkably little use for God or gods." The goal of Stoicism and Epicureanism, Jennifer Hecht writes, "was practical happiness, and they were not merely theoretical about it: they provided community, meditations, and events" that would deepen and enrich the individual's daily life experience.[18]

Early Jewish, Confucian, and Buddhist teachers also spent little time discussing immortality. According to Stephen Batchelor, the Buddha accepted the Hindu idea of reincarnation but emphasized that spiritual practice should never take a back seat to metaphysical speculation.[19] Without encouraging belief in a postmortem paradise, these religions constructed a psychologically protective "canopy of meaning" for their adherents and developed practical mechanisms for human beings to achieve peace of mind.

During my own long tenure in the ministry, I've presided at hundreds of funerals and memorial services, and I've spoken with and sat beside many people as the end approached. Very few of these individuals possessed faith of the conventional sort. Many admitted that they didn't know what fate held in store for them and were willing to be surprised. A few said they would *like* to believe but not at the cost of their intellectual integrity. Most of the men and women I've ministered to have been anxious about death (how could one not be?), but abject fear or panic has been notably absent. People often say they really don't mind dying but are concerned about suffering they might have to endure or any excessive prolongation of the process.

So in the absence of conventional faith, what sustains such people as they head toward the final frontier? Philip Simmons, a Unitarian Universalist diagnosed with ALS (Lou Gehrig's disease) in his forties, worked hard to come up with an answer. Realizing that if the condition ran its normal course he would die within a few years, Simmons retired from a college teaching career and moved back to his native New England when the symptoms of ALS became increasingly disabling. He spent his remaining years in a rustic cabin surrounded by his supportive family and learning to "attend." Like those ancient Epicureans, Simmons tried to connect as completely as possible with the here-and-now, letting the next life—if there was to be one—take care of itself. "Our very presentness is our salvation," he wrote in one of several insightful essays. "The present moment, entered into fully, is our gateway to eternal life. ... You might say I want eternal life now, before it's over with."[20]

I share those sentiments. Individuals should try to live as honorably and honestly as they can, with as much sensitivity as they can muster, striving by turns to savor and serve the world. From what I have witnessed, it is possible to shuffle off this mortal coil pretty well satisfied if those conditions have been met. For George Bernard Shaw, the point was "to be thoroughly used up" when he died. Future existence held no appeal to him whatsoever. He "rejoiced in life for its own sake" and described immortality as an "unimaginable horror."[21]

Experience has taught me that dying without regret is what really matters. Individuals who have lived generously, attentively, enthusiastically—who have loved and been loved—face death with remarkable aplomb. What seems to be essential is the secure knowledge that this life counted for something and that others are now better off for our having lived.

Cary Fowler is the executive director of the Global Crop Diversity Trust, an organization whose mission is to gather specimens from about two million varieties of food plants for a global seed bank. Having survived two bouts with cancer, he admits that the first one really shook him up. But the fate of his soul after death wasn't the primary issue for Fowler. "I was scared that I hadn't done anything—I hadn't contributed constructively to society, and that was frightening."[22]

In later life, the pioneer feminist Betty Friedan began an inquiry of the aging process that causes so much dread in our youth-oriented culture. After numerous interviews with elders and careful study of the pertinent literature on aging, Friedan concluded that those who feel confident that their life has been the product of their own work and choices will have attained a sense of satisfaction that will be "strong enough to offset the psychological pull of inevitable physical disintegration." On the other hand, Friedan wrote, if this conviction is absent, "despair, depression, ...

or a deep fear of old age and death" will likely be the result.[23] One needn't have been awarded a Nobel Prize in medicine, won a Super Bowl ring, or accumulated an unblemished record of saintly service to experience end-of-life serenity. The average person's accomplishments are likely to be much more modest—their lives distinguished and redeemed by small but meaningful acts of creative expression and unbidden gestures of genuine kindness. The important thing is to stay on point, trying as best we can to improve the quality of other people's experience while deepening our own appreciation of all that this good, green planet has to give. "If one can find out what the full meaning of living is," Krishnamurti wrote, "... then one is capable of understanding the wholeness of death. But one usually inquires into the meaning of death without inquiring into the meaning of life."[24]

The Optimal Attitude

I believe that to live is a privilege, and for that privilege I always feel grateful. I have never felt entitled or especially deserving of the good fortune that has come my way. Although I've had the gumption to avail myself of certain opportunities, I also realize that I was not myself their author. There have also been setbacks and disappointments along the way. But even if this is not, as Dr. Pangloss would say, "the best of all possible worlds," it is the one into which I have been deposited, and I can choose either to lament or to celebrate it.

I choose celebration because the alternative just doesn't make any sense. As Anne Lamott has observed, "The [real] secret to joy and equanimity is gratitude."[25] This, then, is the attitude that we should make every effort to adopt and that must, if we aim to be happy, inform our relationship with the world.

Almost every grateful person I've encountered is less competitive, more secure in his or her identity, and basically satisfied with what he or she already has. These people don't begrudge others their position or possessions and seldom complain of being shortchanged. Of wealth and power they generally have little, but somehow they know that these really aren't reliable or sustainable sources of human happiness. One hesitates to characterize such people as "content" because they do not typically lack for motivation; many are eager to do more and to be more. Gratitude is a feeling that causes us to give and to serve freely because we already feel rich and well provided for ourselves.

Tim Jeffery owns a management consulting firm in Madison, Wisconsin, teaches at UW–Madison, and formerly held high-level positions with both the city and the unified school district. He has enjoyed a notably successful career, but he now spends a great deal of time doing volunteer work. Jeffery helps with prairie restoration, sits on several nonprofit boards, and helps organizations improve their volunteer services. His reasons for putting forth all this extra effort are plain and simple. "This community has been such an important part of my life and the life of my family since 1975," Jeffery says, "and I feel an obligation to give back." He also reports that the internal rewards he receives from helping others as a volunteer exceed anything he experienced in his professional career.[26]

"The feeling of wealth is enhanced when you give," Robert Thurman writes, "since subliminally giving means you have enough to share, while taking means you may not be getting enough. Giving is a relief. Taking is a burden."[27]

I'm not saying we are obliged to be grateful for every facet of existence or suggesting that every dark cloud is naturally endowed with a silver lining. Occasionally the wind blows ill, and all we can do is to be patient until the direction shifts. Gratitude teaches that where there is life, there is still hope; that even in the face of misfortune, redemptive possibilities still exist. "Comedy ends in happiness, while tragedy yields wisdom," Philip Simmons says. To be happily wise and wisely happy should be our ambition because "only then can we know the full blessings of our imperfect life."[28]

Though painful, grief can act as a solvent, softening the stubbornly hard heart and giving us access to the compassionate side of our nature. And despite the damage it inflicts on the ego, if it doesn't lead to bitterness, failure helps perfect the personality; for in the muck of disappointment, humility, patience, and self-awareness have a chance to take root.

The more grateful a person is, the more likely that person is to be happy. The two sentiments complement and reinforce each other. Think about it: have you ever met an ungrateful person who was happy? In fact, research shows that people who keep a daily "gratitude journal" experience all sorts of positive benefits, physical as well as psychological.[29] By themselves, physical pleasure, social stature, and privilege don't deliver the goods. In fact, the pursuit and acquisition of such "worldly" objectives often affects people in just the opposite way. Envy, inadequacy, worry, insecurity, and chronic dissatisfaction are their unanticipated by-products, sullying our successes and contaminating whatever happiness we might have won.

A sustainable future is conceivable and more probable if we can manage to instill in people a deeper sense of gratitude. In the final analysis, sustainability is as much a spiritual as a practical matter because it requires both a thorough reorientation of our relationship to the world and a radical revision of certain assumptions we have made about good and meaningful living.

I believe it all boils down to openness: senses open to all that is, a mind open and receptive to new ideas, and a heart open and willing to embrace a world in which joy and woe are woven fine, and in which we must discover our proper place.

Notes

Preface

1. Sy Safransky, "Sy Safrasky's Notebook," *The Sun*, January 2009, p. 47.
2. Bill Moyers, "This Is the Fight of Our Lives," *Timeline*, September/October 2004, p. 6.

Introduction

1. Christina Roessler, "Changing Water Policies in the Dry Southwest," *The American Prospect*, June 2008, p. A-10.
2. "Crisis Feared as Freshwater Supplies Dwindle," *The Capital Times*, Oct. 27, 2007.
3. Thomas Friedman, *The World Is Flat*, Farrar, Straus and Giroux, 2005, p. 495.
4. Bill Berry, "Conservation Principles Don't Deserve Ridicule," *The Capital Times*, Jan. 8, 2008, p. A7.
5. Jonathan Rowe, "Our Conservative Allies," *Yes!* Summer 2007, p. 12.
6. Curt Meine, *Aldo Leopold: His Life and Work*, University of Wisconsin Press, 1991, p. 323.
7. Aldo Leopold, *A Sand County Almanac*, Oxford University Press, 1968, pp. 224–225.
8. Paul Hawken, *The Ecology of Commerce*, HarperCollins, 1993.
9. Myles Dannhausen, "Treading Lightly," *Door County Living*, Summer 2007, pp. 28–37.
10. Scott S. Smith, "The Boutique Mystique," *My Midwest*, September/October 2008, pp. 107–110.
11. Dana Perrigan, "It Takes a Village," *Sierra*, July–August 2007, p. 47.
12. Natasha Abbas et al., "25 Ways to Green the World," *Coop America Quarterly*, Fall 2008, p. 9.
13. Yi Fu Tuan, *The Good Life*, University of Wisconsin Press, 1986, pp. 52, 53.

14. Ibid., p. 21.
15. Ibid., p. 23.
16. Ibid., pp. 28, 36.
17. John McPhee, *Encounters with the Arch-Druid*, Farrar, Straus and Giroux, 1971, p. 83.
18. Bill McKibben, "Planet at the Crossroads," *Yes!* Spring 2006, pp. 26–30.
19. James Lardner, "The Specter Haunting Your Office," *New York Review of Books*, June 14, 2007, p. 62.
20. Sam Roberts, "25th Anniversary Mark Elusive for Many Couples," *The New York Times*, Sept. 20, 2007.
21. Bo Lozoff, interview in *The Utne Reader*, November–December 1996.
22. Paul Raeburn, "Dropping Weight, and Keeping It Off," *Scientific American*, September 2007, pp. 66–67.
23. H. H. The Dalai Lama and Howard C. Cutler, *The Art of Happiness*, Riverhead, 1998, pp. 283–284.
24. Andrew Hacker, "Avner Offer, 'The Challenge of Affluence,'" *New York Review of Books*, Oct. 11, 2007, pp. 31–34.
25. Matthew Fox, *A New Reformation*, Wisdom Inner Traditions, 2005, Thesis #19.

Chapter 1

1. Wendell Berry, *What Are People For?* North Point Press, 1990, p. 210.
2. Lisa M. Hamilton, "Faith in the Land," *Utne Reader*, July–August 2004.
3. Quotations from Chuang Tzu by Thomas Merton, www.terebess.hu/english/merton.html.
4. David Abram, *The Spell of the Sensuous*, Vintage Books, 1997, p. 69.
5. John Gray, *Straw Dogs: Thoughts on Humans and Other Animals*, Farrar, Straus and Giroux, 2002, p. 199.
6. Wallace Stegner, *The Sense of Place*, Random House, 1992.
7. Scott Russell Sanders, *Staying Put: Making a Home in a Restless World*, Beacon Press, 1994.
8. Terry Tempest Williams, *The Sun*, June 2006, p. 48 and www.the-sunmagazine.org/issues/366/sunbeams.
9. Joe Bageant, *Deer Hunting with Jesus*, Three Rivers Press, 2007, p. 28.
10. John Price, "Dear Young Iowan," *The Land Report*, Summer 2007, pp. 22–23.
11. Steven Wright. *The Sun*, August 2007, p. 48 and hwww.thesun-magazine.org/issues/380/sunbeams.

12. Mark Slouka, "Quitting the Paint Factory," *Harper's Magazine*, November 2004, p. 57.
13. Frederick and Mary Ann Brussat, *Spiritual Literacy*, Scribner, 1996, p. 231.
14. Sigurd Olson, *Reflections from the North Country*, University of Minnesota Press, 1998, p. 29.
15. Thich Nhat Hanh, The Path of Emancipation: Talks from a 21-Day Mindfulness Retreat, Parallax, 2000, pp. 7–9.
16. Bill McKibben, *Maybe One*, Plume, 1999, p. 149.
17. Ibid., "The Choice," *The New Yorker*, Oct. 13, 2008, p. 52.
18. Lao Tse, *The Tao Te Ching*, chap. 29, translated by Stephen Mitchell, HarperCollins, 1998.
19. E. F. Schumacher, *Small Is Beautiful*, Harper & Row, 1973.
20. Van Rensselaer Potter, "Getting to the Year 3000: Can Global Bioethics Overcome Evolution's Fatal Flaw?" *Perspectives in Biology and Medicine*, vol. 34, 1990, pp. 89–98.
21. Corey Robin, *Fear: The History of a Political Idea*, Oxford University Press, 2004, p. 36.
22. Bill Moyers, "On Receiving Harvard Medical School's Global Environment Citizen Award," commondreams.org/ views04/1206-10.htm, Dec. 6, 2004.

Chapter 2

1. John Gray, *Straw Dogs: Thoughts on Humans and Other Animals*, Farrar, Straus and Giroux, 2002, pp. 7, 17.
2. Charles C. Mann, *1491: New Revelations of the Americas Before Columbus*, Knopf, 2005. ("In the current view, the Western Hemisphere before 1492 was a thriving, stunningly diverse place ... where tens of millions of people loved and hated and worshipped as people do everywhere. Much of that world vanished after Columbus, swept away by disease and subjugation ... so thorough that within a few generations neither conqueror nor conquered knew that this world had existed." p. 27)
3. Judith Thurman, "First Impressions," *The New Yorker*, June 23, 2008, pp. 62–63.
4. Mark Pinsky, "Leaders See Warming as Biblical Offense," *The Monterey County Herald*, Feb. 23, 2008,
5. David Abrams, *The Spell of the Sensuous*, Vintage Books, 1996, p. 94.
6. Loren Eiseley, *The Invisible Pyramid*, Scribner, 1970, p. 143.
7. Verlyn Klinkenborg, "Trying Times Ahead: The Prospect of 60 Million Californians," *The New York Times*, July 18, 2007.
8. Mark Beliles and Stephen McDowell, "Thy Kingdom Come," *Harper's Magazine*, February 2005, p. 20.

9. Valerie Saturen, "Evangelicals' Faith Leads Them to Issues of Environmental, Social Justice," *Yes!* Fall 2008, p. 44.

10. Bart Jones, "Green Pope Takes on Climate Change," *The Capital Times*, Apr. 11, 2008.

11. Sallie McFague, *A New Climate for Theology*, Fortress Press, 2008, p. 96.

12. Barbara Kingsolver, "Sunbeams," *The Sun*, July 2008, p. 48.

13. David Ehrenfeld, *The Arrogance of Humanism*, Oxford, 1981, see esp. pp. 77–82. (Ehrenfeld's exposure of modern secular/scientific humanism's excesses continues to be relevant.)

14. Mark Twain, "Damned Human Race," *Letters from the Earth*, Harper Perennial, 1974, p. 176.

15. Gray, *Straw Dogs*, pp. 7, 17.

16. Ando Arike, "Owning the Weather," *Harper's Magazine*, January 2006, pp. 72–73.

17. Berry, *What Are People For?* p. 209.

18. Peter Hessler, "The Wonder Years," *The New Yorker*, Mar. 31, 2008, p. 74.

19. Richard Lewontin, "The Wars Over Evolution," *The New York Review of Books*, Oct. 20, 2005.

20. Charles Mann, *1491: New Revelations of the Americas Before Columbus*, Knopf, 2005, pp. 300–308.

21. Marcia Bjornerud, *Reading the Rocks*, Basic Books, 2005, p. 98.

22. Paul Krugman, "The Big Squeeze," *The New York Times*, Oct. 18, 2005.

23. Wallace C. Peterson, *Silent Depression: The Fate of the American Dream*, W. W. Norton, 1995, pp. 115–157.

24. Jared Bernstein, "Median Income Rose as Did Poverty," *Economic Policy Institute*, Aug. 26, 2008 (online).

25. James Loewen, *Sundown Towns: A Hidden Dimension of American Racism*, New Press, 2005.

26. World Population News Service, September/October 2005.

27. David Korten, *The Great Turning: from Empire to Earth Community*, Berrett-Koehler, 2006, pp. 66–67.

28. Quoted by Jim Hightower in "Hightower," *Tucson Weekly*, Oct. 13–19, 2005.

29. Charles Derber, *Corporation Nation*, St. Martin's Griffin, 2000, p. 305.

30. Eiseley, *The Invisible Pyramid*, p. 62.

31. Thomas Geoghegan, "Going Nowhere Fast," *The American Prospect*, March 2008, p. 44.

32. Curtis White, "Hot Air Gods," *Harper's Magazine*, December 2007, p. 15.

33. Karen Armstrong, *The Great Transformation*, Knopf, 2006, p. 234.

34. John Mackey, "The Omnivore's Dilemma," *Harper's Magazine*, December 2007, pp. 32, 33.
35. Robert C. Solomon, *Spirituality for the Skeptic*, Oxford, 2002, p. 68.
36. Reed McManus, "Green and Greed, Can They Get Along?" *Sierra*, January/February 2008, p. 31.
37. Ann Crittenden, "Faster and Faster," *The American Prospect*, July 2007.
38. Robin Shepard, "Co-ops for Hops," *The Isthmus*, Nov. 7, 2008, pp. 35, 36.
39. "Interview with Don Shaffer," conducted by Steve Kemper, *American Forests*, Spring 2007, p. 37.
40. Barry Adams, "Working to Revive Main Streets," *Wisconsin State Journal*, June 1, 2008.
41. Jess Worth, "Buy Now, Pay Later," *The New Internationalist*, issue 395, November 2006 (online).
42. Paul McLeary, "John Carroll on Winning Pulitzers While Losing Circulation," *The Columbia Journalism Review*, July 22, 2005 (online).
43. Michael Massing, "The Enemy Within," *The New York Review of Books*, Dec. 15, 2005.
44. Lardner, "The Specter Haunting Your Office," p. 62.
45. Bill McKibben, *Deep Economy*, Henry Holt, 2007, p. 124.
46. Ibid., p. 187.
47. Curt Meine, *Aldo Leopold: His Life and Work*, University of Wisconsin Press, 1991, p. 303.
48. Marcia Angell, "Health Reform You Shouldn't Believe In," *The American Prospect*, May 2008, p. A-15.
49. Neal Halfon, "The Primacy of Prevention," *The American Prospect*, May 2008, p. A-7.
50. Michael Specter, "What Money Can Buy," *The New Yorker*, Oct. 24, 2005, p. 59.
51. George Soros, *The Age of Fallibility*, Public Affairs, 2006, p. 171.
52. Korten, *The Great Turning: From Empire to Earth Community*, pp. 34, 35.
53. Ann Grauvogl, "Living Small," *The Isthmus*, Apr. 11, 2008, p. 13.
54. White, "Hot Air Gods," pp. 13–15.
55. Eric Sorensen, "Seven Wonders for a Cool Planet," *Sierra Magazine*, March/April 2008, p. 49.
56. Joseph Romm, "The Technology That Will Save Humanity," *Salon*, Apr. 14, 2008, pp. 1, 2 (online).
57. Philip Shabecoff, "Sunbeams," *The Sun*, June 2006, p. 48.
58. Robert Aitken, "The Long View," *Turning Wheel*, Summer 2004, pp. 12–14.

59. Lewis Mumford, "Sunbeams," *The Sun*, October 2006, p. 48.
60. John Seabrook, "Sowing for the Apocalypse," *The New Yorker*, Aug. 27, 2007, pp. 60–71.
61. John Seabrook, "Harper's Findings," *Harper's Magazine*, February 2005, p. 96.
62. Sara Fishkin, "From the Roots Up," *Turning Wheel*, Winter 2003–2004, pp. 32–33.
63. McKibben, *Deep Economy*, p. 68.
64. Jason Epstein, "A New Way to Think About Eating," *The New York Review of Books*, Mar. 20, 2008, pp. 23–24.
65. David Shipley and Will Schwable, *Send: Why People Email So Badly and How to Do It Better*, Knopf, 2007, pp. 10–11, 175–198.
66. Marilynne Robinson, *Gilead*, Farrar, Straus and Giroux, 2004, p. 126.
67. Luke Mitchell, "The Black Box," *Harper's Magazine*, December 2007, p. 50.
68. Edward Hoagland, "Endgame: Meditations on a Diminishing World," *Harper's Magazine*, June 2007, p. 42.
69. McPhee, *Encounters with the Arch-Druid*, p. 84.
70. "Yearning for Balance, Views of Americans on Consumption, Materialism and the Environment," a report prepared for the Merck Family Fund by the Harwood Group, 1995 (online).
71. "81% in Poll Say Nation Is Headed on Wrong Track," *The New York Times*, Apr. 4, 2008 (online).

Chapter 3

1. Abram, *The Spell of the Sensuous*, pp. 62–63.
2. Marcia Bjornerud, *Reading the Rocks*, Basic Books, 2005, p. 190.
3. Robert Fulghum, "All I Ever Really Needed to Know I Learned in Kindergarten," Teacherweb.com (online).
4. Heather Sellers, "The Wizard in the Closet," *The Sun*, December 2007, pp. 17–19.
5. Larry Rosenberg, *Breath by Breath*, Shambhala, 1998, p. 39.
6. See Diet and Disease, National Cancer Institute website; also "WHO/FAO Independent Expert Report on Diet and Chronic Disease," World Health Organization website, Mar. 3, 2003.
7. Bee Wilson, "The Last Bite," *The New Yorker*, May 19, 2008, pp. 76–80.
8. Stephen Shapin, "Eat and Run," *The New Yorker*, Jan. 16, 2006, p. 82.
9. Will Johnson, "Full Body, Empty Mind," *Tricycle*, Fall 2007, pp. 34–39.
10. Atul Gawande, "The Way We Age Now," *The New Yorker*, Apr. 30, 2007, pp. 50–59.

11. Jack Kornfield, *After the Ecstasy, the Laundry*, Bantam Books, 2000, pp. 100–101.
12. Chogyam Trungpa, *Shambhala: The Sacred Path of the Warrior*, Shambhala, 1988, p. 119.
13. Philip Simmons, *Learning to Fall*, Bantam Books, 2006, p. 126.
14. H. H. The Dalai Lama, *Ethics for a New Millennium*, Riverhead Books, 1999, p. 62.
15. "Heart Attack Survivors Half as Likely to Suffer Further Attacks if They Have Love and Friends," *Medical News Today*, Apr. 14, 2004 (online).
16. Mary Pipher, *The Shelter of Each Other*, Ballantine Books, 1996, p. 116.
17. Judith Wallerstein, *Second Chances*, Houghton-Mifflin, 1996, p. 19.
18. William Doherty, *The Intentional Family*, Addison-Wesley, 1997, p. 14.
19. Pipher, *The Shelter of Each Other*, p. 228.
20. John Anderson, "Bowling for Columbine," *Newsday*, Oct. 11, 2002 (online).
21. Scott H. Forbes, "Krishnamurti and His Insight into Education," *Infed*, Apr. 11, 2008 (online).
22. Malcolm Gladwell, *The Tipping Point*, Little, Brown, 2002, p. 45.
23. Andrew C. Revkin, "A New Measure of Well-Being from a Happy Little Kingdom," *The New York Times*, Oct. 4, 2005.
24. Robert Bellah et al., *The Good Society*, Knopf, 1991, p. 273.

Chapter 4

1. Susan Kepecs, "Table Talk," *The Isthmus*, Apr. 4, 2008, p. 40.
2. Jane Jacobs, *The Death and Life of Great American Cities*, Vintage, 1992, pp. 112–140.
3. James Lardner, "The Specter Haunting Your Office," p. 62.
4. Scott Russell Sanders, *Staying Put: Making a Home in a Restless World*, Beacon Press, 1993, pp. 103–107.
5. Frank Watson, "Correspondence," *The Sun*, December 2007, p. 3.
6. Bill Perkins, "Why the Bubble Popped," *Isthmus*, May 9, 2008, p. 10.
7. McKibben, *Deep Economy*, p. 120.
8. Wendell Berry, *Home Economics*, North Point Press, 1987, pp. 188–189.
9. Ibid., p. 54.
10. Anne Matthews, "Commonplace Book," *The American Scholar*, Autumn 2008, p. 143.
11. Margaret Gunning, "Soul Food," *January Magazine*, Oct. 20, 2008 (online).
12. Gary Ferguson, "Outbound," *Wilderness*, 2006–2007, p. 22.
13. John P. Schuster, *Answering Your Call*, Berrett-Koehler, 2003, p. 1.

14. Sam Keene, *To a Dancing God*, Harper & Row, 1970, p. 15.
15. Lev Grossman, "Wise Guy," *Time*, Nov. 24, 2008, p. 48.
16. John R. O'Neil, *The Paradox of Success*, G. P. Putnam's Sons, 1993, p. 114.
17. Parker Palmer, *Let Your Life Speak*, Jossey-Bass, 2000, p. 2.
18. Anne Lamott, *Plan B: Further Thoughts on Faith*, Riverhead Books, 2005, p. 304.
19 Wallace Stegner, *Crossing to Safety*, Penguin, 1988, pp. 103–104.
20. Becky Brun, "Your Stories of the Good Life," *Yes!* Summer 2004, p. 36.
21. Barbara Ehrenreich, *Nickel and Dimed: On Not Getting By in America*, Henry Holt, 2008; and Juliette Schorr, *The Overworked American*, Basic Books, 1991.
22. Robin, *Fear: The History of a Political Idea*, pp. 228–240.
23. Bageant, *Deer Hunting with Jesus*, p. 11.
24. Christopher Kimball, "Hands on the Plough," *Cook's Illustrated*, May/June 2005, p. 1.
25. George Leonard, *Mastery*, Penguin-Plume, 1992, pp. 39–49.
26. Ibid., p. 29.
27. Pema Chodron, *The Places That Scare You*, Shambhala, 2002, p. 85.
28. Paul Raeburn, "Dropping Weight and Keeping It Off," *Scientific American*, September 2007, pp. 66–67.
29. Marion Nestle, "Eating Made Simple," *Scientific American*, September 2007, pp. 60–69.
30. Robert Johnson, *We*, HarperCollins, 1983, pp. 102–103.
31. Richard Holloway, *Looking in the Distance*, Canongate Books, 2004, p. 184.
32. McKibben, *Deep Economy*, p. 101; Sam Roberts, "25th Anniversary Mark Elusive for Many Couples," *The New York Times*, Sept. 20, 2007.
33. Mary Pipher, *The Shelter of Each Other*, Ballantine Books, 1996, p. 90.
34. Jane Smiley, *At Paradise Gate: A Novel*, Simon & Schuster, 1981.
35. Pipher, *The Shelter of Each Other*, p. 243.
36. Doherty, *The Intentional Family*, p. 48.
37. Sanders, *Staying Put*, p. 35.
38. Holloway, *Looking in the Distance*, p. 185.

Chapter 5

1. Andrew Hacker, "They'd Much Rather Be Rich," *The New York Review of Books*, Oct. 11, 2007, p. 31.
2. H. H. The Dalai Lama, *Ethics for a New Millennium*, pp. 105–106.
3. Benjamin Hoff, *The Tao of Pooh*, Penguin Books, 1983, pp. 95–96.
4. Wayne Muller, *Sabbath*, Bantam Books, 2000, p. 3.

5. McKibben, *Deep Economy*, p. 9.
6. Mark Kingwell, "Fast Forward: Our High-Speed Chase to Nowhere," *Harper's Magazine*, May 1998, p. 48.
7. Jonathan Freedland, "Falling Hawks," *The New York Review of Books*, July 17, 2008, p. 26.
8. Thich Nhat Hanh, *Being Peace*, Parallax Press, 2005, p. 68.
9. "National Endowment for the Arts Announces New Reading Study," NEA News Room, Nov. 19, 2007 (online).
10. Ursula K. Le Guin, "Staying Awake," *Harper's Magazine*, February 2008, pp. 33–38.
11. Alan D. Wolfelt, "Blessed Are Those Who Mourn Quickly," *Frontline*, Summer 2008, p. 4.
12. Louise Dunlap, "Walks Far Woman," *Turning Wheel*, Winter 2002–2003, pp. 24–26.
13. Robert Coles, *The Call of Service*, Houghton Mifflin, 1993, p. 80.
14. "Ten Most Dangerous Foods to Eat on the Road," *MSN Money*, July 2008 (online); Eric Schlosser, *Fast Food Nation*, Harper Perennial, 2002, p. 261.
15. Stephen Mitchell (translator), *Tao Te Ching*, Harper &Row, 1988, Chapters 67, 64.
16. Willa Cather, "Sunbeams," *The Sun*, August 2007, p. 48.
17. Amby Burfoot, *The Runner's Guide to the Meaning of Life*, Skyhorse Publishing, 2007, p. 14.
18. Robert Taylor, Letters, *Utne Reader*, May–June 2006.
19. Robert Johnson, *We*, HarperCollins, 1983, pp. 195–196.
20. Pipher, *The Shelter of Each Other*, p. 202.
21. Jim Malusa, "As Low as You Can Go," *Sierra Magazine*, March–April 2008, p. 1 (online).
22. Dena Wortzel, "Of Love and the Material World," *Wisconsin People & Ideas*, Summer 2006, p. 41.
23. David Noel Freedman, *The Nine Commandments*, Doubleday, 2000, p. 60.
24. Muller, *Sabbath*, p. 30.
25. Martin Marty, "Keep Convenient the Sabbath," *Context*, January 2004, p. 5.
26. Gary Snyder, *Sierra*, March–April 2007, p. 60.
27. McKibben, *Deep Economy*, p. 169.
28. Carolyn McConnell, "Deliberation Day," *Yes!* Winter 2003 (online).
29. Ronald A. Heifetz, *Leadership without Easy Answers*, Belknap Harvard, 1994, p. 141.

Chapter 6

1. Roger D. Hodge, "Findings," *Harper's Magazine*, February 2005, p. 96.

2. McPhee, *Encounters with the Arch-Druid*, p. 74.
3. Bjornerud, *Reading the Rocks*, p. 149.
4. Wingspread Statement on the Precautionary Principle," Global Development Research Center Urban Governance Link, July 5, 2008 (online).
5. E. J. Dionne, "Capitalism's Reality Check," *The Washington Post*, July 11, 2008.
6. Fred Clark, "Forest Sustains Family, Family Sustains Forest, *Landscapes* (newsletter of the Thousand Friends of Wisconsin), Fall 2005, p. 3.
7. Thomas Frank, *What's the Matter with Kansas?* Macmillan, 2004, pp. 59–61.
8. "Wal-Mart 1st in State Aid Enrollees," *Arizona Daily Star,* Oct. 1, 2005.
9. McKibben, *Deep Economy,* Henry Holt, 2007, pp. 106–107.
10. Tami Abdollah, "A Strict Order for Fast Food, *Los Angeles Times,* Sept. 10, 2007, *p. A-1.*
11. Larry Eriksson, *Business Decisions,* Quarter Section Press, 2002, pp. 61–65.
12. Linda Brewer, "More Than Coffee," *The Desert Leaf,* November 2005, p. 40.
13. Dan Barber, "Change We Can Stomach," *The New York Times,* May 11, 2008 (online). (According to World Watch, the ingredients for an average American meal typically travel between 1,500 and 2,500 miles, a 25 percent increase from 1980 alone. Seventeen times more petroleum products are consumed to provide that meal than one that is locally sourced.) Alisa Smith and J. B. MacKinnon, "Living on the 100-Mile Diet," *The Tyee*, June 28, 2005.
14. David Kupfer, "Judy Wicks on Her Plan to Change the World, One Restaurant at a Time," *The Sun*, August 2008, pp. 5–13.
15. Matt Ridley, *The Origins of Virtue*, Penguin, 1998, p. 133.
16. Herman Daly and John Cobb, *For the Common Good*, Beacon Press, 1989, pp. 138–141.
17. Steven Stoll, "Fear of Fallowing," *Harper's Magazine*, March 2008, pp. 90–91.
18. Hawken, *The Ecology of Commerce*, p. 140.
19. McKibben, *Deep Economy*, p. 190.
20. Kendrick Frazier, *People of Chaco*, Norton, 1999, p. 104.
21. Margaret Atwood, "A Matter of Life and Debt," *The New York Times*, Oct. 22, 2008 (online).
22. Daniel Gilbert, *Stumbling on Happiness*, Knopf, 2006, pp. 217–220; Tal Ben-Shahar, *Happier*, McGraw-Hill, 2007, p. 56.
23. Jared Diamond, "What's Your Consumption Factor?" *The New York Times*, Jan. 2, 2008 (online).

24. McKibben, *Deep Economy*, p. 35.
25. Revkin, "A New Measure of Well-Being from a Happy Little Kingdom."
26. Peter Block, *Stewardship*, Berrett-Koehler, 1996, pp. 9, 10, 181.
27. McKibben, *Deep Economy*, p. 38.
28. Epstein, "A New Way to Think about Eating," pp. 23–24.
29. Joan M. Naughton, Kerin O'Dea, and Andrew Sinclair, "Animal Foods in Traditional Australian Aboriginal Diets," *Lipids*, November 1986 (online).
30. Barry M. Popkin, "The World Is Fat," *Scientific American*, September 2007, pp. 88–95.
31. Marc David, *Utne Reader*, November–December 2005, p. 96.
32. Mark Bittman, "Rethinking the Meat-Guzzler," *The New York Times*, Jan. 27, 2008 (online); McKibben, *Deep Economy*, pp. 62–63.
33. David Medaris, "Chasing after Chi," *The Isthmus*, July 18, 2008, p. 46.
34. Lindsey Tanner, "Fit to Be Eyed," *Wisconsin State Journal*, July 13, 2008.
35. McKibben, *Long Distance*, p. 24.
36. Judith Wallerstein, *Second Chances*, Houghton Mifflin, pp. 8–9.
37. McKibben, *Maybe One*, pp. 36–37.
38. Arnie Cooper, "Peak Experience: The Age of Oil Is Coming to an End (interview with Richard Heinberg)," *The Sun*, July 2006.
39. Mihaly Csikszentmihalyi, *Flow: The Psychology of Optimal Experience*, HarperCollins, 1990, p. 3.
40. Thomas Merton, *The Way of Chuang Tzu*, Shambhala, 1992, pp. 88–89.
41. Ram Dass, *Still Here*, Riverhead Books, 2000, p. 79.
42. Randolph E. Schmid, "Giving Better Than Getting," *Salon*, Mar. 20, 2008 (online).
43. Robert Inchausti, *The Ignorant Perfection of Ordinary People*, SUNY Albany Press, 1991, p. 129.

Conclusion

1. Karen Armstrong, *The Spiral Staircase*, Anchor Books, 2004, p. 270.
2. Curtis White, "The Spirit of Disobedience," *Harper's Magazine*, April 2006, p. 38.
3. Huston Smith, *Why Religion Matters*, Harper & Row, 2001, p. 33.
4. Larry Rosenberg, *Breath by Breath*, Shambhala, 1998, p. 147.
5. Robert Inchausti, *Thomas Merton's American Prophecy*, SUNY Albany Press, 1998, pp. 132–133.
6. Edward Mendelson, "Auden and God," *The New York Review of Books*, Dec. 6, 2007, pp. 70–75.

7. Palmer, *Let Your Life Speak*, p. 82.
8. Richard Holloway, *Looking in the Distance*, Canongate, 2004, p. 28.
9. Rosenberg, *Breath by Breath*, p. 170.
10. Robinson, *Gilead*, p. 245.
11. Parker Palmer, *To Know as We Are Known*, HarperCollins, 1993, pp. 11–12.
12. H. H. The Dalai Lama, *An Open Heart: Practicing Compassion in Everyday Life*, Little, Brown, 2001, pp. 95, 96.
13. Parker Palmer, "Finding Your Soul," *Spirituality and Health*, September/October 2004, pp. 38–43.
14. Loren Eiseley, *The Unexpected Universe*, Harcourt Brace Jovanovich, 1969, pp. 67–92. (In this essay, Eiseley describes a man who regularly patrolled a lonely beach retrieving starfish that had washed ashore and heaving them back into the surf. The essay underscores the cosmic significance of such small acts of compassion.)
15. William Elliott, *Tying Rocks to Clouds*, Doubleday, 1995, p. 141. (Of course, Mother Teresa believed in the spiritual efficacy of suffering. In her efforts to emulate the Gospel's suffering servant, she actively inflicted pain on herself.)
16. Gail Straube, *The Rhythm of Compassion*, Charles Tuttle, 2000, p. 5.
17. Nina Utne, "A Conversation with Robert Gass & Nina Utne about Spiritual Activism," *Utne Reader*, January–February 2006, p.3. (online)
18. Jennifer Hecht, *Doubt: A History*, HarperCollins, 2003, p. 29.
19. Stephen Batchelor, *Buddhism without Belief*, Riverhead, 1998, pp. 34–38.
20. Philip Simmons, *Learning to Fall*, Bantam Books, 2003, p. 145.
21. George Bernard Shaw, "A Treatise on Parents and Children,", 1910 (online).
22. Seabrook, "Sowing for Apocalypse," pp. 60–71.
23. Betty Friedan, *The Fountain of Age*, Simon & Schuster, 1993, p. 122.
24. J. Krishnamurti, "Words on Taking Leave, *Parabola*, Summer 2002, p. 60.
25. Lamott, *Plan B: Further Thoughts on Faith*, p. 295.
26. Andy Hall, "Know Your Madisonian: Tim Jeffery," *Wisconsin State Journal*, Oct. 12, 2008.
27. Robert Thurman, *Infinite Life*, Riverhead Books, 2004, p. 140.
28. Simmons, *Learning to Fall*, p. xvi.
29. Stephen Post and Jill Neimark, *Why Good Things Happen to Good People*, Broadway Books, 2007, p. 28.

Acknowledgments

Any decent book (and I trust this one qualifies) is ultimately the product of more contributors than can possibly be named. Some who deserve credit for this work include Trina, my wife, who read the manuscript several times, made corrections, and reminded me of ways in which the four keys figured in our own life. She was extraordinarily supportive of the project, tolerated the intrusion of work on vacations and days off, and provided frequent, welcome backrubs! No author could wish for a better partner. Our son, Kyle, also provided feedback and, as an illustrator, helped me think about the "look" of the book. The "keys" that grace the first page of four of the book's chapter are of his design. Sasha, our affectionate papillon, sacrificed her playtime and comforted me with her presence during long spells of writing.

Special thanks to Jack and Phoebe Lewis for making their lovely Tucson home available to us for the sabbatical leave during which the book was conceived, and to Liz Wessel, Bill and Nan Cronon, and Morris and Carolyn Waxler whose vacant vacation homes were invaluable in helping to move forward the editing process.

As University of Wisconsin faculty members and friends, Bill Cronon and Alan Knox offered encouragement and direction as I undertook the project, while Mary Bergin, Alan Knox, and Pamela Johnson were kind enough to read an early version of the manuscript and provide candid feedback. Other readers included Douglas Dupler, Pam Gordon, Carol Metzker, and EN. I am grateful to all of them and believe that because of their insight, Making the Good Life Last is more concise and cogent than it would otherwise have been. I also need to thank my ministerial colleagues at First Unitarian Society, Kelly Crocker and Karen Gustafson, who assumed extra responsibilities so that the manuscript would be finished on deadline. The congregation as a whole tolerated my periodic absences while evincing enthusiasm about the enterprise. And special thanks to John Woods, who worked with me from the beginning on this book, for providing his continuous encouragement and for making the book both attractive and more coherent. Finally, thanks to Judy Duguid for copyediting the final manuscript, Marg Sumner for her proof-reading, and especially thanks to Scott Russell Sanders for agreeing to compose the book's Foreword, and to Johanna Vondeling, Jeevan Sivasubramaniam, and all the good folks at Berrett-Koehler for taking a chance on an unknown, first-time author from the heartland.

Index

About the Author

A fifth-generation native of Dixon, Illinois, a modest town straddling the Rock River, Michael A. Schuler returned with his family to the upper reaches of the same watershed in 1988, after an absence of twenty years. Since then, they have made their home in Madison, Wisconsin, where Michael has served as senior minister of the First Unitarian Society of Madison, a congregation that has grown from 500 to 1,500 adult members during his tenure. In the fall of 2008 the Society completed a sustainably designed, LEED-certified, 23,000-square-foot addition to its original Frank Lloyd Wright–designed Meeting House in keeping with the organic principles that America's greatest architect once championed.

Michael Schuler spent his early years on a 200-acre family farm before moving with his parents to Naples, Florida, in 1967. There he had the great good fortune to meet the love of his life, Trina, in a high school algebra class. Following a six-year courtship and four years of college, they were joined in marriage in an intimate sunset ceremony overlooking the Gulf of Mexico. In 2008 they celebrated their thirty-fifth wedding anniversary.

Michael earned a bachelor of arts degree in political science from Eckerd College in 1973 and in 1976 a master of divinity from Starr King School for the Ministry, a Unitarian Universalist seminary in Berkeley, California. While preparing for a career in ministry, he served with the Unitarian Universalist Migrant Ministry, assisting seasonal farmworkers in California's central valley, and also studied Tibetan Buddhism with Tarthang Tulku at the Nyingma Institute in Berkeley. Following graduation, Michael and Trina moved to Sioux City, Iowa, where he served a small congregation for several years before entering Florida State University's interdisciplinary Ph.D. program in the humanities. Having completed a dissertation on American humanism, Michael received his doctorate in 1982.

After much deliberation, Michael elected to return to the ministry rather than pursue an academic career. He and Trina accepted an offer to serve the Unitarian Universalist Church of Binghamton, New York, where he enjoyed a successful seven-year tenure. During their time in Binghamton, Michael and Trina were blessed with their first and only child, Kyle. It was also a period during which Michael, a lifelong long-distance runner, began competing seriously in road races. In 1984 he was recognized as the Triple Cities Runner of the Year and achieved a career-best 2:36 time in the 26.2-mile marathon.

Despite the fondness they felt for New York's Southern Tier, Michael and Trina decided that Madison, Wisconsin, would provide an ideal environment in which to settle and raise a child. In addition to parenting and serving a busy, growing parish, for the past two decades Michael has pursued other interests and served the community in a number of areas. He was tapped by the University of Wisconsin to sit on the All-Campus Human Subjects Committee and on the Advisory Board of the Pathways to Excellence initiative. He has been a Planned Parenthood and Urban Open Space Foundation Board member, a member of the Steering Committee of Dane County United, and a Cub Scout Pack Master. For several years Michael was a regular "Faith and Values" feature writer for the *Capital Times* newspaper and has often been invited to speak at local and regional environmental, and peace and justice events. He has been published in two collections of essays, *Salted with Fire* and *Everyday Spiritual Practices*, and in *Dharma World* magazine.

Recognizing the importance of self-care, twelve years ago Michael undertook a disciplined study of hatha yoga and tai chi and maintains these practices along with recreational running. With their papillon (toy spaniel) Sasha, he and Trina travel extensively, and at home they make time for daily togetherness. They are gratified to have developed a lifestyle that feels balanced and sustainable. They feel confident that you can too.

About Berrett-Koehler Publishers

Berrett-Koehler is an independent publisher dedicated to an ambitious mission: Creating a World That Works for All.

We believe that to truly create a better world, action is needed at all levels — individual, organizational, and societal. At the individual level, our publications help people align their lives with their values and with their aspirations for a better world. At the organizational level, our publications promote progressive leadership and management practices, socially responsible approaches to business, and humane and effective organizations. At the societal level, our publications advance social and economic justice, shared prosperity, sustainability, and new solutions to national and global issues.

A major theme of our publications is "Opening Up New Space." They challenge conventional thinking, introduce new ideas, and foster positive change. Their common quest is changing the underlying beliefs, mindsets, and structures that keep generating the same cycles of problems, no matter who our leaders are or what improvement programs we adopt.

We strive to practice what we preach—to operate our publishing company in line with the ideas in our books. At the core of our approach is *stewardship*, which we define as a deep sense of responsibility to administer the company for the benefit of all of our "stakeholder" groups: authors, customers, employees, investors, service providers, and the communities and environment around us.

We are grateful to the thousands of readers, authors, and other friends of the company who consider themselves to be part of the "BK Community." We hope that you, too, will join us in our mission.

A BK Life Book

This book is part of our BK Life series. BK Life books change people's lives. They help individuals improve their lives in ways that are beneficial for the families, organizations, communities, nations, and world in which they live and work. To find out more, visit www.bklife.com.

Be Connected

Visit Our Website

Go to www.bkconnection.com to read exclusive previews and excerpts of new books, find detailed information on all Berrett-Koehler titles and authors, browse subject-area libraries of books, and get special discounts.

Subscribe to Our Free E-Newsletter

Be the first to hear about new publications, special discount offers, exclusive articles, news about bestsellers, and more! Get on the list for our free e-newsletter by going to www.bkconnection.com.

Get Quantity Discounts

Berrett-Koehler books are available at quantity discounts for orders of ten or more copies. Please call us toll-free at (800) 929-2929 or email us at bkp.orders@aidcvt.com.

Host a Reading Group

For tips on how to form and carry on a book reading group in your workplace or community, see our website at www.bkconnection.com.

Join the BK Community

Thousands of readers of our books have become part of the "BK Community" by participating in events featuring our authors, reviewing draft manuscripts of forthcoming books, spreading the word about their favorite books, and supporting our publishing program in other ways. If you would like to join the BK Community, please contact us at bkcommunity@bkpub.com.